A Fatherly Eye

A Fatherly Eye

Indian Agents, Government Power, and Aboriginal Resistance in Ontario, 1918–1939

Robin Jarvis Brownlie

OXFORD
UNIVERSITY PRESS

OXFORD
UNIVERSITY PRESS

70 Wynford Drive, Don Mills, Ontario M3C 1J9
www.oup.com/ca

Oxford University Press is a department of the University of Oxford.
It furthers the University's objective of excellence in research, scholarship,
and education by publishing worldwide in

Oxford New York
Auckland Bangkok Buenos Aires Cape Town Chennai
Dar es Salaam Delhi Hong Kong Istanbul Karachi Kolkata
Kuala Lumpur Madrid Melbourne Mexico City Mumbai Nairobi
São Paulo Shanghai Taipei Tokyo Toronto

Oxford is a trade mark of Oxford University Press
in the UK and in certain other countries

Published in Canada
by Oxford University Press

Copyright © Oxford University Press Canada 2003

The moral rights of the author have been asserted

Database right Oxford University Press (maker)

First published 2003

National Library of Canada Cataloguing in Publication

Brownlie, Robin, 1963–
A fatherly eye: Indian agents, government power, and aboriginal resistance
in Ontario, 1918–1939 / Robin Jarvis Brownlie
Includes bibliographical references and index.
ISBN 0–19–541891–3

1. Canada. Dept. of Indian Affairs—History. 2. Daly, John McLean.
3. Lewis, Robert J. 4. Indians of North America—Ontario—Georgian Bay Region—History.
5. Indians of North America—Canada—Government relations—1860–1951.
6. Indian agents—Ontario—Georgian Bay Region.
7. Paternalism—Canada—History. I. Title.
E92.BK74 2003   353.534'97071   C2003–901119–4

1 2 3 4 – 06 05 04 03

This book is printed on permanent (acid-free) paper ∞.
Printed in Canada

Contents

'Its [*sic*] a great work, its [*sic*] a thankless task, but behind all the seeming indifference of the Indian for the officials of the Department, I am glad to say that in their heart, they know the Department is watching with a fatherly eye to their care and protection.'

—John Daly, Indian agent, 1930

'The rhetoric of power all too easily produces an illusion of benevolence when deployed in an imperial setting.'

—Edward Said, *Culture and Imperialism* (New York: Knopf, 1993), xvii.

Acknowledgements

The process leading to this book has taken many years, and I have had a lot of help along the way. The book began as a doctoral dissertation, and the members of my thesis committee all provided considerable support and expertise. My supervisor, Sylvia Van Kirk, was particularly helpful in developing a coherent organization and in furthering my analysis of the material. She has also generally offered strong backing for my work from my early graduate years to the present. I am most grateful to my other two committee members as well, Ian Radforth and Mark McGowan. Ian Radforth has been a reliable source of encouragement, knowledge, and sound advice for many years. For his part, Mark McGowan exceeded his official role as 'third' committee member, investing significant time, energy, and intellectual engagement. All my committee members also made valuable suggestions about additions that would improve the work as it proceeded towards becoming a publishable book.

There were other scholars who helped me as well. The late Franz Koennecke, Aboriginal claims researcher and historian of the Wasauksing (formerly Parry Island) Reserve, helped me generously in the early stages of my research. In addition to offering useful advice and his own considerable historical knowledge, Mr Koennecke made his personal collection of Indian Affairs documents available to me, which became one of the most important sources of material for the work at hand (these materials are housed at the office of Wasauksing First Nation, where Mr Koennecke was the claims researcher for many years). He also assisted in my attempts to contact potential interview candidates for oral history interviews. In this connection, I would like to thank Rosamund Vanderburgh for the information she provided about possible interviewees.

Special thanks go to my interview subjects for sharing their time and knowledge with me: Nonie Bristol of Syracuse, New York, granddaughter of John Daly, who tempered my view of her grandfather's character; Verna Johnston of Cape Croker, who made time for a telephone interview when she was struggling with health issues; Don Fisher of Wikwemikong, Lyle Jones of Parry Sound, and Aileen Rice of Wasauksing, all of whom offered all the information they had that they thought might help me out. I would like to thank Verna Johnston, Don Fisher, and Aileen Rice with an Ojibway *meegwetch* as well.

Two other women deserve recognition for their part in helping me begin to understand what it means to be Aboriginal in this society. Susan Beaver, a Mohawk of the

Six Nations reserve, and Karen Huska, a Mohawk through the maternal line, shared their friendship with me during the tense summer of 1990 when the Sécurité de Québec and then Canada's armed forces confronted their people at Kanesatake and Kahnawake. That experience, which occurred just before I entered the doctoral program, was decisive for me, as it was for many other Canadians. The Oka crisis reaffirmed my commitment to understand the history of colonialism in Canada and to work towards justice, equality, and full Aboriginal rights for First Nations people. For their friendship and comradeship in that time, I thank Susan and Karen: *nia:wen*.

All the women in the Inter-Library Loan department at Robarts Library earned my gratitude for their good humour and patience in processing dozens of microfilm reels from the National Archives. The staff at Wasauksing Community Centre showed equal goodwill in photocopying reams of paper from Franz Koennecke's collection. And Father Patrick J. Boyle, SJ, of the Jesuit Archives, has been unfailingly helpful and interested in my project.

I wish to acknowledge the generous support of the Social Sciences and Humanities Research Council of Canada while I originally researched and wrote this work. And while their support took a different form from that of the SSHRC, Valerie Korinek and Elspeth Heaman helped temendously with their friendship, camaraderie, and humour as we went through the doctoral program together and worked to finish our dissertations.

Kate McPherson, who supervised my postdoctoral work at York University, was instrumental in getting me started on the revision process, engaging meaningfully with the dissertation and making a series of valuable suggestions for transforming it into a book. Arthur Silver picked up the ball after her, reading the thesis in his turn, making many useful observations about the early revised chapters, and encouraging me in a way that made a great difference. Their assurance that the project was worthwhile carried me a long way in the early stages of revision.

In the last phase of creating this book, I was fortunate enough to land at the History Department of the University of Manitoba, where I joined a community of active, productive, intellectually engaged scholars. Here I found an academic home that has far exceeded my expectations for collegiality, encouragement, and generosity of spirit. My colleagues from History, Native Studies, English, and other departments have given me useful feedback on sections of the book I gave as papers, as well as on the other work I have pursued here. For their support and commentary on Chapter 6, thanks to the members of my Canadian history writing group: Julie Guard, Esyllt Jones, Tamara Myers, and Adele Perry. I would also like to thank the anonymous readers for their comments, particularly the final reader, whose observations were very thoughtful and knowledgeable.

Finally, I would like to thank my partner Roewan for eight years of love, work, and joy. At every stage of this book's development, she was there—listening, challenging, reading draft chapters, helping me work out the tough bits, offering initiating energy when I seemed to have none. Her caring heart, big soul, unfailing sense of perspective, and enthusiasm for intellectual endeavour carried me through the difficult times and helped me sustain the momentum I needed to complete this project. This book is dedicated to her.

Introduction

In the spring of 1933, Indian agent John Daly summoned to his Parry Sound office the chief and both councillors of the nearby Parry Island band (now Wasauksing First Nation).[1] These men—Chief John Manitowaba, his son Stanley Manitowaba, and Francis Pegahmagabow—were three of the most prominent challengers to his authority the Indian agent faced. His purpose in assembling the men was to read them a letter from the Department of Indian Affairs (DIA), ordering them not to write to the department any more. All contact with Indian Affairs was to pass through the agent, and he alone would take care of any issue that arose on the reserve. In other words, the elected representatives of the people of Parry Island were blocked from direct access to the government office that managed all their affairs. The only permitted interaction with the all-powerful department would be through its local agent, whether they were satisfied with his work or not. While the DIA had always shown considerable reluctance to engage in direct contact with First Nations people, in 1933 the mediating position of the Indian agent became official policy.[2] The effect of this practice was to entrench Indian agents as power brokers between the department and its 'wards', while insulating internal, decision-making officials from the inconvenience of negotiating with the real people affected by their choices.

Both the policy itself and the manner of its announcement were characteristic of Aboriginal-government relations at the time. Indeed, while this study deals with the period between the two world wars, many of the problems it identifies predated this era and persisted at least until the 1960s. Indian Affairs was very much a 'top-down' colonial system designed to concentrate decision-making power in the hands of non-Native bureaucrats. While Aboriginal leaders repeatedly challenged the department's right to manage their affairs, the Indian department maintained its supremacy until the 1960s, when a new political climate made it possible for First Nations people to begin expelling their Indian agents.[3]

Parry Sound Agent Daly was a World War I veteran and fond of the simple military chain of command. Upon learning, shortly after their meeting, that Francis Pegahmagabow had gone home and promptly written another letter to the DIA,

Daly again called the band councillor into his office. The agent then informed Pegahmagabow, who was himself a highly decorated war veteran, that an 'order' from the Department of Indian Affairs 'must be carried out.' It was Daly's duty to explain this 'the same as the officers in the field explained orders from head-quarters to the troops in the field.'[4] Although not all Indian agents took such a dog-matic view, Daly was expressing an essentially universal sentiment among department officials, in keeping with their colonizing role: First Nations people held a subordinate rank and were supposed to defer to DIA authority. The Indian Affairs system was designed to ensure that control of First Nations communities, resources, and politics remained firmly in the hands of federal officials.

This book addresses the destructive legacy of the Indian Affairs system in Canada. It does so by examining a significant and little-scrutinized area of Aborig-inal-government relations: namely, the interaction between Indian agents and Abo-riginal people. From the 1830s, when the assimilation policy was adopted, to the 1960s, this was where the government and its wards met face to face. The Indian agent was the local DIA official who represented the federal government on Cana-dian reserves. His job was to implement federal policy, enforce the Indian Act, and manage First Nations communities. During the era under consideration, the Indian agent was always Euro-Canadian. While decisions on important matters were made by officials in Ottawa, their conclusions were based on information and advice pro-vided by the agents on the ground. Relatively less important questions were often decided directly by the agent. This official was thus a pivotal figure in Aboriginal-government relations. His views, attitudes, and personal qualities decisively influ-enced the experiences of First Nations people in their interactions with government. The Indian agent system had a deep psychological impact on Aborig-inal people, one that appears to be almost entirely negative. That impact is most starkly revealed in present-day comments on Indian agents, which uniformly depict these officials as agents of oppression, neglect, and injustice. What has remained, then, is the memory of a government-sponsored tyranny that deprived Aboriginal people of virtually all of their autonomy.

The application of Indian policy is examined here in the form of two case stud-ies of Ontario Indian agents, John Daly and Robert Lewis, who served in the inter-war period. John McLean Daly was appointed to the Parry Sound agency, on the eastern shore of Georgian Bay, in 1922 and remained there until his retirement in 1939. Robert J. Lewis, of the Manitowaning agency on Manitoulin Island, was agent from 1915 to 1939. Both occupied their postings for relatively long periods—17 years and 24 years, respectively—and served in a single agency throughout their tenure.[5] Although Lewis began his work earlier than Daly, their careers cover sub-stantially the same era. Their agencies were adjacent to each other, meeting on the north shore of Georgian Bay, and were closely similar in topography and climate. These similarities make the two agents appropriate subjects for comparison. At the same time, Lewis and Daly were very different in character—Daly, a committed paternalist, took a proactive and controlling approach to his job, while Lewis leaned much more towards liberal individualism and a non-interventionist practice. Their differences permit an analysis of the varying styles that could be brought to the work, and of the effects of personality differences on policy implementation and on Native people themselves. Moreover, political conditions were quite different in the two agencies and provide interesting contrasts. The body of this work, then, pursues the theme of Indian department fieldwork on its most intimate and practical level. It details the decisions, actions, and attitudes of two individual field officials who operated in Ontario in the interwar period, and demonstrates their impact on the Native communities under their jurisdiction.

Using a case-study approach in which the careers and activities of the two Indian agents are carefully analyzed, this study asks a series of questions about the impact of government policies on the everyday lives of First Nations people. How did Indian agents use the powers delegated to them by the Indian department? What happened when abstract policies met real-life situations in all their complexity and specificity? How did Indian agents reconcile federal goals with the needs and interests of Aboriginal people whom they knew personally? In the face of the woeful inadequacy of federal Indian policy to cope with twentieth-century realities, did the agents in the field develop new strategies better suited to the contemporary situation, or did they continue to apply outdated principles and methods? How did First Nations people influence the process, and what goals can be discerned from their actions? Why does the issue of agents refusing various kinds of assistance loom so large in community memory?

There is some attention here, too, to the role of officials located in Ottawa. Internal officials such as secretaries J.D. McLean and A.F. Mackenzie wielded an astonishing amount of power, in spite of the modest titles they bore. These men (they were all men)[6] made decisions on a daily basis, from the trivial to the profoundly important, that affected First Nations people and communities. Although they received a steady flow of information filtered through the Indian agents, they had little direct experience with First Nations people and were insulated by geography and government structure from a more intimate knowledge of the department's wards. What was their role in applying federal policy? Did they demonstrate any adaptation to changing conditions, or any self-consciousness about their part in stifling Aboriginal political development? What was their relationship with Indian agents, and how did the Ottawa bureaucrats and field agents work together?

The Indian department in this period operated in a context of substantial public indifference towards Aboriginal affairs. With Euro-Canadian concerns about land apparently settled and First Nations people largely confined to their reserves, most mainstream Canadians turned a blind eye to other matters relating to Aboriginal peoples.[7] Thus, DIA officials could safely assume that their actions would not attract much attention from the general public. When major disputes arose, as when the department forcibly imposed an elected council on the Six Nations reserve in 1924, the newspapers tended to be sympathetic to the Aboriginal side.[8] But media interest was never sustained enough to have an impact. There were still missionaries working with Aboriginal people who intervened with the Indian department on specific issues and who, potentially, could keep an eye on the department's activities. But even the Jesuits at Wikwemikong, who were skeptical of the federal government's intentions and opposed Agent Lewis on several occasions, spoke out only on certain issues, and typically they demanded more, not less, government interference.[9] In any event, missionaries usually supported most of the department's methods and the general assimilative thrust of Indian policy. On the whole, then, First Nations people had no reliable allies in efforts to check the power of the Department of Indian Affairs.

The Indian Agent's Legacy

Like so much of First Nations history, the concerns addressed here have relevance to the contemporary situation. In current Aboriginal writings, Indian agents are often viewed as front-line enforcers of colonial oppression. They appear in phrases such as 'the all-powerful Indian agent' and 'nobody got help from the Indian agent.'[10] Histories authored by Aboriginal people invariably mention this official, and always in negative terms.[11] Burton Jacobs, former chief of the Walpole Island First Nation, has written about agents in an article on his campaign to expel the Indian agent from his reserve.[12] Jacobs had few positive words to say about the system, which he viewed as ensuring the direct control of the agent over all important matters related to the reserve. He noted that the chief and council were 'virtually powerless' and that 'in all the years that the agents had been acting for the Indian people, they made no significant advancements.' He also stated succinctly, 'The agent was the top dog, and there was no mistaking it.'[13] In Jacobs's experience, the expulsion of the Indian agent and move to self-rule were preconditions for a series of positive developments on Walpole Island.

DIA records strongly support the argument that Indian agents in the twentieth century were a primary source of oppression for Aboriginal people. These officials acted in ways that reinforced the subordination, marginalization, and disempowerment of First Nations people. This outcome was a direct result of the paternalistic Indian Affairs system, which relegated all meaningful authority over local Aboriginal affairs to the Indian agent. Agents justified their actions, and indeed their jobs, on the grounds that they provided necessary services that First Nations communities could not provide for themselves. This belief underscores the racist assumptions on which the system was based and the inability of the officials responsible for it to envision Aboriginal self-determination. The agent was one of the primary means by which federal officials secured and maintained government domination over First Nations peoples.

The ideological position of an individual Indian agent powerfully shaped his response to the Aboriginal predicament of the period, and thus the nature of his impact on his clients. To a large extent, this ideological position was a function of his understanding of race and the place that Aboriginal people ought to take in Canadian society. The two agents examined here took distinctive approaches towards their work and Aboriginal people. Agent John Daly of Parry Sound tended to view the people as a culturally and racially distinct group with their own lifestyle, economic pursuits, and rights. Particularly in the early years of his career, he endeavoured to influence Indian policy in the direction of facilitating the people's pursuit of 'traditional' economic activities.[14] For example, he advocated designating a large fishing ground for the people of Shawanaga, and sought more than once to enlarge hunting rights. He also condemned the practice of forcing Aboriginal guides to pay for guiding licences, arguing that they had fished and hunted in the area from time immemorial and therefore had a prior right to do so. Thus, there was room in Daly's world for the retention of 'traditional' Aboriginal skills and cultural traits, as well as a dimly recognized prior claim to certain occupations and resources.

Agent Robert Lewis of Manitowaning, on the other hand, evinced little sympathy for the notion of maintaining Aboriginal ways. Those who lived in the bush, far from Lewis's home and the reserves where they were members, were merely an administrative inconvenience to him. He was not interested in facilitating their retention of bush skills and ways of life. Lewis argued for permitting the people to fish for personal use, but never spoke in terms of an Aboriginal or prior right to natural resources. On the whole, this agent gave no indication that he viewed the people as a distinct cultural group. Rather, in keeping with his official role as assimilative agent, he viewed them simply as individuals who needed to live according to the values of Euro-Canadian society. Those who did so ceased to be 'Indians' in his eyes, and this he viewed as a positive development. Although he did not undertake active measures to suppress Aboriginal cultures or force the assimilation process, Lewis wished to see increasing numbers assimilating entirely to mainstream world views and occupations.

In part, the variance in perspectives between these two agents probably reflects diverging economic realities in their respective agencies. On Manitoulin Island, hunting was no longer a viable pursuit, and guiding tourists was not a readily available option for Aboriginal men unless they travelled to the mainland to do so. Instead, many men of the Manitowaning agency performed wage labour for much of the year, primarily in the forest and transportation industries. A significant number of the Manitoulin Island people also farmed. Thus, although some people at Wikwemikong and elsewhere still fished, in their paid work the people did not make extensive use of the kinds of skills Euro-Canadians regarded as typically Aboriginal, especially hunting and canoe tripping skills. Around Parry Sound, by contrast, there was much greater scope for these skills. For one thing, there was still game in the area and some men retained an identity as hunters. Perhaps more importantly, the thriving tourist industry of the 1920s relied heavily on Aboriginal guides to satisfy the tourists' desire for a wilderness experience offering hunting, fishing, camping, and canoeing. Thus, a reasonably respectable economic role for Aboriginal skills was integrated into the local Euro-Canadian economy. Indeed, the locals needed Aboriginal people with this particular skill set to help attract the wealthy tourists who bolstered the economy. This reality created a market for the sale of wilderness skills and an appreciation of their value among Euro-Canadians. Neither of these factors was present on Manitoulin Island.

In addition to these local differences, the two agents differed greatly in their personalities. Daly, an active man himself, had a healthy respect for a successful hunter, which was reflected in his comments on certain men of his agency. As a proud war veteran, he clearly admired the scouting and sharpshooting skills that hunters developed, and that had distinguished many Aboriginal soldiers during the Great War (including Francis Pegahmagabow, one of Daly's foremost adversaries). He also had a romantic streak that predisposed him to value traditional or pre-modern cultures, including his own Scottish Highlander roots. Thus, despite his habit of disparaging Native people in his correspondence, Daly was not committed to erasing their cultural difference, especially their adherence to long-practised subsistence strategies. He did not seem to prefer one type of economic strategy over another, so long as the people provided for themselves. In other words, Daly was not personally committed to the principle of assimilation.

In all these ways Daly differed significantly from his fellow agent. Lewis, although old enough to do so, did not choose to enlist during World War I. He never spoke admiringly of outdoorsmanship or Aboriginal bush skills. He never made reference to Native people's prior occupation of Canada, and his correspondence is largely devoid of sentiment. Lewis gave no indication of valuing Aboriginal cultural traits. When he spoke favourably of his clients, it was invariably because he recognized them as hard workers or because they had successfully adopted Euro-Canadian occupations and attitudes towards work. He was conspicuously more reluctant than Daly to extend aid, especially monetary aid. In his first years, Lewis apparently supported the policy of enfranchisement, although he retreated from this position when he observed that previous enfranchisees had fared poorly. Nevertheless, he continued to favour their assimilation into Euro-Canadian society, through erasure of their differences. Most of the time his efforts seemed narrowly oriented towards promoting the people's successful adaptation to the liberal individualistic ethic of his time. Much of the present study will be devoted to analyzing the ways in which these and related differences affected the First Nations people whose lives these men administered.

Assimilation and Control

In his study of the history of Canadian Indian policy, historian John L. Tobias stated that between 1933 and 1945 Indian Affairs relied on ad hoc decisions and showed 'an obvious lack of policy or policy goal'.[15] It is true that, even by the 1920s, the department lacked clearly stated policies and did not seem to guide itself by well-defined goals. At the same time, there were two unmistakable policy orientations in the period: assimilation and control. Assimilation was championed particularly vehemently by Deputy Superintendent General Duncan Campbell Scott, whose well-known poetry depicted Aboriginal people as a 'weird and waning race'.[16] Although his poems were full of romanticized, often tragic, portrayals of Aboriginal people, Scott was not interested in preserving their cultural distinctiveness, and his administrative work was explicitly geared to stamping it out. He pursued his goal of assimilation mainly by means of compulsory education and new legislation simplifying the enfranchisement process. Assimilation, then, was an explicit element of federal policy. Control, by contrast, was never acknowledged as an official aim of policy or legislation. Yet the intent to maintain political control over First Nations communities was obvious both in the Indian Act and in the behaviour of

Indian agents and other department officials. In fact, while assimilation remained a distant goal in the interwar period, the objective of maintaining control was readily attainable. Much of the time it appeared to be the real first principle of Indian policy.

Initially, control was ostensibly intended to serve the larger goal of moulding Aboriginal people into assimilated, working-class members of Euro-Canadian society with a commitment to middle-class values. But by the interwar period, control had become a goal in itself, especially since it both justified and facilitated the agents' own work. The ideal that hovered before the officials' eyes was a quiet, hard-working, co-operative set of clients who offered no opposition to the agent's or the Indian department's authority. Agents did not want to hear about unfulfilled treaty provisions, unresolved grievances about lands and unsurrendered islands, or the argument of some that an outsider was not required to run the reserve. They did not want to see band councils used as political instruments to empower First Nations communities—the councils were designed merely as convenient hand-maidens of DIA policy. Whenever the elected leaders attempted to reach beyond their extremely limited jurisdiction to matters of political importance, they ran headlong into the department's restrictive regulations and the determined opposition of its agents.

Leadership Roles and Expectations

One of the most significant factors shaping the interaction between Indian agents and First Nations people was the cultural gulf. The agents were certainly conscious of differences between themselves and their involuntary clients, which they generally ascribed to a combination of individual character and racial/cultural traits. But, like their fellow Euro-Canadians, they underestimated the social and philosophical differences between the two cultural systems and assumed the superiority of their own belief system. The agents expected Aboriginal people to make choices based on goals and values substantially similar to their own. In the light of more recent analysis, however, it is clear that Aboriginal priorities were significantly different. Cultural disparity meant, among other things, that Indian agents were bound to offend First Nations people in a number of important ways and to violate certain Aboriginal standards. Their cultural transgressions were particularly significant in regard to the expectations placed on Aboriginal leaders, expectations that were clearly transferred to Indian agents.

It is unlikely that most Indian agents thought of themselves as leaders, except in the sense that they were expected to exert moral leadership and provide positive role models. Although they were clearly aware of exercising authority, in Euro-Canadian terms they were not leaders, for they operated largely according to instructions from above. Yet their presence, their power, and the system they represented displaced and largely destroyed indigenous systems of leadership and authority, as more recent Aboriginal commentators have noted.[17] The elected band council imposed by the Indian Act was not used to replace the old leaders with new ones who would have similar authority among their people. But someone had to be found to exercise certain essential functions formerly performed by chiefs, such as dispute mediation and assistance to those in need. From the perspective of First Nations people, the agents were often the most obvious successors to the chiefs for such tasks, particularly in view of their access to band funds and DIA money.

Aboriginal concepts of the leadership role were markedly different from the European model of hierarchical, class-based, coercive authority. The Ojibway, Odawa, and Mohawks (the main nations living in the agencies studied here) had disparate cultures and systems of government, but they shared the principle that leaders generally did not have the power to impose obedience on anyone. Chiefs made decisions, but the people abided by these decisions of their own free will and could choose at any time to disregard them or stop following a chief. Further, when chiefs made important decisions they generally did so in close consultation with their people. At treaty negotiations, for example, there were frequent pauses to permit the main negotiators to discuss matters with each other and with the rest of their people. These leaders sought to obtain consensus before agreeing to a treaty.

Among the Ojibway, there was often provision for passing the chief's position within a certain family line, but leaders were still chosen for displaying certain desirable qualities. The qualities typically sought were wisdom, generosity, good judgement, hunting ability, and courage and success in war. The Reverend Peter Jones, whose mother was Ojibway, wrote the following words in the mid-nineteenth century about the Ojibway system of government:

> The chiefs are the heads or fathers of their respective tribes; but their authority extends no further than to their own body, while their influence depends much upon their wisdom, bravery, and hospitality. . . . they govern more by persuasion than by coercion. Whenever their acts give general dissatisfaction their power ceases.[18]

Hospitality and generosity were among the most important requirements for a chief. As a commentator wrote in the 1930s, '[t]he people demanded from their chiefs liberality above all things.'[19] This required not only skill in hunting, but also willingness to share the bounty freely (a culturally approved trait generally). An Ojibway man in the 1920s, for instance, described how his father, a chief, deliberately obtained surplus food to distribute among his people.[20] It was clearly considered part of his role. In addition to habitual largesse, leaders were expected to supply food when individuals were in need, as well as collect contributions from other members of the group. As we will see, this expectation was probably transferred to Indian agents.

In contrast, the role and expectations of Indian agents within their own society, and particularly within the Indian department, were founded on fundamentally different premises. These officials operated in a race- and class-based hierarchical framework that assigned First Nations people one of the lowest positions. Unlike the chiefs before them, they assumed the right to exercise compulsion, and they had the means to do so. There was no question of seeking consensus or consulting with Aboriginal people about policy issues. The autocratic manner in which they asserted their authority is one of the most common complaints about these officials today. As a Mohawk elder recently remarked, 'When we used to have Indian agents, they were the dictator. . . . I was glad when we got rid of them once and for all.'[21]

Another obvious distinction between the chiefs and the Indian agents was the selection process. Native people were not asked about their wishes when agents were appointed, and in the few instances when they suggested candidates, these were rejected.[22] Once an agent was hired, he was practically immune from the criticism of his clients.[23] Vigorous complaints about certain issues might mean the official was required to make further explanations, but this was typically the end of the matter. Unpopular agents frequently retained their positions for many years, and when agents were fired it was due to their superiors' dissatisfaction, not to any Aboriginal concerns. The department's selection criteria did not include wisdom, generosity, or ability to provide; if some agents had these qualities, this was coincidental. Agents were generally hired because they had connections with the political party in power in Ottawa at the time.

Above all, the two systems diverged on the issue of generosity. In contrast to Aboriginal traditions, the Indian department expected its agents to exercise 'strict economy' (a favourite phrase), spending no more than was absolutely necessary. The department's watchword was 'training the Indians to be self-sufficient'. This often meant turning down those who asked for help. The refusal of help is another frequent motif in current reminiscences about Indian agents. On the Tobique Reserve in New Brunswick, for example, the Indian agent from the 1920s and 1930s is remembered primarily as someone who failed to help those in need.[24] It should be noted that the agents' correspondence frequently records instances of assistance, and that careful attention was paid to aiding the sick and elderly (though at a bare subsistence level). But in the Aboriginal tradition, one who was in a position to help was bound to do so when asked. It was here that the agents violated the traditional culture, for they helped some and not others. These officials were also perceived as stingy in the help they did give, especially since they were always wealthier than their clients and, in addition, had access to government resources as well as the band funds. Perceiving this, First Nations people clearly expected behaviour that matched their own standards. Their disappointment on this score is deeply inscribed in the community memory of Indian agents.

The Cultural Gulf

Misunderstandings occurred in other areas as well. Here it is useful to explore briefly the areas of culture not accounted for by material needs or political power, that is, social and spiritual beliefs, and those attributes—sense of self, sense of community, purpose, meaning—that derive from those beliefs and form the basis of our actions and expectations. These more intangible aspects of culture—world view, ideas, patterns of interaction, values, aspirations, perceptions, habits—are probably the least susceptible to change, and here, even in the present day, the gulf between Aboriginal and newcomer cultures has remained.

One of the most prominent writers on this subject is Rupert Ross, a Euro-Canadian Crown attorney who works with many First Nations teachers.[25] Ross has been criticized for generalizing his conclusions to First Nations people all across Canada, but he has worked most closely with Ojibway and Oji-Cree people from northern Ontario whose cultural traits would have much in common with the Georgian Bay Ojibway who are the main focus here.[26] Ross's analysis reveals important insights for an understanding of how the Indian agents violated First Nations cultural principles. He notes several basic characteristics of Aboriginal cultures, which include a central ethic of non-interference as well as rules about avoiding public anger and public expressions of praise and gratitude.[27] The ethic of non-interference, originally identified by Mohawk psychiatrist Dr Clare Brant, prescribes that it is rude, arrogant, and culturally unacceptable to interfere 'in any way with the rights, privileges and activities of another person'.[28] For the same reasons, it is impolite and inappropriate to give advice or even comment on someone's behaviour when not specifically requested to do so. It does not require a great deal of imagination to recognize the degree to which Indian agents typically violated this code: indeed, the central purpose of their job was to interfere in the communal, social, and personal lives of the people.

Ross has also identified other rules that are equally foreign to the Indian agents' own cultural patterns. He suggests, for example, that in Ojibway and Oji-Cree societies, anger should generally be kept to oneself and not displayed in public; similarly, praise should not be expressed in public, since it involves singling someone out and suggesting, by implication, that the one praised is valued more highly than others. Both these principles are geared towards maintaining community harmony. This sort of reticence in public behaviour is undoubtedly one source of the belief within the DIA that the people were undemonstrative 'ingrates' who failed to appreciate the officials' work. Ross states that the Ojibway and Oji-Cree cultures do not expect people to show gratitude or express thanks for acts such as sharing food or other resources: it is simply understood that sharing is the correct thing to do. In fact, many Aboriginal languages lack an equivalent to the English word 'please'.[29]

As a result of these cultural differences, Indian agents clearly acted in ways that were frowned upon among their clients. An Indian agent who was dutiful and conscientious within his own framework would appear to Aboriginal people as a rude, arrogant meddler who had the bad manners to show anger, disagree publicly with others, and damage community harmony by openly expressing criticism and praise. The agents, for their part, were often disappointed in their interactions with First Nations people. They did not always receive the expected gratitude for the help they extended or for the other work they did as officials. Given the importance placed in the Euro-Canadian context on showing gratitude even for small favours, the agents often concluded that their services were not appreciated because they received no overt thanks. In consequence, the agents might become less inclined to offer help, since they did not receive the reward of gratitude and increased co-operation that the Euro-Canadian world view taught them to expect.

The major cultural differences between First Nations people and DIA personnel raised a significant barrier to understanding between the two groups. They were also, no doubt, an important factor in the failure of Indian policy to attain its goals. As Ross has pointed out, Indian policy was based on the unexamined assumption that Aboriginal people would respond to a given situation in the same manner as Euro-Canadians.[30] Yet many times they did not. The often-expressed frustrations of the Indian agents about the people's choices were a measure of this cultural dissonance. Lacking awareness of the differing principles that motivated Aboriginal choices, the agents were inclined instead to draw negative conclusions about their clients. In turn, they acted on these conclusions in approaching their work. In this way the cultural gulf resulted in a climate of mutual distrust and incomprehension.

Sources and Parameters

This book examines a neglected period in the history of these First Nations through the lens of the servants of the Indian department. It is thus a study in Aboriginal-white relations, and particularly in Aboriginal-government relations. Virtually all the records on which it is based were written from a Euro-Canadian perspective, in a time when racist ideas were accepted as truth. They convey a sense of race relations when First Nations people were ill-equipped to influence government or public perceptions. They describe the means by which Indian agents attempted to control Aboriginal communities and to further the 'civilization' and assimilation of First Nations people. Read 'against the grain', these records can be used to reconstruct some aspects of Aboriginal lives in the period. They also allow some limited insights into the resistance waged individually and collectively by First Nations people.

The focus here is on Ontario, where so much of Canadian Indian policy was developed and pioneered. Upper Canada witnessed the institution of treaty-making to obtain the surrender of Aboriginal land; the reserve system with its emphasis on settlement and agriculture; and the official government program of Christianizing First Nations people and assimilating them into Euro-Canadian society. Aboriginal people in this region of Canada have a long history of interaction with non-Aboriginals: first with the fur traders and missionaries who were the advance guard of the European invasion, and later with government officials. Yet in spite of this extended period of European and Euro-Canadian influence, cultural assimilation was as unsuccessful in Ontario as elsewhere in Canada. In the 1920s, approximately 21,000 recognized or 'status' Indians lived in Ontario, representing about 20 per cent of the status Indian population of Canada.[31] Significant numbers of 'non-status' and 'non-treaty' Indians lived there as well, some of them on the reserves, but no statistics on their numbers are available. The people embraced by this study are largely those who lived on reserves.

The information presented here is primarily based on the records of the Indian agents themselves and their superiors in Ottawa. Attempts to employ oral history in First Nations communities did not prove fruitful, largely because of the relative shortage of elders of sufficient age to have lived in the 1920s and 1930s.[32] Younger individuals seemed to have few detailed memories of Indian agents.[33] I also experienced difficulty in accessing potential interview candidates as an outsider who was not directly involved in these communities. The absence of oral history in this work thus does not indicate a dismissal of its relevance or validity; rather, it is indicative of the challenge confronting researchers in their attempt to integrate oral testimony into traditional, document-based historical scholarship.

The letterbooks of Robert Lewis, agent at Manitowaning on Manitoulin Island, are available for the years 1915 to 1934 in Record Group 10 at the National Archives. The original agency records of John Daly of the Parry Sound agency apparently no longer exist.[34] The bulk of the information on Daly contained in this study is derived from the extensive material collected by the late historian Franz Koennecke, who examined Daly's correspondence at the Department of Indian Affairs and Northern Development in the 1970s. Mr Koennecke very kindly allowed me access to his photocopies and notes, which are housed on Wasauksing (Parry Island) Reserve.[35] In addition, I consulted a wide variety of DIA records: reports of inspectors of Indian agencies; departmental circulars; the case files of the Soldier Settlement program; files organized according to different topics, such as 'Roads and Bridges', 'Minutes of Band Council Meetings', and other themes.

These materials provide an abundance of information, but they have obvious shortcomings that should be noted at the outset. Above all, they were generated as official documents that would become part of the public record. Although some of the letters in Franz Koennecke's collection are exchanges with people who were not DIA employees, all of the letters relate to agency matters, and Daly had included them in his files in the agent's office. Lewis's available letters are also exclusively official correspondence. Moreover, in his case they include only the letters he wrote, not those sent to him by others. Such communications, of course, would normally omit information that reflected badly on department officers. As Stan Dragland has remarked of DIA annual reports, 'self-justification is a convention of the genre.'[36] The agents constructed their accounts to the department in such a way as to justify their own position, excluding information they thought would contradict their viewpoint. Although Daly frequently recorded the actions and statements of his Native clients in his letters, these are naturally very selective, biased portrayals of events and must be read with great caution and skepticism. When analyzed with care, they offer some evidence about the Aboriginal side of interactions. They are, however, at best partial, fragmented depictions of Aboriginal points of view; at worst, they might be egregious distortions.

In the case of the Parry Sound agency, some documents generated by First Nations individuals have been preserved. These include letters written to Daly and to the department by some of the agent's most active opponents. Thus, Daly's accounts are supplemented to some extent by information stemming from the people themselves. For the most part, these communications correspond quite well with the agent's portrayal of conflict situations. They also provide a fuller picture of the interactions between Daly and his clients. Lewis's correspondence, by contrast, is limited to the agent's own writings, but some conclusions may be drawn through comparisons of his letters to Aboriginal people themselves, to the department, and to other individuals who contacted the agent. It has been possible in some instances to supplement Lewis's correspondence with the records of the

Jesuit missionaries at Wikwemikong. Generally, it has been necessary to analyze the sources judiciously and with due regard to their bias and incompleteness. Unfortunately, the records contain gaps, so it was not always possible to discover the outcome of specific situations.

Finally, this study's account of the Parry Sound agency concentrates heavily on one reserve in this agency, Parry Island (now Wasauksing First Nation). This focus is again a consequence of the available sources, for Mr Koennecke collected his records in the course of conducting research on the Parry Island Reserve.[37] Other bands receive mention from time to time in these documents, so they are not entirely absent, but they are significantly under-represented. At the same time, Daly's agency diaries reveal that this reserve, which was located close to his home, occupied a substantial portion of his time. Parry Island, along with Shawanaga, was one of only two reserves in the agency that Daly could reach in a single day, and he visited there often. Moreover, political opposition to the agent seems to have been particularly strong and persistent among this band, as well as among the Shawanaga band, which was not far distant from Parry Island and had close links with its residents. A letter written by Daly in 1924 suggests that the agent himself perceived these two bands as his most vigorous opponents. He submitted the minutes of a Parry Island band council meeting to the department and complained, 'I would like to take this opportunity of drawing the attention of the Department to the tone of these minutes, and to state that the same feeling exists at Shawanaga. In other words, these two bands have the idea that what is passed by the Council should be accepted by the Dept.'[38] There is no indication that the focus on Parry Island creates a distorted picture of Daly's activities as agent, but it should be remembered that the present account is partial in this respect as well.

It is necessary to say a few words about the use of language in this study. As a Euro-Canadian scholar writing about First Nations history, I have had to make choices about language, particularly in selecting the preferred terms to use when referring to First Nations people themselves. I have rejected the word 'Indian' because of its pejorative connotations (past and present), and also because so many First Nations people today reject it. This word appears here only in direct quotations, or when referring specifically to questions of status under the Indian Act. The terms that are presently most acceptable among the people themselves are 'Aboriginal', 'Native', and 'First Nations' people.[39] For this reason, I have employed these three terms interchangeably. By using 'First Nations' I do not intend to exclude those who have some white ancestors, nor have I attempted to differentiate among people according to such criteria. In southern Ontario, Aboriginal people with *no* non-Aboriginal ancestors are relatively rare, and the term 'First Nations' is widely used for those of Aboriginal descent and/or culture. Where possible, I have also used the word 'Anishinabek', which usually refers to the descendants of the Ojibway, Odawa, and Potawatomi.[40]

In referring to those representing the dominant, Euro-Canadian society, I have used Euro-Canadian, white, non-Aboriginal, or non-Native, despite the awkwardness of all these terms. Immigrants to Canada have never been exclusively European, but in the Georgian Bay area white people, or Euro-Canadians, made up the vast majority of the non-Aboriginal population, and they certainly monopolized social and economic power. I have most often used the term 'white' when addressing issues of race and racial constructs. The expression 'Whiteman' (often written as one word) appeared frequently in the agents' correspondence and functioned as a racial-cultural concept that was extremely important to them. All of these dilemmas around terminology are, of course, part of the colonial legacy. Euro-Canadians invented most of these terms and invested them with their own meanings, which haunt the language to this day.

I make use of terms such as 'race', 'racism', and 'class' in this book as well, so it is appropriate to explain what these terms mean in the present context. 'Race' is a notoriously difficult concept to define, but I use it here to refer to the socially constructed categories by which Canadians (especially Euro-Canadians) differentiated among social groups distinguished mainly by their physical appearance, language, social behaviour, and cultural characteristics.[41] Despite the many differences of language, nation, and cultural practice among First Nations people in Canada, Euro-Canadians perceived them as a single race, which they denoted as 'Indians' and treated as essentially homogeneous. 'Racism' is the practice of making invidious distinctions based on perceived 'race', a practice that operates (consciously or unconsciously) in the interest of preserving the dominance of a single 'racial' group and maintaining the marginalization of the rest. 'Class' is an economic and social categorization based on a complex of factors such as income level, type of occupation, cultural values, and relationship to the means of production. Those belonging to the working class do not own the means of production, have only their own labour power to sell, usually perform physical or manual labour, and typically have little access to formal avenues of power. As I have noted, the intent of Indian policy was to integrate Aboriginal people into working-class status and occupations. At the same time, they were supposed to adopt values associated with the middle class, such as an endorsement of work for its own sake (not as an instrumental means of making a living), conformity to social and sexual respectability, and above all, a liberal individualism that rejected Aboriginal forms of collective property ownership, economic co-operation, and community reciprocity.

A brief overview of the book's structure and content is in order. Chapter 1 introduces the people of the Manitowaning and Parry Sound agencies, outlining their histories, treaty relations with government, and economies. It also introduces the geographic areas and some background information about non-Aboriginal settlement and the Euro-Canadian economy. Chapter 2 looks at the administrative structure of the Indian department, the powers of the agents, and the duties they were expected to fulfill. The remaining chapters examine particular topics that emerged from the records. Chapter 3 looks at the activities of the band councils and explores the most overtly political contests between agents and their local challengers. Chapter 4 takes up a theme that is of particular importance today: the ways in which agents handled questions about treaty and Aboriginal rights, land claims, and other issues related to lands and resources. Chapter 5 examines the assistance provided to Aboriginal people by the agents and how this role magnified their power. Finally, Chapter 6 considers the means adopted by department officials to put the policy of assimilation into practice.

On one level, this book can be seen as a study of the 'micro-physics' of power relations, informed by a Foucauldian analysis of the exercise and daily negotiations of power.[42] At its heart, however, it is not a theoretical project. The intent here is to provide a wide readership with a detailed understanding of the dynamics of the colonial relationship between Aboriginal people and government. I have asked questions of the sources based on my own feminist, anti-racist, and anti-colonial perspective. For me this project is an attempt to engage meaningfully with my country's colonial past and to examine how a particular group of Euro-Canadians—Indian agents—exercised power in the service of the state and of white dominance. Ironically, my first studies in the history of imperialism and colonialism concerned other parts of the world, not Canada. I was studying these issues in West Berlin in the late 1980s when I found myself facing repeated questioning from German students about Canada's treatment of First Nations people. Their inquiries taught me two important lessons: first, I realized that I had learned practically nothing about Aboriginal people in my many years of education; and second, I was forced to recognize that I had located colonialism outside Canada, despite the fact that the process was still ongoing there. This experience set me on my path of working to understand colonialism in my own backyard, the kind I had been taught not to see and from which I benefited personally. I chose southern Ontario because it was close to my Toronto home and I hoped to pursue oral as well as documentary history; the choice of agents arose organically from the fact that theirs were the most complete records available for interwar Ontario.

Through illuminating the details of the DIA system, I hope to shed light on the psychological, social, financial, and political impact of wardship and tutelage on Aboriginal peoples. In addition, the colonial encounter analyzed here reveals in microcosm the mutual misunderstandings that have taken place in Canada since the beginning of contact. Those misunderstandings became more damaging to Aboriginal people as their powers of self-determination were progressively weakened. Present-day efforts to forge a more positive relationship between Canada and first peoples can only benefit from examining the errors and harmful premises of the old colonial order.

1

Homeland:
The Area and the People

'Do not consider us helpless wards, we now feel we have sufficient intelligence to hold and voice our rights.'[1]

This study focuses on the experiences of some of the First Nations people who moved onto small reserves around Georgian Bay after signing treaties with Canada in the mid-nineteenth century. In particular, it examines their experiences with the federal government. The Georgian Bay area is probably best known for its unforgettable natural beauty, immortalized in some of Canada's most famous paintings. Popular as a summer playground for urban Ontarians, the region otherwise attracts relatively little attention, particularly from academic historians. But in many ways the story of the First Nations here can be seen as a microcosm of Aboriginal-government relations in the interwar era. By this period, most First Nations people in the southern portions of Canada had been confined to reserves and lived under the Indian agent system. Despite considerable local variations in climate, economy, and Aboriginal culture, the Indian department's primary orientation towards control was consistent wherever Aboriginal people had entered treaties and formed permanent settlements. At the same time, the Indian agent system made First Nations people vulnerable to variations in the attitudes and practices of individual Indian agents. The relatively sympathetic or unsympathetic approaches of these men affected the degree to which they would mediate the harsher aspects of policy. A study of Indian agents in Ontario, then, has implications for communities across the country.

In the Georgian Bay area, as elsewhere, Aboriginal people struggled to adapt to the economic realities established by Euro-Canadians and quietly but firmly resisted many aspects of federal Indian policy. As reserve populations began to increase, the inadequacies of federal planning were revealed in the growing poverty and marginalization of First Nations people. Indian agents doggedly exhorted Aboriginal people to adopt Euro-Canadian values and work habits, integrate into non-Aboriginal society, and forget the treaty rights enshrined barely three generations earlier. Ironically, though, federal policies contributed to the separation from

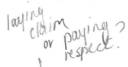

laying claim or paying respect?

Dreamer's Rock, located on Manitoulin Island at the tip of the La Cloche peninsula (north of Little Current), was a sacred site for the Odawa and Ojibway of the island and a favoured spot for the young people's vision quests. This photo, showing a white man lying on top of the rock, was taken in 1904. Archives of Ontario, RG 1-448-1, Box 84; AO 6118.

mainstream society that maintained Aboriginal people in poverty and simultaneously helped to preserve their cultural distinctiveness, including their awareness of their special treaty relationship with the federal government. This chapter outlines the people of the two agencies studied here, their origins, the treaties they signed with government, and the impact of settlement on their communities.

Aboriginal Origins

At the time of contact with Europeans, the area around Georgian Bay was inhabited by the Huron (Wendat) and various Algonquian ancestors of the present-day Anishinabek. 'Anishinabek' is the common self-designation chosen by the descendants of the Ojibway, Odawa, and Potawatomi peoples, who spoke closely related languages and shared other cultural characteristics.[2] Manitoulin Island was an ancient home of the Odawa, while the Huron, Nipissing, Ojibway, and other Algonquians lived on the southern, eastern, and northern shores of Georgian Bay. The Potawatomi were based around Lakes Michigan and Superior, particularly in present-day Michigan and Wisconsin.[3]

In the mid-seventeenth century all these groups scattered west and north before the depredations of Iroquois (Haudenosaunee) warriors, temporarily relocating to the areas around Lakes Michigan and Superior. By 1701, a lengthy military campaign mounted by Ojibway and Odawa warriors had helped to exhaust the overextended Iroquois and drive them out of the lands north of Lake Ontario, thus allowing the Anishinabek to wrest back their ancestral hunting grounds.[4] These nations returned gradually to reoccupy their lands. The Odawa reclaimed Manitoulin Island as early as 1670, although they returned westward shortly after this.[5] A more permanent wave of resettlement began in the 1830s, and by 1839 the island's Odawa population was about 350 people, living mainly at Wikwemikong.[6] Some Ojibway were also living on the island at this time. Potawatomi people fleeing from the US removal policy of the 1830s and 1840s contributed to Manitoulin's mix, along with more Ojibway, mostly from the north shore of Lake Huron. In the Parry Sound region the Ojibway predominate, although here too some Odawa and Potawatomi found their homes in the mid- and late nineteenth century. In the ensuing years the three nations have intermarried and become less distinct.

Treaties

Three major treaties were signed by the peoples of this study: the Bond Head Treaty of 1836, the Robinson Huron Treaty of 1850, and the Manitoulin Island Treaty in 1862. The Bond Head Treaty was a unique arrangement under which Sir Francis Bond Head, then Upper Canada's Lieutenant-Governor, promised eternal protection from Euro-Canadian settlement on Manitoulin Island in exchange for an agreement to make the island a refuge for any First Nations people who wished to move there. The Robinson and Manitoulin Island treaties were more standard land surrenders through which the Crown extinguished Aboriginal title in exchange for an initial payment, further annual payments, and reserves. All of these treaties arose from pressure exerted on the government by settlers and businessmen to make more land available for settlement and economic exploitation. By the mid-nineteenth century, practically all the good farming land of southern Ontario was occupied by the newcomers, and farm families were looking for more land for their offspring. In addition, mineral finds on the American side of the Great Lakes sparked hopes of similar deposits under Canadian soil. The treaties provided an orderly mechanism by which, without resort to military force, governments acquired Aboriginal lands and resources for the incoming whites.

In 1836 Sir Francis Bond Head visited Manitoulin Island to attend the annual gift distribution to Britain's Aboriginal allies from the Great Lakes region. During a whirlwind tour of Upper Canada's Aboriginal settlements, Bond Head had become convinced that First Nations people could not adapt to the new order and would inevitably die out. He therefore proposed to the Odawa and Ojibway who claimed Manitoulin Island that their island become a permanent sanctuary for all First Nations people who decided to move there. This agreement was highly unusual in that it was a spontaneous action by Bond Head, without prior authorization, and without following the usual procedures for land surrenders.[7] Even more unprecedented was its purpose of retaining all of the surrendered land for permanent occupation by its Aboriginal owners and other First Nations people, a feature that makes it unlike any other treaty signed in Canada.

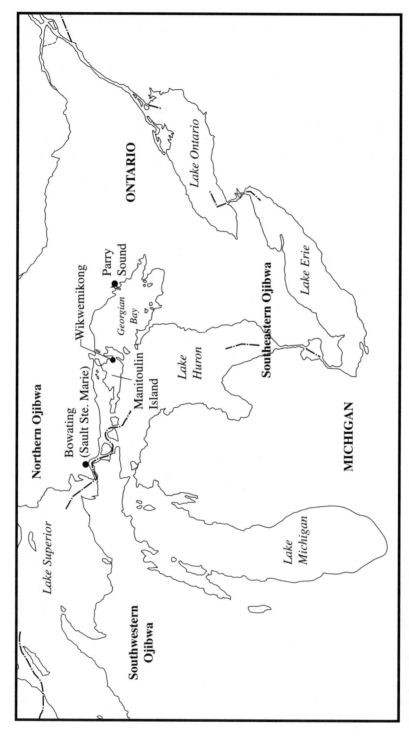

Ontario Indian agencies and their location.

Bond Head justified the agreement as a means of allowing the people to live out their final days in peace. Another major motivation, however, was to effect the removal to Manitoulin Island of all the First Nations people of southern Ontario, thus clearing the way for Euro-Canadian settlement on their more fertile and accessible lands.[8] This treaty did not include any payments, nor did it make any reference to harvesting rights. But Bond Head had chosen the island in part because of its abundant fisheries, specifically mentioning the 'innumerable Fishing Islands' around it in his speech proposing the treaty.[9] At the time the fish were harvested exclusively by Native fishers.[10] All parties presumably accepted that the people would continue their usual means of supporting themselves, which included hunting and fishing and selling the products of these harvesting activities. The Bond Head Treaty was superseded by the 1862 Manitoulin Island Treaty, but the Wikwemikong group (by far the largest community on the island) refused to sign the latter treaty. Thus, the Wikwemikong Unceded First Nation maintains that it is still covered by the treaty of 1836.

In 1850, the Ojibway living on the northern and eastern shores of Lake Huron signed the Robinson Huron Treaty. This treaty and its twin, the Robinson Superior Treaty,[11] became necessary when mining interests began to probe the area for mineral wealth in the mid-1840s. Beginning in 1845, the united Province of Canada unwisely granted mining leases north of Lakes Huron and Superior without consulting the Ojibway. The province initially attempted to avoid a treaty despite Ojibway complaints about prospecting, hoping that it could deny the legitimacy of their claims to the land.[12] But it began to investigate these claims in 1848 and proceeded with added urgency after some of the Ojibway took action to defend their territory in what became known as the Mica Bay Incident. In November 1849, a group of Ojibway, Métis, and two Euro-Canadians seized the operations of the Quebec Mining Company at Mica Bay on Lake Superior in a clear assertion of Aboriginal rights and title.[13]

The incident underlined the need to arrange a treaty as quickly as possible, a process for which the government had already laid the groundwork in the summer of 1849. The treaties of 1850 were the result, negotiated by William Benjamin Robinson and including, in the case of the Lake Huron group, an estimated 1,422 people.[14] The Robinson Huron Treaty covered 10 of the bands of this study.[15] In return for the surrender of their land, the signatories received reserves, an initial cash payment of £2000 to be divided among themselves, and a perpetual annuity of £600 divided among all the bands, the latter amount to be increased later if the income from the surrendered lands made this possible.[16] The treaty also guaranteed to the Ojibway the 'full and free privilege to hunt over the territory now ceded by them and to fish in the waters thereof as they have heretofore been in the habit of doing'.[17] The sole restriction on these rights was the provision that the Ojibway could not hunt or fish on lands sold or leased to others and actually occupied by them.

In 1862, the Province of Canada attempted to gain title to Manitoulin Island, contrary to Bond Head's promise only 26 years earlier of eternal protection from Euro-Canadian settlement. Canada was motivated by the lure of additional farming land, the suspected presence of oil and gas on the island, and the exceedingly rich fisheries around Manitoulin and its numerous satellite islands. The commissioners who negotiated this treaty explained the apparent inconsistency with Bond Head's treaty by arguing that the government had expected about 9,000 Aboriginal people to relocate to the island. Because only small numbers had actually moved there (less than a thousand), the government now claimed that the Manitoulin Island First Nations had 'not fulfilled their part of the contract'.[18] The people of Wikwemikong, supported by their Jesuit missionaries, strongly opposed the new treaty and attempted to prevent the rest from signing. In response, the treaty commissioners excluded Wikwemikong from the negotiations and obtained the agreement of the other groups to the surrender.

Those who signed received reserves (six were eventually established) and an initial payment totalling $700. Further, the government agreed to establish an investment fund from the proceeds of land sales and to distribute the interest from this fund on an annual basis. Hunting rights were not mentioned in the treaty, and fishing rights were to be the same as those accorded to Euro-Canadians.[19] Four of the bands in the Manitowaning agency were established under the 1862 treaty: Sheguiandah, South Bay, Sucker Creek, and Sucker Lake. As for the Wikwemikong people, they retained their peninsula on the southeast end of the island as unceded territory, officially called the Manitoulin Island Unceded Territory and occupied by the Manitoulin Island Unceded band (since renamed Wikwemikong Unceded First Nation). Although the 1862 treaty contained an option for Wikwemikong chiefs to sign at a later date, the people have never chosen to exercise this option, and they remain the possessors of unceded territory.[20] Thus the only treaty ever signed by Wikwemikong was the agreement with Sir Francis Bond Head in 1836.

The Impact of Settlement

Non-Aboriginal settlement and development began soon after the treaties were signed. Both Manitoulin Island and the Parry Sound region had attracted small numbers of homesteaders by the late 1860s, and increasing numbers of Euro-Canadians came to the region in the 1870s. Those who settled in the Parry Sound-Muskoka area soon discovered that it was poor agricultural land, but there were compensating advantages, the foremost among them timber. Parry Sound was founded as a lumbering town and remained so well into the twentieth century.[21] By the early twentieth century it had begun to profit from tourism as well, which grew into a significant industry. On Manitoulin Island, initial hopes of locating deposits of oil and natural gas proved illusory. Yet the island contained pockets of good arable land (some on the reserves), mixed with the rocky land typical of the Canadian Shield. More importantly, it offered access to a rich fishery that was commercially exploited from about the 1840s on.[22] The economy developed by the settlers here was based on a combination of relatively marginal agriculture, sheep and turkey farming, commercial fishing, and the forest industry.[23]

In the 1920s and 1930s, the years of interest here, the Georgian Bay region was an economic hinterland providing raw materials and natural resources to the

Canadian urban heartland. The North American economy had an insatiable appetite for the area's timber and for the fish that had always been a mainstay of the local Aboriginal diet. Both resources had already been severely reduced—the formerly abundant sturgeon and other important fish almost wiped out by commercial over-fishing, and significant areas stripped of large trees—but fishing and lumbering remained important economic activities. Local Euro-Canadians supported them-selves through a mixed economy that included seasonal wage labour related prima-rily to the forest and tourist industries. On Manitoulin Island the fishing industry provided jobs and there was still a significant farm economy. Euro-Canadians also maintained gardens, hunted, and trapped fur-bearing animals to sell their pelts.

The economy on the reserves was not that different from that of the surrounding white settlements. Aboriginal people based their livelihoods on a combination of hunting, trapping, some gardening, and wage labour. Opportunities for wage employment for First Nations men centred on three main industries: lumbering and sawmills; loading and unloading rail and ship freight; and tourism, which required Aboriginal guides. A few men were also involved in shipping on the Great Lakes. Women sold crafts and wild berries in the summer, and some performed domestic labour for wages. Trapping remained a part of Aboriginal life since there was still a market for furs. On Manitoulin Island, some Anishinabek had farms.

It is difficult to know how much interaction there was between Aboriginal people and the newcomers. Early pioneers on Manitoulin Island later recorded fond

Local white people visiting an Aboriginal camp (probably Ojibway) on Oak Island, Parry Sound District, in the late nineteenth century. Archives of Ontario, Acc. 6287, S 8250.

memories of their Aboriginal neighbours (coloured by nostalgia, no doubt) and in some cases even developed friendships with them.[24] Especially in the early days, a mutually beneficial interdependent economy could develop, with First Nations men providing meat, fish, and sometimes labour in exchange for items such as tobacco, fishnets, potatoes, and flour. The pioneers were impressed by Aboriginal men's hunting ability, forest skills, and feats of strength and endurance.[25] They had considerably less to say about First Nations women, who may have had less occasion to meet Euro-Canadian settlers. Pioneer days were long over by the 1920s, but the men continued to meet through their work in the lumber camps and sawmills.

In Parry Sound there were many occasions for contact. The various opportunities for wage labour brought Aboriginal and non-Aboriginal workers together, particularly in the Parry Sound tourist industry and the freight-loading work at Depot Harbour, a major Great Lakes port and railway depot located right on Parry Island.[26] According to one local historian, Depot Harbour provided 'plentiful' work and meant that the Parry Islanders had increased contact with the ethnically diverse residents of the 'bustling, progressive shipping port'.[27] Through guiding, First Nations men met Parry Sounders and the wealthy tourists who stayed at resorts such as the Belvedere Hotel. Even the famous made their way to the Belvedere on occasion, including US President Theodore Roosevelt and Hollywood actress Bette Davis.[28] Affluent families such as the Christies of the well-known cookie and biscuit company owned cottages in the area and employed local Native people in various capacities.

According to Franz Koennecke, historian of the Parry Island Reserve, jobs in the railroad and tourist industries were lucrative enough to lure many non-band members to Parry Island in search of work.[29] An additional attraction was the proximity of Parry Sound, which provided a market only two miles distant from the reserve. The Christian Island band members who lived for generations on Parry Island specifically mentioned this fact as a major reason for preferring their adopted home.[30] Limited as they were by non-Aboriginal standards, the unusually plentiful economic opportunities for First Nations people on Parry Island were the reason for its high population of residents and Native visitors who technically belonged to other bands.

On the other hand, despite the existence of certain kinds of economic interaction, there was still a well-established social and physical separation of the Aboriginal and non-Aboriginal worlds.[31] As Franz Koennecke found in his investigation of Parry Island's history, '[t]he relationship of the Parry Island band with the inhabitants of Parry Sound seemed to have been restricted to the religious and economic sector.'[32] No doubt this statement applies to the entire Georgian Bay area.

There were, of course, many barriers to understanding between the two groups. Communication was difficult for a number of reasons. English was a second or even third language for most First Nations people, and many were unable to speak it with any fluency, much less write it. Practically no Euro-Canadians spoke Aboriginal languages unless they were missionaries, although both Lewis and Daly understood some spoken Ojibway.[33] Virtually all the First Nations people around Georgian Bay had been converted at least nominally to Christian religions, but in other respects they retained many features of their traditional cultures, including the philosophical beliefs and values that made their approach to life and other people distinct. No doubt Euro-Canadians frequently misinterpreted the actions they witnessed, judging them by Euro-Canadian standards. First Nations people must have made similar mistakes judging Euro-Canadians by Aboriginal standards. Euro-Canadians were also burdened with persistent beliefs about the supposed superiority of European culture, and in some cases by more virulent forms of racism, which discouraged attempts to form interracial friendships or even to interact at all. They did not seek opportunities to revise their views or learn about Aboriginal cultures. At the time, hierarchical ideas about 'race' were widely accepted, and few mainstream Canadians considered racism to be a problem.

Among non-Aboriginal people, a superficial curiosity about 'Indians' remained, as indicated by the staging of Aboriginal people in exhibits at the Canadian National Exhibition in Toronto and other similar fairground performances across the country.[34] There were related local events around Georgian Bay: for example, in the 1920s the owners of a tourist lodge on the French River engaged local Aboriginal men to perform as 'Indian guides' accompanying Samuel de Champlain and Etienne Brulé in a historic re-enactment of the Frenchmen's trip down the river.[35] But this show, like all the others, was intended to depict 'historic Indians', with the Aboriginal actors conforming to a script shaped by Wild West shows and other images from American popular culture.[36] Exhibition engagements were chiefly a matter of generating a sense of local colour and history. The public's interest focused on First Nations people of the past—or rather, as Euro-Canadian culture imagined them in the past. By contrast, fair goers and members of the general public were usually not much interested in modern-day Aboriginal people, who probably appeared disappointingly unlike prevailing stereotypes. Exhibition-style appearances helped to confine 'Indians' safely in the past, where non-Aboriginal viewers did not have to grapple with the contemporary state of their descendants.

Much had changed for First Nations people since their first contact with the European strangers. From a highly mobile life based on seasonal shifts of settlement to harvest the land's resources, they had been confined to small reserves. Their former food sources were drastically depleted and they had increasingly adopted wage labour to make up the shortfall. While their early adaptations to the newcomers' presence had involved active participation in trade, including a near-monopoly on the fish trade, they were increasingly excluded from the Euro-Canadian commercial economy. Their health continued to suffer from formerly unknown diseases and from the susceptibility to illness caused by poverty.

Perhaps the most significant change was their loss of political independence. Aboriginal chiefs had signed the treaties as representatives of independent nations. Although they contracted to abide by the Queen's laws, no doubt they envisioned a future of continuing self-determination, which some leaders pursued with great energy and vision.[37] The Canadian government, however, consigned First Nations people to a state of wardship in which the Indian department held almost unhindered political power over band governments, exercising the final authority over such crucial matters as band membership, resource use, and band funds. The department's control was progressively tightened through an endless series of additions to the Indian Act, a set of laws that applied only to Aboriginal people. The Indian Act itself was first passed in 1876, after the region's treaties were signed. Noel Dyck has highlighted the involuntary nature of the Aboriginal-government tutelage relationship:

> the tutelage that Canadian Indians have experienced has been based neither upon a contractual agreement nor a negotiated understanding but upon the power of one side to regulate the behaviour of the other in accordance with a set of unilaterally selected purposes.[38]

Moreover, the Canadian government did not live up to all the obligations it had undertaken under the treaties, particularly those related to harvesting rights.[39] The Robinson treaties of 1850 guaranteed that Native people could continue to hunt and fish in their traditional manner. The Manitoulin Island Treaty of 1862 stated merely that the signatories would have the same fishing rights as white settlers; but it is not clear that the chiefs had actually agreed to cede any rights to fish or game. The people of the unceded territory at Wikwemikong never surrendered their land or their harvesting rights. Securing continued access to these resources had been a priority for most chiefs in the treaty negotiations.[40] Yet fishing and hunting rights were quickly eroded by the commercial fishing and game conservation regimes developed by successive governments.

In general, the creation by Confederation of the Ontario provincial government in 1867 (after the treaties were signed) was a fateful development for First Nations people in a number of ways. The new division of powers assigned the federal government responsibility for 'Indians and lands reserved for Indians', so that the provincial government lacked any constitutional obligation to protect First Nations interests. In practice, it showed a consistent tendency to disregard those interests and frequently denied the existence of Aboriginal or treaty rights.[41] After 1892 the Ontario government imposed a host of new regulations on hunting and fishing, including closed seasons and additional licensing procedures, without First Nations consent. In spite of a clause in the early game laws that exempted First Nations people, game wardens repeatedly prosecuted them and confiscated their take and equipment. The Indian department made weak initial protests, but was rebuffed by the Ontario government. Thwarted by the increasing political power of the provinces, by the early twentieth century the department had abandoned all efforts to protect First Nations treaty rights. In effect, it can be said that the Indian Act superseded the treaties, becoming the sole legal document by which the department was guided in its relations with First Nations.

The Manitowaning and Parry Sound Agencies

The First Nations people investigated here are those who lived in two administrative areas of the Department of Indian Affairs: the Manitowaning and Parry Sound agencies. The Manitowaning agency comprised the eastern portion of Manitoulin

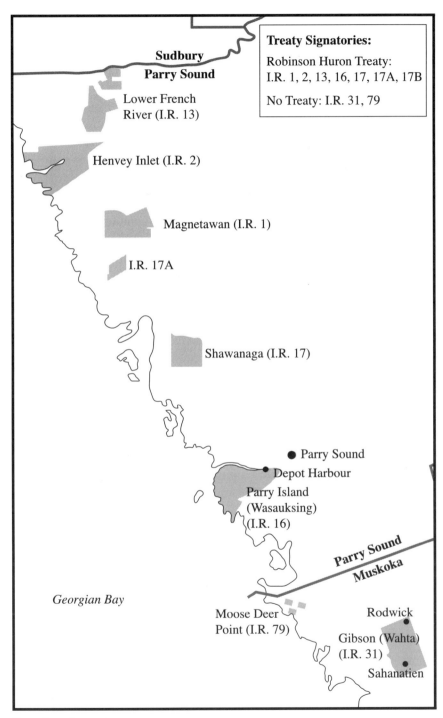

Sudbury
Parry Sound

Lower French
River (I.R. 13)

Henvey Inlet (I.R. 2)

Magnetawan (I.R. 1)

I.R. 17A

Shawanaga (I.R. 17)

Parry Sound

Depot Harbour

Parry Island
(Wasauksing)
(I.R. 16)

Parry Sound
Muskoka

Georgian Bay

Moose Deer
Point (I.R. 79)

Rodwick

Gibson (Wahta)
(I.R. 31)

Sahanatien

Treaty Signatories:
Robinson Huron Treaty:
I.R. 1, 2, 13, 16, 17, 17A, 17B

No Treaty: I.R. 31, 79

Parry Sound agencies.

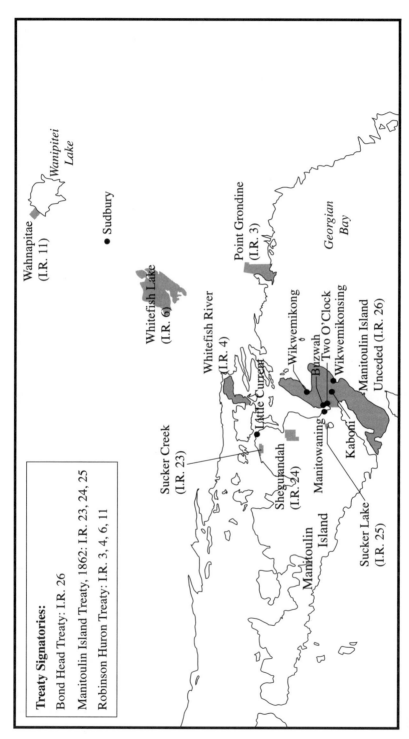

Treaty Signatories:

Bond Head Treaty: I.R. 26

Manitoulin Island Treaty, 1862: I.R. 23, 24, 25

Robinson Huron Treaty: I.R. 3, 4, 6, 11

Manitowaning agency.

Treaty pay day at Shawanaga, 1907. The annual payment of treaty annuities was conducted with ceremony (note the flags, the men's suits, and the women's hats) and was often accompanied by festivities. Archives of Ontario, RG 1-488-1, Box 106; #502A; AO 6126.

Island, along with a number of reserves on the islands north of it and on the north shore of Georgian Bay. There were nine bands[42] in this jurisdiction: Manitoulin Island Unceded, Point Grondine (Indian Reserve No. 3), Sheguiandah, South Bay, Sucker Creek, Sucker Lake, Tahgaiwenene (or Wahnapitae IR No. 11), Whitefish Lake (IR No. 6), and Whitefish River (IR No. 4). The Parry Sound agency consisted of the seven reserves along the eastern shore of Georgian Bay. From north to south, these were: Lower French River (IR No. 13, often called Pickerel River by the agents), Henvey Inlet (IR No. 2),[43] Magnetawan (IR No. 1), Shawanaga, Parry Island (Wasauksing),[44] Moose Deer Point, and Gibson (Wahta). As noted in the Introduction, the vagaries of record preservation have meant that this study covers the Parry Island band almost to the exclusion of the other Parry Sound reserves. Shawanaga receives some attention, while the others, unfortunately, remain shadowy presences.

As we have seen, the Robinson Huron Treaty of 1850 was the single most important treaty for the two agencies. It created five of the reserves in the Parry Sound agency (all but Gibson and Moose Deer Point) and five of those in the Manitowaning agency.[45] The First Nations selected relatively small areas for their reserves, and in many cases experienced disputes over the size of the land to be reserved when surveying began. Often the sites chosen for reserves were the best fishing stations or garden locations. Although the written treaty plainly states that the islands in Lake Huron and Georgian Bay were included in the surrender, it is equally clear that the Aboriginal understanding was different. According to the Aboriginal view, the islands had not been discussed during negotiations and the people had never intended to surrender them. Shortly after the treaty was signed, the people heard that non-Aboriginals were claiming rights to the islands, and a number of chiefs immediately began to assert their conviction that the islands had not been surrendered. Especially in southern and eastern Georgian Bay, islands contained the best land for growing crops and, most importantly, were the best fishing stations.[46] The chiefs and their people had strong motivations for retaining their ownership of the islands. Some First Nations, including Wasauksing (Parry Island), have continued to assert their ownership of islands to the present day, although to date the federal government has continued to deny their claims.

One result of the inadequacies of records is that the story of the Gibson or Wahta First Nation, the only Mohawk reserve in the two agencies, remains to be told elsewhere.[47] Its origins, however, should be noted here. The Gibson Reserve was formed in the early 1880s by Methodist Mohawks who had been resident at Oka (Kanesatake) until that time. These Mohawks had been converted to Methodism in the 1870s and were part of the conflict with the Sulpician order over the ownership of the Kanesatake lands.[48] At their request, the Department of Indian Affairs began negotiations in 1880 to purchase a 25,582-acre plot of land from the Ontario government so that the Methodist Mohawks could move there. In the 1880s, 32 families moved to the Gibson Reserve.[49] In 1924 the Gibson band counted 192 members.[50]

Moose Deer Point was also founded later than the other reserves, and was not covered by any treaty. It was a small community of families, mostly of Potawatomi

By the early twentieth century, First Nations men already had a long tradition of wage labour, especially in resource extraction industries such as fur and lumber. This 1901 photo shows Iroquois (Haudenosaunee) men, perhaps including some men from the Gibson Reserve, in a lumber gang on the Ottawa River. Archives of Ontario, C 120-3, Acc. 2271, S 5186; AO 6127.

and Odawa descent, that had simply settled in the area with the permission of the local Ojibway. The Potawatomi and some of the Odawa had arrived in Canada in the 1830s and 1840s, fleeing the removal policy of the United States and answering a call from the British to seek refuge in Canada. They believed they had been promised treatment similar to that of their northern cousins, but they found a chilly welcome in Canada. The Moose Deer Point people had spent some time living on Christian Island and had then moved to their current location on a peninsula jutting into the southeast corner of Georgian Bay. The local Ojibway had granted them the right to hunt and fish in the surrounding area, but they were never permitted to become part of any treaties.[51] In the 1920s the federal government purchased the small plots of land on which their houses sat and set them aside as reserve land. Their homes were thus protected, but they did not receive interest money as those in other parts of the agency did. The place was isolated and in Daly's time could only be reached by boat. As a result, the people of this reserve interacted relatively little with their agent, who generally visited once or twice a year.

Manitoulin Island's treaty history has already been described. The mid-1830s to 1850s witnessed a major government project to settle the island's First Nations people. Beginning in 1835, the Upper Canada government sponsored an Anglican mission and settlement at Manitowaning on Manitoulin Island, hoping to 'civilize' the Ojibway and Odawa through religious conversion and instruction in farming and trades.[52] The Anglican missionaries were soon countered by the Jesuits, who established a mission 18 miles away at Wikwemikong.[53] There was bitter rivalry between the two, but the Jesuits were far more successful in gaining adherents: in 1918 there were 252 Anglicans in the Manitowaning agency and 1,886 Roman Catholics (Table 1).[54] The religious rivalry spawned destructive tensions, sowing hatreds among formerly friendly groups and leading the Odawa to avoid the government settlement because of its Anglican character. There were other problems, too: population pressures due to in-migration of displaced Anishinabek from the US and the north shore of Lake Huron; poor soil; and finally, the fact that hunting and fishing could still supply the people's needs.[55] The latter fact may have been most important, for the Ojibway simply continued their seasonal migration: 'Secure in the possession of fishing stations, sugar bushes and hunting grounds, the Ojibway of Manitoulin Island had no need of the white man's civilization.'[56] By 1854 government officials were reporting that the Manitowaning settlement was a failure, and the experiment was abandoned. Government interest and financial support had evaporated, but the people remained.[57]

Both geographically and demographically the Manitoulin Island Unceded Territory was by far the largest reserve in the area of this study. The long-standing Jesuit mission station at Wikwemikong provided valued services to the Catholic members, and the settlement there was large and well-established. Good fisheries were located close by, especially off the neighbouring islands. The territory had attracted substantial numbers of people from bands all over the region, as well as most of the members of four bands: Manitoulin Island Unceded band itself, South Bay, Spanish River No. 3, and Tahgaiwenene.[58] According to government statements at the time of the 1862 treaty, the unceded band was obliged to retain its role of admitting

Table 1
Manitowaning Agency: Population and Religion

1918: Band	Catholic	Anglican	Total
Manitoulin Island Unceded	1,136		1,136
Point Grondine	46		46
Sheguiandah	38	83	121
South Bay	86		86
Spanish River No. 3	214		214
Sucker Creek	10	124	134
Sucker Lake	10		10
Tahgaiwinine	131		131
Whitefish Lake	176		176
Whitefish River	31	45	76
Total	1,878	252	2,130

1924: Band	Catholic	Anglican	Methodist	Total
Manitoulin Island Unceded	1,283			1,283
Point Grondine	42		10	52
Sheguiandah	48	71		119
South Bay	75			75
Spanish River No. 3	215			215
Sucker Creek	12	88		100
Sucker Lake	10			10
Tahgaiwinine	146			146
Whitefish Lake	153		6	159
Whitefish River	55	36		91
Total	2,039	195	16	2,250

(continued)

Table 1 *(continued)*

1929: Band	Catholic	Anglican	United	Total
Manitoulin Island Unceded	1,369			1,369
Point Grondine	32		11	43
Sheguiandah	50	64		114
South Bay	51			51
Spanish River No. 3	140			140
Sucker Creek	14	65		79
Sucker Lake	12			12
Tahgaiwinine	130			130
Whitefish Lake	139		3	142
Whitefish River	72	35		107
Total	2,009	164	14	2,187

1934: Band	Catholic	Anglican	United	Total
Manitoulin Island Unceded	1,378			1,378
Point Grondine	23		10	33
Sheguiandah	40	68		108
South Bay	45			45
Spanish River No. 3	107			107
Sucker Creek	12	57		69
Sucker Lake	7			7
Tahgaiwinine	110			110
Whitefish Lake	125		5	130
Whitefish River	89	37		126
Total	1,936	162	15	2,113

all First Nations people who wished to settle on its territory. This arrangement was basically inequitable, since it permitted members of treaty bands (especially other Manitoulin Islanders) to benefit from the money earned by selling their land, while living on the unceded territory as if they had not surrendered. Members of the unceded band, by contrast, received no money from the treaty but for many years were obliged to share their resources, such as their land and timber, with members of the treaty bands. Roughly three-quarters of the agency's 2,100 people lived on their territory in the interwar period.[59]

Wikwemikong experienced major divisions within its ranks because of the disparities of band membership. The many non-band members living in the unceded territory differed from the members most noticeably through the fact that they received treaty and annuity money, unlike those belonging to the Manitoulin Island Unceded (MIU) band.[60] Some members of the MIU band resented this inequality, particularly because their own resources were shared equally with non-members. The non-members even enjoyed voting rights in council elections until 1912, when the band changed to the more usual pattern of limiting these rights to members. By the 1920s, resentment had built to the point where serious dissension broke out and a series of confrontations ensued. The MIU band moved to limit timber use on its territory to band members, hoping to convince resident non-members to transfer their membership and their funds to the MIU jurisdiction. The struggles over this new policy were labelled 'The Great Trouble' by the Jesuits, and are described in more detail later in this volume.

Parry Island had similar troubles for the same reason—a significant presence of resident non-band members. Many Anishinabek who were officially members of bands further south, especially Christian Island and Cape Croker, had moved to Parry Island in the late nineteenth century and settled there permanently. In addition, some non-treaty Anishinabek, including Potawatomi, had made their homes on the island. At times, the resident non-members actually formed a majority of the population. For instance, of the 292 people Daly reported in 1924 as Parry Island residents, 170 were non-members.[61] In this band, non-members had no voting rights in council elections.

Other factors also contributed to friction in the Parry Island community. One significant difference was religion: a majority of the residents were Methodists (later United Church), but a substantial minority were Catholics—at times the Catholic group was nearly equal in size to the Methodist group (see Table 2). The two religious factions lived in separate villages, the Upper Village at the northeastern corner of the island being Methodist, the Lower Village at the south end Catholic.[62] There was clearly competition between the two, and Daly claimed that this was reflected in band politics.[63] In fact, Daly may have manipulated the two factions to help solidify his own position, a strategy suggested in his comment that a Catholic chief, Frank Judge, was attempting to fill all the band's official positions with Catholics. If he had succeeded, wrote the agent, 'Chief Judge would have been the power on the Parry Island Reserve, not the DIA.'[64] As a final divisive factor, several families of Potawatomi and Odawa each lived in their own separate settlements on the island (the settlements were called King and Nanibush, respectively, after the families' surnames). These families retained a certain distinctness from the majority Ojibway population.[65] Such divisions of religion, band affiliation, and Indian status contributed to political factionalism and disunity among Parry Islanders, probably exacerbated by their residential segregation in separate settlements.

These sorts of fault lines were important because they worked against the kind of solidarity that might have made resistance to DIA control more effective. On the unceded territory some people obviously hoped to create more unity by adding

Table 2
Parry Sound Agency: Population and Religion

1918: Band	Methodist	Catholic	Pagan	Total
Gibson/Wahta	132	1		133
Henvey Inlet	41	126		167
Magnetawan		30		30
Parry Island	60	55	1	116
Shawanaga	65	54		119
Total	298	266	1	565

1924: Band	Baptist	Methodist	Presbyterian	Catholic	Other Christian	Total
Gibson/Wahta	1	188	3			192
Henvey Inlet		47		162	7	216
Magnetawan	2		2	27		31
Parry Island		185		103	4	292
Shawanaga		75		72		147
Total	3	495	5	364	11	878

1929: Band	Anglican	United	Catholic	Other Christian	Total
Gibson/Wahta		133			133
Henvey Inlet			151		151
Magnetawan		5	45		50
Moose Deer Point		33	10		43
Parry Island		165	87	1	253
Shawanaga	1	76	48		125
Total	1	412	341	1	755

1934: Band	United	Catholic	Other Christian	Total
Gibson/Wahta	240	3	11	254
Henvey Inlet	100	59		159
Magnetawan	33	4		37
Moose Deer Point	23	22		45
Parry Island	70	50	2	122
Shawanaga	62	33		95
Total	528	171	13	712

resident non-band members to the unceded band. Parry Island, too, had attempted to consolidate its membership, but an application to accept long-time resident outsiders into the band had been disallowed by the DIA (many were accepted into the band later, in the 1940s).[66] Despite efforts to resolve differences, then, the two communities experienced significant internal conflict. The Indian department may not have intentionally applied a 'divide and rule' strategy to create these problems, but it benefited from their tendency to channel frustrations into internal clashes instead of into a united challenge to department rule.

Economic Realities of the 1920s and 1930s

First Nations people around Georgian Bay had a workable economic strategy, but they were not wealthy. Due to the importance of wage labour in their lives, they were vulnerable to movements of the national and international economies, which affected them even in the 1920s and became painfully apparent in the 1930s. On Manitoulin Island they pursued a subsistence strategy based on a mixed economy, as outlined above. Men earned wages working in lumber camps off the reserve during the winter, on river drives in the spring, and in sawmills in the summertime. Members of bands with timber resources could earn income on the reserve during the winter by cutting pulpwood, lumber, railroad ties, or whatever kinds of wood products were in demand. These were sold to the highest bidder, who purchased the wood and also paid timber dues, which were added to the band funds. Women

Many Aboriginal men in the Georgian Bay area worked on river-driving crews like this one, of the Graves and Bigwood Co., taking lumber down the Magnetawan River in 1914. Archives of Ontario, RG 1-448-1, Box 106, #497.

could generate income through the sale of berries, bark work, baskets, and other crafts.[67] Gardens of potatoes and vegetables seem to have been maintained by most people, while many also grew wheat and hay, which made a substantial contribution to the total income of the agency.[68] Finally, the traditional pursuits of fishing, hunting, and trapping contributed to the diet and brought additional income through the sale of fish and pelts. Thanks in part to the seasonal availability of labour, and perhaps also as a cultural pattern, many of these people were highly mobile, particularly those on the more isolated reserves.

In the annual report of the DIA, figures on the total earnings of each agency were published (see Tables 3 and 4).[69] Although the numbers are undoubtedly approximate, they lend some insight into the local means of subsistence, as well as indicate economic trends throughout the period. For the Manitowaning agency (Table 3), the figures show that the two most significant forms of cash income were wage labour and the sale of farm produce. In 1919, for instance, wage labour contributed 35 per cent and farm produce 33 per cent of the total income.[70] The remaining third came from a variety of sources—6 per cent from fishing, hunting, and trapping; 8 per cent from annuities and interest payments (paid only to members of treaty bands); 11 per cent from other industries and occupations. On a per capita basis, the total 1919 income of $267,235.57 works out to $125 per person—hardly a princely sum. This would mean that a family of five would have, on average, an income of $625 for the year, or about $52 a month. By comparison, the Veterans' Allowance Act provided $40 a month to a single veteran and $70 to one who was

First Nations people in southern Ontario embraced farming wherever the soil was sufficiently fertile, as on parts of Manitoulin Island. In this photo from the 1920s, a First Nations woman works in the field with her team. Archives of Ontario, RG 1-448-1, Box 105, #273B; AO 6119.

Table 3
Income, Manitowaning Agency, 1918-1938

Year	Value of Farm Products incl. Hay	Value of Beef Sold and Used for Food	Wages Earned	Received from Land Rentals	Received from Timber	Earned by Fishing	Earned by Hunting and Trapping	Earned by Other Industries and Occupations	Annuities Paid and Interest on Trust Funds	Total Income of Indians**
1918	$50,408	$8,290	$27,450	$20,525*		$4,360	$3,730	$39,250	$11,284.42	$165,297.42
1919	$88,615	$14,130	$93,780	$4,450*		$9,050	$7,280	$29,585	$20,345.57	$267,235.57
1920	$70,460	$16,705	$266,100	$2,300*		$8,050	$12,750	$19,360	$20,345.57	$416,070.57
1921	$63,180	$20,495	$284,000	$4,165*		$10,595	$11,500	$25,050	$22,529.73	$441,514.73
1922	$23,259	$18,640	$129,485	$2,550*		$6,860	$12,125	$16,550	$22,574.33	$232,043.33
1923	$29,769	$16,140	$115,710		$2,541.79	$6,350	$12,750	$17,290	$22,270.53	$222,821.32
1924	$22,870	$7,190	$125,000		$2,628.05	$4,885	$7,625	$14,545	$22,054.20	$206,797.25
1925	$26,690	$9,865	$88,150	$155	$8,596.31	$7,265	$6,760	$16,350	$22,593.81	$186,425.12
1926	$26,620	$9,360	$76,800	$30	$6,195.82	$9,260	$4,600	$16,350	$22,967.47	$172,183.29
1927	$30,390	$10,100	$83,300	$162.50	$4,339.93	$7,675	$4,525	$17,200	$23,180.17	$180,872.60
1929	$46,990	$12,650	$93,400	$80	$3,764.02	$7,725	$3,060	$20,725	$24,715.28	$213,109.30
1930	$33,370	$10,810	$64,800	$80	$3,446.11	$5,295	$2,370	$13,300	$24,208.71	$157,679.82
1931	$25,002	$8,130	$25,800	$80	$1,882.41	$4,110	$1,820	$5,270	$24,444.36	$96,538.77
1932	$22,185	$5,800	$14,010	$100	$452.63	$3,375	$1,980	$2,355	$24,539.51	$74,850.04
1933	$26,918	$4,770	$15,785	$150	$3,272.83	$3,925	$1,960	$2,455	$24,294.06	$83,543.89
1934	$21,310	$6,230	$21,595	$100	$2,607.76	$4,210	$3,320	$4,755	$25,010.12	$89,570.98
1935	$19,255	$5,320	$24,530	$80	$2,752.94	$3,260	$4,840	$6,360	$25,400.55	$92,112.49
1936	N/A	N/A	N/A	N/A	N/A	N/A	N/A	N/A	$25,504.96	N/A
1937	$22,880	$5,035	$51,910	$465	$4,492.93	$2,940	$3,960	$10,380	$25,762.06	$128,211.54
1938	$17,665	$5,155	$49,830	$215	$4,101.69	$2,590	$2,170	$13,975	$35,850.22	$131,954.56

Note: Figures for each year are derived from the reports of the succeeding year, i.e., those for 1918 are compiled from the annual report for 1919. Figures for 1928 are not available.

*These figures include income from land rental and timber combined.

**Total income includes small amounts received for mining for the years 1932–5 and 1937–8, as follows: 1932: $52.90; 1933: $14; 1934: $433.10; 1935: $314; 1937: $386.55; 1938: $402.65.

Table 4

Income, Parry Sound Agency, 1918-1938

Year	Value of Farm Products incl. Hay	Value of Beef Sold and Used for Food	Wages Earned	Received from Land Rentals	Received from Timber	Earned by Fishing	Earned by Hunting and Trapping	Earned by Other Industries and Occupations	Annuities Paid and Interest on Trust Funds	Total Income of Indians**
1918	$4,970	$900	$8,600			$400	$700	$6,900	$4,111.24	$26,581.24
1919	$7,450	$1,375	$36,000	$1,000*			$1,125		$9,534.23	$56,484.23
1920	$8,210	$2,100	$39,500				$6,000		$9,534.23	$65,344.23
1921	$8,450	$2,100	$38,500				$3,300		$12,123.12	$64,473.12
1922	$8,885	$2,100	$38,500	$15,371*		$750	$3,800		$12,736.54	$82,142.54
1923	$7,450	$1,375	$36,000	$390	$38,648.97		$1,125		$12,245.57	$97,234.54
1924	$7,450	$1,375	$36,000	$535	$52,903.64		$1,125		$11,589.02	$110,977.66
1925	$7,450	$1,375	$3,600	$300	$26,415.18		$1,125		$15,738.69	$56,003.87***
1926	$7,450	$1,375	$36,000	$560	$13,278.01		$1,125		$16,820.68	$76,608.69
1927	$7,450	$1,375	$36,000	$355	$3,441.54		$1,125		$16,840.97	$66,587.51
1929	$7,450	$1,375	$36,000	$255	$3,660.03		$1,125		$17,494.73	$67,359.76
1930	$7,450	$1,375	$36,000	$160	$5,614.61		$1,125		$17,517	$69,241.61
1931	$7,450	$1,375	$36,000	$100	$137.98		$975		$18,315.57	$64,353.55
1932	$1,500			$264	$458.67				$18,135.69	$20,358.36
1933	$1,500		$2,450	$54	$38.30		$425		$17,444.18	$21,912.18
1934	$1,500		$7,578	$80	$2,757				$17,245.65	$29,160.65
1935	$1,500		$1,430	$170	$2,211.65				$17,369.44	$22,686.53
1936	N/A	N/A	N/A	N/A	N/A	N/A	N/A	N/A	$17,298.80	N/A
1937	$1,500	$1,500		$430	$1,857.20		$300	$1,100	$17,361.25	$22,883.04
1938	$1,120	$300	$15,280	$432.50	$1,565.25	$200	$375	$800	$17,310.65	$38,293.93

Note: Figures for each year are derived from the reports of the succeeding year, i.e., those for 1918 are compiled from the annual report for 1919. Figures for 1928 are not available.

*These figures include income from land rental and timber combined.

**Total income for the years 1933, 1935, 1937-8 includes a small amount received from mining, as follows: 1933: $0.70; 1935: $5.44; 1937: $334.59; 1938: $340.53.

***Wage labour income for 1925 is reported as $3,600, but this is probably a clerical error, given that the figure of $36,000 is given consistently for every other year from 1923 to 1931. If the actual amount of wages earned was approximately $36,000, as in the other years, the total income for 1925 was $88,403.87.

married.[71] Agent Lewis received an annual salary of $1,440 in 1919, or $120 a month, in addition to rent-free accommodation in the agency house.[72] Duncan Campbell Scott, head of the DIA, earned $5,000 a year.[73]

The people of Manitoulin experienced shifting fortunes in this period, but overall they underwent a brief period of plenty between 1919 and 1921, followed by a steady downward trend in the 1920s and a collapse in incomes after 1929. In 1920 and 1921 earnings from wage labour suddenly peaked, presumably as a result of the brief post-war boom: the reported wage earnings for 1921 were triple those of 1919. Incomes in some other areas also rose, so that per capita incomes increased by 1921 to roughly $206 annually per person, or about $85 per month for a family of five. Thereafter wage income dropped back almost to the 1919 level, while the value of farm products plunged in 1922, reflecting the national collapse in agricultural prices. Agricultural prices remained low throughout the rest of the period.

After the peak of 1921, incomes plummeted in 1922 to about 53 per cent of the previous year's level. Thereafter, apart from a slight recovery in the late 1920s, they slid inexorably downward, to the nadir in 1932 when the total income reported was $74,850. This represents barely more than a quarter of the 1919 total and a mere 17 per cent of the bountiful year of 1921. In per capita terms, the earnings of 1932 meant that there were approximately $35 for each man, woman, and child for the entire year, or less than $15 per month for a family of five.[74] By comparison, in the Depression year of 1936 the city of North Bay provided a maximum monthly relief allowance of $21.66 for a five-person family. This amount was calculated to provide only the absolute essentials and was for food only, additional amounts being allowed for fuel and rent.[75]

Although the department's figures for the Manitowaning agency moved gradually upward again from 1933 on, the increases were quite slight and can hardly be designated as a recovery. By 1938 they were recorded at almost $132,000, still only half of the 1919 total. The shortfalls occurred in all categories except annuities and interest payments, which remained constant. If the cash income levels of 1919 and the two years that followed may be seen as years of moderate comfort, they were succeeded by two decades of increasing impoverishment. In the Depression of the 1930s, the people of Manitowaning were desperately poor, probably poorer than many non-Natives of the area. Moreover, their agent was exceedingly reluctant to give relief to the able-bodied. For the most part, he restricted his intervention to distributions of flour and other foodstuffs, and often denied even this form of aid to able-bodied single men. This was the economic picture facing the people of the Manitowaning agency in the years with which this study is concerned.

Although the Parry Sound agency was large compared to those further south in Ontario, all its dimensions appear relatively small beside Manitowaning. Its seven reserves were home to a total of 878 people in 1924, compared to the 2,253 reported for the Manitowaning agency in the same year (see Tables 5 and 6). None of the bands occupying these reserves was particularly large: the greatest population at any time was that of Parry Island in 1924, with 292 people. While Parry Island was located close to Parry Sound, some of the other reserves were far

Table 5
Manitowaning Agency Population by Band and Year

Band	1918	1924	1929	1934
Beausoleil	8	3	N/A	N/A
Manitoulin Island Unceded	1,136	1,283	1,369	1,378
Point Grondine	46	52	43	33
Sheguiandah	121	119	114	108
South Bay	86	75	51	45
Spanish River No. 3	214	215	140	107
Sucker Creek	134	100	79	69
Sucker Lake	10	10	12	7
Tahgaiwinine	131	146	130	110
Whitefish Lake	176	159	142	130
Whitefish River	76	91	107	126
Total	2,138	2,253	2,187	2,113

Table 6
Parry Sound Agency Population by Band and Year

Band	1918	1924	1929	1934
Gibson/Wahta	133	192	133	254
Henvey Inlet	167	216	151	159
Magnetawan	30	31	50	37
Moose Deer Point	N/A	N/A	43	45
Parry Island	116	292	253	122
Shawanaga	119	147	125	95
Total	565	878	755	712

from population centres, and thus isolated. Moose Deer Point, a small band with 45 members in 1934, was apparently accessible only by boat.[76]

As on Manitoulin Island, fish and game resources underwent a rapid decline following non-Aboriginal settlement of the area. Complaints about diminishing fish and game for food—particularly the fish, an important item in the diet—are recorded as early as the mid-nineteenth century.[77] Agriculture was not a viable alternative: this land is mostly hilly and rocky, unsuited to the growth of substantial crops, although many people maintained small gardens.[78] Livestock production was never undertaken to any great extent. As we have seen, tourism, lumbering,

From the beginning of white settlement around Georgian Bay, First Nations people faced growing competition from the newcomers who hunted the diminished supplies of game. Archives of Ontario, RG 1-448-1, Box 106, #464.

and loading freight were the industries in which First Nations men found sources of income. The women's industries were similar to those of the Manitowaning agency, with the addition of some domestic work in the homes of local white settlers. In contrast to the high mobility among people of the Manitowaning agency, reserve residence seemed to be the typical pattern in the Parry Sound agency for much of the year. This was probably a result of the greater employment opportunities located nearby, which allowed more people to earn income while based on their reserves.

The movements of the local economy cannot be discerned as well as those in Manitowaning because the Indian department's statistics for this agency are inadequate. After the first year of his tenure, agent John Daly reported identical figures in most categories from 1923 to 1931.[79] The only figures that varied from year to year were receipts from land rentals and timber sales, and interest and annuity payments, statistics that Daly's other duties forced him to track regularly (see Table 4).[80] These records can thus be used only in certain ways. The figures given for wage earnings are practically useless until 1932, when they start to vary. The same may be said of the statistics on farm produce, except that they demonstrate the insignificant place of farming in the area, in contrast to Manitoulin Island.[81] Nevertheless, certain conclusions can be drawn from these data.

Per capita incomes show a slightly different pattern compared to the Manitowaning agency, though it was really just a matter of postponing the decline.

In Daly's agency incomes peaked in 1924 instead of 1921, and then showed a similar relentless downward trend. The difference resulted from a considerable inflow of timber money between 1922 and 1926, peaking at nearly $53,000 in 1924. Most of this cash would have gone into the band fund rather than into individual earnings.[82] Since it is impossible to know how much of the timber money went into the people's pockets, we can only calculate this income as part of individual earnings. Unfortunately, this undoubtedly results in an inflation of Parry Sound incomes, and the reader should bear this in mind.

Based on Daly's figures, the per capita income in 1918 (a very poor year) was $47 per person, or less than $20 per month for a family of five. Earnings from wage labour improved dramatically in 1919, but then remained roughly constant, without showing the boom Manitowaning experienced in 1920 and 1921. The highest recorded income occurred in 1924, when the people earned about $126 per person, or $52.50 monthly for a five-person family. This amount is probably inflated by the timber statistic, yet it is still less than two-thirds of the earnings for Manitowaning in the same year. After 1924, incomes fell off fairly steadily year by year to 1931[83] and then plummeted in 1932 when the wage labour market collapsed. In this year, the worst of the period, incomes were cut to less than a third of the previous year, falling to the equivalent of $11.25 monthly for a five-person family. Incomes remained at this drastically low level throughout the rest of the 1930s, and it is likely that earnings came almost exclusively from the road labour the men performed as relief work. In 1938 a slight improvement in conditions is indicated, as wage labour income increased significantly, but these earnings still totalled well under half of what they had been in the 1920s.

In short, this was a bleak period for the people of the Parry Sound agency. Even in the relatively buoyant economy of the 1920s, they lived on significantly less than their counterparts in the Manitowaning agency, who were themselves far from rich. The declining fortunes of the late 1920s gave way to the near-destitution of the 1930s, when many people were clearly desperate for food, clothing, and other essentials. In a contrast that must have been glaringly obvious to the people, both Lewis and Daly were earning $2,040 per annum in the 1930s, or $170 a month.[84]

It is not surprising, then, to see that anthropologists who visited Parry Island in the 1920s perceived the people as living poorly. Their accounts lend some insight into the daily reality of the island's residents. Frederick Johnson, for instance, described their housing and economy in terms that clearly suggested poverty. He wrote that some lived in log cabins, and a larger group in 'poorly constructed' tarpaper shacks. In outlining their economic pursuits, Johnson declared that fishing and hunting had been reduced to 'sport' thanks to the depletion of stocks, and that, in general, the people were 'forced to rely on their small gardens, poor cows, and a few odd jobs that they can pick up about the towns in order to secure a livelihood.'[85] Curiously, Johnson did not mention other wage-earning opportunities in the lumber industry and at Depot Harbour. Another anthropologist did, however, while still depicting the community as relatively disadvantaged. Diamond Jenness, one of the most prominent anthropologists of his day, conducted interviews on Parry Island in the late 1920s and later published a book about the reserve and its people. He cited a wider range of jobs, corresponding to those we have already listed, but added, 'Steady employment all the year round practically does not exist.' Jenness also stated that the people gardened and collected wild fruits, but that 'for most of their food supply they depend, like their white neighbours, on the stores.'[86] Thus, although the DIA liked to claim that First Nations people could get some of their food for free by gathering it locally, clearly the people required cash to feed themselves, and they had great difficulty maintaining or creating a cash income during the Great Depression. Its only available replacement was relief rations from the agent.

Conclusion

The interwar period saw a steady and then steep decline in First Nations people's incomes in the area of this study. By the 1930s, most were merely eking out a precarious existence and were heavily dependent on relief. While Euro-Canadians in the region were also badly affected by the near-disappearance of wage-earning opportunities, they at least received higher levels of relief from the municipalities. When the DIA instituted standardized relief issues in the 1930s, it prescribed $4 monthly for a single person and allowed only tiny increments for larger families, capping monthly amounts at $10 even for the largest households.[87] This was drastically below the amounts required to sustain people. We have seen that North Bay's relief rates for a five-person family were more than twice as high. Daly objected repeatedly that the department's relief was insufficient, but his protests fell on deaf ears. Even if one takes as a basis the relatively low calculation for 1932, that at least $6–$7 per week were required to provide a balanced diet for a family of five, the department's relief rates fell terribly short.[88] In 1932, the First Nations people of this study subsisted on incomes barely over half this amount.

No doubt the people in both the Parry Sound and the Manitowaning agencies made up the shortfall as much as possible by hunting, fishing, and trapping. But income from wage labour and timber sales had been important to both economies, since fish and game stocks had long been insufficient to feed First Nations people. Moreover, local Euro-Canadians were also endeavouring to supplement their diets from these sources. The impact on the people's livelihoods was severe.

The immediate post-war period and the mid-1920s were relatively good times, and First Nations people apparently participated modestly in the benefits. In the 1930s, they faced hard times, harder even than those experienced by many of their non-Native neighbours. Meanwhile, the Indian agents were among the lucky ones whose standard of living improved, since their incomes remained stable while prices fell. The 1930s were clearly the period in which Indian agents enjoyed the most power. The progressive disappearance of cash-earning possibilities forced more and more First Nations people to turn to the agent for help, simply to survive and feed their families. This meant that political agitation against the agent or the DIA became riskier than ever, because it could result in the denial or withdrawal of much-needed relief. Daly openly used the denial of rations to punish political opponents, especially once he had the ability to dispense roadwork instead of simply handing out rations. The resulting interactions, conflicts, and disputes are a major theme of this study.

2

'A Particularly Authoritarian Organization': The Administrative Context

'If anything is responsible for the backwardness of the Indians today it is the domineering, dictating, vetoing method of the Indian Department.'[1]

'There is hardly any matter that an Indian can undertake that is not dependent for its outcome on the whim of some official who probably has the most casual knowledge or no knowledge whatever of the circumstances to be considered.'[2]

Aboriginal people who lived on reserves in the interwar period inhabited a physical and administrative world defined by the Indian department. Their lives and plans were controlled by DIA officials in ways most Canadians would have found intolerable. Harold Cardinal has expressed the situation in stark language: 'If you are a treaty Indian, you've never made a move without these guys, these bureaucrats . . . saying yes or no.'[3] The reserve itself was an invention of colonialism, the Indian department decided who was entitled to live there, and the elective band council system had been imposed by the Indian Act to replace traditional systems of government. Sales of land and resources had created 'band funds' owned collectively by the band, which in some cases contained considerable sums, but access to this money was strictly controlled by federal officials. The agents ran the schools, the band councils, and the reserve economies. Aboriginal poverty and marginalization strongly reinforced the importance of the agent, who could offer part-time jobs on the reserve, mediation with the dominant society, and access to food rations and relief in time of need. Given his potential to help those in difficulty, he was not someone to cross lightly.

The degree to which individuals were compelled to interact with the agent varied from one person to the next. Those living off-reserve or on small, isolated reserves usually had minimal contact. Those who were financially stable had less need of the agent's services. But on a large reserve like Parry Island or Wikwemikong, where the agent visited frequently, he was a tangible presence. He influenced important economic matters such as lumbering, construction, and farming on the reserve.

Above all, he was a central figure for individuals who wished to play a political role in their community, who desired greater freedom from government control, or who sought to address unresolved treaty issues. One of the agent's most important roles was to block such activists and minimize their political effectiveness. Moreover, in his routine interactions with First Nations people the agent was a constant reminder of their wardship status, of their social inferiority and subjection to government control. This pervasive message of the agent's presence may have been one of the most lasting legacies of the system. Officials in Ottawa further drove the message home in their condescending letters permitting or denying people's requests—and undoubtedly also in the personal encounters that do not appear in the written record. It was always a power-laden encounter when First Nations people dealt with DIA officials. This chapter examines the administrative context of the interwar period, the tasks and qualities of Indian agents, and the attitudes of department personnel.

Establishment of the Indian Agent System

The Indian agent was a field officer of the Department of Indian Affairs whose role and responsibilities began to be defined in the early nineteenth century. Since the seventeenth century Britain had employed men, referred to as Indian agents or superintendents, to maintain diplomatic relations with First Nations. But until about 1815, the role of these men was essentially that of ambassador, distributing presents to Aboriginal people in order to maintain military alliances. After the War of 1812, this role became obsolete, since the British no longer needed First Nations military support to defend their North American territory.

As a result, a fundamental revisioning of Indian Affairs took place. By 1828, a new set of policies had been developed, and its implementation began in 1830 with the transfer of Indian Affairs from military to civilian control. Nineteenth-century British and British-Canadian authorities envisioned a homogeneous society in Canada modelled on the mother country. Thus began a campaign of settlement and 'civilization' (directed acculturation) of First Nations people, with the aim of integrating them into Euro-Canadian society.[4] The ultimate goal of Indian policy became the gradual elimination of First Nations people as a distinct group, an aim that persisted long past the interwar period with which this study is concerned.[5] Duncan Campbell Scott, Deputy Superintendent General of Indian Affairs from 1913 to 1932, summarized this unchanged objective a hundred years after it was first formally adopted: 'the government will in time reach the end of its responsibility as the Indians progress into civilization and finally disappear as a separate and distinct people, not by race extinction but by gradual assimilation with their fellow-citizens.'[6]

In pursuit of this policy, the Indian department established experimental Aboriginal settlements in Upper Canada in the 1830s with the goal of inculcating British values and habits into First Nations people. Responsibility for this acculturation was divided between Christian missionaries and Indian agents (still called Indian superintendents at this time). The latter were, for the most part, individuals who had already been involved with First Nations, making Britain's annual gift distributions and reporting on conditions. Since they were considered to have invaluable experience in dealing with Aboriginal people, they were retained in their positions. But the nature of their tasks underwent a substantial transformation, as agents became empowered to intervene more and more directly in the internal workings of Aboriginal communities.

The machinery of Indian Affairs became increasingly elaborate after Confederation. Canada passed the first Indian Act in 1876, consolidating previous laws relating to Aboriginal people and extending an intricate net of formerly piecemeal legislation over Aboriginal people across the country. In 1880 the Indian Affairs Branch achieved department status and became the Department of Indian Affairs, overseen nominally by the Department of the Interior but maintaining considerable autonomy in everyday operations. By 1913, when Duncan Campbell Scott was appointed Deputy Superintendent General of Indian Affairs, the department had become a highly centralized bureaucracy with power concentrated in the hands of a select group of officials at headquarters. As department head, Scott was known for his insistence on thrift and hierarchical authority.[7] Agents were required to submit a monthly diary detailing their daily activities, as well as a bewildering variety of monthly, quarterly, and annual reports. This was symptomatic of the growing degree of supervision and control the department exercised over its employees. By the 1920s and 1930s this control had reached a high level of elaboration. Agents carried on a regular correspondence with headquarters in which they reported their activities in detail, accounting for every penny spent and every decision made. The agent occupied one of the lowest positions in the departmental hierarchy and was chiefly responsible for carrying out the decisions and instructions of others. Between agents and the internal officials in Ottawa stood an agricultural representative and an inspector of Indian agencies, both responsible for a number of agencies. They visited occasionally to report to Ottawa on the efficiency and competence of the agents, among other things.[8]

The most important figures within the Indian department were the internal officials, designated as clerks and secretaries, who made most of the daily decisions. These men typically began their careers in the department as clerks, which was simply a form of apprenticeship preparing them for higher positions. They moved on to become secretaries, a position of much greater authority than the term implies today. A key figure for the first two or three decades of the twentieth century was John D. McLean, who carried on the lion's share of the correspondence with the agents during the 1920s. McLean had worked in the DIA since 1876, and although he tended to be referred to as a secretary, he was also the Assistant Deputy Superintendent General.[9] This was a post of considerable power, second in command to the Deputy Superintendent General. The fact that such a high-ranking official was involved in minor daily decisions and routine correspondence is indicative of the small size and scope of the department, and also of its micromanagement of the agents in the field.

The internal DIA officials were a small, insular, inward-looking group, and their plans for the future were more or less those developed in the nineteenth century. This essentially meant continuing to administer First Nations people's money and band affairs until they became enough like Euro-Canadians to be enfranchised. There were no special programs and no employees trained in long-range economic development. In fact, apart from a few engineers and surveyors, the department's staff had little training for their work. They learned from senior officials both their job skills and their attitudes towards First Nations people, which made for a good deal of continuity not only in personnel but also in work culture and beliefs about their clients.

These men were the ultimate arbiters and decision-makers. They were the audience whom the agents addressed in their correspondence, whom agents such as John Daly attempted to persuade and sway to their own way of thinking. For a less assertive agent like Robert Lewis, they were the people who determined the path to be pursued in a given situation. The agents formed, in a sense, a third party in the power struggle between Indian Affairs and First Nations people. On the one hand, they brokered the power of the DIA, acting as the source through which any benefits from the federal government flowed. Their personal knowledge of reserve conditions and individual Native people meant that they could act on behalf of First Nations people as well, even to the extent of attempting to alter Indian policy or specific decisions. Though they had no power to change key policies, agents could moderate their effects. By the same token, they were the only means of access to federal officials. The Indian department generally refused to correspond directly with First Nations people, and most other government bodies passed on any Aboriginal-related problems to Indian Affairs. In addition, the multiplicity of the agents' roles endowed them with considerable power over Aboriginal people, who needed to cultivate good relations with the agent if they wished to retain him as a potential resource. Although they were DIA employees and under the direct control of internal officials, as men in the middle the agents were not simply passive instruments of central authority, but could play their own considerable part.

Functions and Selection of Agents

Indian agents had two primary functions: to implement DIA policies and to keep its officials informed of conditions and developments on the reserves. In effect, both functions were simply aspects of maintaining control over reserve communities. Another major area of responsibility was the enforcement of the Indian Act. In addition to these broader functions, field officials had a wide variety of tasks to attend to, most of them administrative matters relating to the political and economic affairs of the reserves. Every reserve matter that involved interaction with the outside world was handled by the Indian agent.

Indian agents also had an impact in various ways on individual Aboriginal people. They had some role in policing morality on the reserves, they settled disputes, and they provided social services such as rations, relief, and organizing care of the elderly. This kind of activity could be helpful, but it was a double-edged sword. The social functions performed by these officials significantly broadened their ability to exercise power. When agents wished to curtail the political activities of Aboriginal activists, for instance, they could use their social power as an effective control mechanism. Native activist Harold Cardinal has outlined some of the ways in which an agent could do this:

> The Indian agent . . . actively worked against the leaders of the day. . . . He had many weapons. . . . Sometimes he openly threatened to punish people who persisted in organizational efforts. More often he used more subtle weapons such as delaying relief payments or rations to show the Indians which way the wind was blowing. . . . By spreading gossip or falsifying facts, the government officials often were able to undermine the leaders through their own people. It was made quite obvious to people on the reserve that it was not wise to talk to certain Indians.[10]

This description accords with some of the complaints Francis Pegahmagabow made about Daly's behaviour, claiming that the agent had discredited the council, taken sides among the band, and discouraged people from associating with Pegahmagabow himself.[11]

The criteria for selecting Indian agents varied over time. The early superintendents, up to about the 1830s, were military men, employees of the Indian Affairs Branch attached to the British army. In most cases these men had fought side by side with Aboriginal warriors; they spoke Aboriginal languages, and often married First Nations women. Certain families even established dynasties within Indian Affairs, ensuring that their sons and other relatives obtained employment with the branch.[12] With the transfer of Indian Affairs to civil control in 1830, this tradition died out. In the mid- and late nineteenth century, Indian agents were sometimes local missionaries who were already involved with the Aboriginal groups concerned. This arrangement can be explained by the fact that the missionaries had succeeded soldiers as the Euro-Canadians who knew First Nations people best and might even speak one or more of their languages. Both military and missionary Indian agents had pre-existing personal relationships with Aboriginal people, and at times the missionaries had their own agendas, which might conflict with that of officials at headquarters. Thus agents of these types were capable of acting as a counterbalance to the power of the department.

Increasingly, however, Indian agents were political appointees who took the job as a livelihood. They no longer had prior experience with Aboriginal people or knowledge of their languages, much less wives of Aboriginal descent. They obtained their positions through patronage, which meant that the major selection criterion was their affiliation with the political party currently in power. Although in the early 1930s the records begin to refer sporadically to 'competitions' for appointments, the nature of these is unclear.[13] It appears that patronage continued to operate, perhaps slightly more covertly, up to World War II.[14] For twentieth-century agents, the primary allegiance was to the Indian department. Although agents often showed more sympathy for Aboriginal people than did the internal officials, where Aboriginal and government interests conflicted, the agents were likely to throw their weight behind the government's plans.

It is worth noting that as late as the 1950s, there were few formal qualifications for field officials of Indian Affairs. In 1958 anthropologist R.W. Dunning obtained a letter from a regional supervisor who stated that those hired were simply expected to be familiar with the office procedures and filing system of the Indian Affairs Branch. The desirable qualities listed included knowledge of the local area and technical knowledge of road- and bridge-building. Vacancies were not always publicly advertised, since recruitments were normally from within the branch or related government departments.[15] Such recruitment procedures were in keeping with the branch's reputation for an inward-looking mentality, a feature of its corporate culture that had been established very early.[16]

The Indian Act

As DIA representatives, Indian agents exercised many of the powers the Indian Act vested in the Superintendent General. The provisions of the Indian Act governed many aspects of Aboriginal lives and powerfully shaped the agent's job as well. This legislation covered an immense range of issues: lands, education, band government, band membership, agriculture, timber, mining, illegitimacy, wills and testaments, and liquor, to name a few. It overrode federal legislation in some respects and, as a federal bureaucrat noted soon after its initial passage, it had 'the force of the Criminal Code and the impact of a constitution' on Aboriginal people.[17] This comprehensive Act, first passed in 1876 as an amalgamation of existing laws, was supplemented and amended almost yearly, generally in the direction of weakening Aboriginal self-determination and strengthening the government's coercive powers. It supplied Indian agents, as representatives of the Superintendent General of Indian Affairs, with broad powers to shape individual lives, exert political control over Aboriginal affairs, and apply sanctions to those who dared to defy their authority.

The Indian Act gave government officials significant control over the economic activities of First Nations communities. Perhaps the most important factor was the department's control of band funds, which consisted of money the bands had received for the sale or lease of land, timber, or other resources. These funds were owned in common by the band, but were held in Ottawa and could be disbursed only upon the passage of a band council resolution. Band council resolutions, in turn, were valid only if approved by the department. Thus a council decision to use band funds for any purpose was subject to an absolute DIA veto. The same was true of band resources such as timber—cutting lumber, firewood, and other wood products for sale could make an important contribution to reserve incomes, but access to these resources on their own land was contingent on department approval. On the other hand, the department had the right to grant licences to cut trees on reserve lands without reference to the band council. After 1918 the DIA even had the right to expend band funds against the band's will, although it seems that little use was made of this provision.[18] In general, the deployment of resources was a critical area in which economic and political power was transferred by law from First Nations communities to the federal government.

Other provisions of the Indian Act were equally significant in economic terms. Status Indians were protected from seizure of their property for debt, a feature based on their presumed incompetence to manage their affairs. While this provision sometimes saved them from personal losses, it also had the effect of blocking Aboriginal people from practically any access to bank loans because their property could not be used for collateral. The only remaining sources of loans were band funds or the DIA itself. Similarly, title to the reserves themselves was vested in the Indian department. Not only were band members unable to mortgage their land or sell it to outsiders, but even leasing land for various purposes tended to be the prerogative of the department. Typically, department officials insisted on negotiating contracts for leases, timber permits, woodcutting contracts, and other such matters, rather than letting First Nations people handle these themselves. Under the Indian Act, the department also had the right to lease 'unused' reserve land against the will of the band.

The department exercised extensive political power over First Nations as well. By the interwar period, the elective band council system had been imposed on most southern Ontario First Nations, superseding traditional government. Although the band council was elected by all the adult male members of the band, the illusion of democracy stopped there. The department's veto power over council resolutions has already been mentioned. This power, which was routinely employed, allowed federal officials total control of band funds and nearly complete control over the council's activities. The chiefs and councillors themselves could be deposed by the department for 'dishonesty, intemperance, immorality or incompetency', and the department was known, on occasion, to veto the nomination or election of chiefs who opposed its policies.[19] The powers and responsibilities of the councils were in any case defined in highly restrictive terms. The only significant power assigned to the councils was that of distributing land within the reserve. A single line in the Indian Act made the priorities of federal policy abundantly clear: 'In the event of any conflict between any regulation made by the Superintendent General and any rule or regulation made by any band, the regulations made by the Superintendent General shall prevail.'[20]

Indian agents could exercise authority over meetings of band councils in important ways. It was their role to call council meetings, act as the chair, and express their own views in deliberations. They were excluded only from the voting process. Burton Jacobs has written that, under this system, all administrative matters related to reserves were directly controlled by the agent. In Jacobs's experience, the agent acted autocratically, insisting that council meetings were official only when he was present and arriving at meetings with a list of items he expected the council to pass. The agent might argue with councillors who expressed views he opposed, and he was always in a position to urge officials at headquarters to veto a resolution he disliked.[21]

Perhaps the most decisive power assigned to Indian agents under the Indian Act was their role in dispensing justice. Since 1881, agents had been justices of the peace for the reserves under their charge, responsible for offences under the Indian Act and some sections of the Criminal Code.[22] This meant that for minor offences (most often for alcohol consumption) the agent frequently laid the charges himself, investigated them, examined the evidence, pronounced the verdict, and, if applicable, assigned a penalty. For fines of $10 or less, or 30 days in jail, no appeal was permitted. Such a form of justice could hardly have the appearance of impartiality or due process.

Finally, the Indian Act gave federal officials the power to decide who enjoyed band membership and the other privileges of Indian status. Not only was the Indian department the final arbiter in questions of who belonged to a band, but in practice Indian agents constantly made decisions about which individuals they would assist, regardless of their band affiliation or lack thereof. Some individuals were referred to as 'halfbreeds' or 'non-treaty Indians' but given relief and other assistance by the agents. On the other hand, since non-treaty Indians and those belonging to a different band had no legal right to reside on a reserve, they could be summarily expelled by the agent. DIA officials thus functioned as gatekeepers to Indian status, while Aboriginal communities were robbed of the ability to determine their own membership. Particularly affected were children born out of wedlock, people who lived off the reserves, and those who had no band membership on the reserve where they were living.

Daly provided a telling demonstration of the DIA's power over 'non-treaty Indians' when he expelled a man named Kelso R. from the Parry Island Reserve. Kelso R. was described as a 'half-breed' and did not enjoy membership in the Parry Island band, but he had lived on the island since childhood.[23] The reasons for his expulsion are not entirely clear, except that Daly disliked the man and claimed that he was undermining his authority. The man had been acting as secretary to the band council, and Daly's account of the matter suggests that he was taking an overtly political role. The agent claimed that R. had caused 'a lot of dissatisfaction' on the reserve by 'posing as a Secretary for the Band and advising the Indians that he can get better results from the Dept. than the Agent.' He stated that R. had been trying to discredit him as agent for over two years, and also made some unspecific allegations about possible illegal activities relating to a young woman. Finally, he claimed that R. was 'a dangerous man to have around any Reserve'.[24] DIA secretary J.D. McLean promptly wrote back authorizing Daly to expel Kelso R., and the agent moved fast.[25] Despite a flurry of efforts by the Parry Island chief and some lawyers to protect R., within 13 days Daly could report that he had been permanently removed and banished from the reserve. He had also been banned from returning to any other reserve in the Parry Sound agency and had been jailed for a month, just to drive the lesson home.[26] The Indian Act allowed an agent, band chief, or band constable to eject any non-band member from a reserve. An agent could do so against the band's will, as in this case, and could also authorize anyone to live on a reserve regardless of the band's wishes. An agent's decision to expel someone from the reserve was final and no appeal was allowed.[27]

Indian policy was designed, in addition, to supply incentives to First Nations people to abandon their Aboriginal community and identity through the enfranchisement process. Since 1857, legislation had provided a process whereby anyone of Indian status could apply to become 'enfranchised' and thus admitted to full citizenship. To do so, one had to give up Indian status, which essentially meant renouncing membership in the First Nations community. Enfranchisement meant losing important rights and privileges—the right to live on a reserve, Indian Act protections such as freedom from taxation, and (theoretically at least) access to benefits distributed by the Indian department. Enfranchisees received their proportionate share of band funds and annuities and thereafter ceased to have any right to share in band resources. Men with wives and children received a lump sum representing the whole family's share, which was often a significant financial incentive. The intent of this provision was to achieve the gradual elimination of reserves and First Nations communities, as enfranchisees received parcels of reserve land to hold as private property and, it was assumed, would become assimilated into mainstream Canadian society. If all members of a band enfranchised, their original reserve would disappear into individually owned holdings that could be bought and sold like any other land. In the 1920s and 1930s, achieving the enfranchisement of all Indian status persons in Canada was an official goal of Indian policy.

The Indian Agent:
Sole Route to the Indian Department

Thanks to federal policy and Indian department attitudes, the Indian agent was the sole conduit between the DIA and First Nations people. In the eyes of officials in Ottawa, the agent was acting on the department's behalf. His reports and recommendations were assumed to be accurate and impartial, and if Aboriginal people were displeased with his actions they were likely to be considered troublemakers. For Aboriginal people, there was no avenue for circumventing the agent or for redress if his actions were contrary to their wishes. Complaints sent directly to the department were either ignored or handled by asking the agent for explanations. Rarely was an agent unable to explain a matter to the department's satisfaction.

Moreover, the department had long since developed a fortress mentality with regard to complaints from its Aboriginal clients. In her study of Indian Affairs policies in the Canadian West, Sarah Carter described the department's 'formula response' to Aboriginal grievances: 'Indians were dismissed as chronic complainers and lazy idlers willing to go to any lengths to avoid work. At the same time, nefarious "outside agitators"—usually unnamed—were blamed for any discontent.'[28] Most grievances expressed by Native people could be discounted using this set of explanations. As noted earlier, the Indian department had always preferred to communicate with First Nations people at one remove, that is, through the Indian agent. In 1933, it made this preference into official policy, prohibiting Aboriginal people from approaching the department directly—all inquiries, requests, and complaints had to be made through the Indian agent.[29] The policy was enforced by a humiliating procedure in which the agent confronted anyone who wrote to the department, advising the person that the department would respond only to requests sent through him. Although this did not prevent Aboriginal spokespersons from continuing to write to the department and other agencies, it did mean they faced swift exposure when they tried to campaign surreptitiously against the agent.

Many resourceful people found ways around this system—by complaining to the inspector of Indian agencies, for example, or engaging a lawyer or member of

Parliament to intervene. Such persons could sometimes increase First Nations people's leverage with DIA officials. As a rule, however, the department made every effort to protect its exclusive jurisdiction over Aboriginal affairs and to reinforce the subordinate position of Aboriginal people. Historian Helen Buckley, analyzing the failure of Indian policy in the Prairie provinces, has aptly written that the role assigned to First Nations people 'consisted largely of following instructions and refraining from making trouble.'[30] Leadership and decision-making functions were to be left to the white bureaucrats.

Within this system, the agents exercised power over First Nations people but were themselves strictly controlled by higher-ranking officials. Any suggestion that agents were attempting to usurp the decision-making prerogative of their superiors resulted in sharp reminders of their inferior status. The comments of H.B. Hawthorn after investigating the Indian Affairs Branch in the 1950s and 1960s apply equally well to earlier periods: 'The Branch was, and had a widespread reputation for being, a particularly authoritarian organization . . . characterized by a concentration of decision-making at the top.'[31] The agent's job entailed prompt attention to the voluminous correspondence from the department and the wide range of reports it required. The paperwork also included correspondence with Aboriginal people, tradespeople, clergymen, and a wide variety of others, as well as extensive record-keeping.[32] While the agent's position demanded the exercise of power, it also involved a central function of service provision. These two roles often coexisted in an uneasy and precarious balance.

Official Paternalism and Racial Stereotypes

It should be clear already that the Indian agent's role was strongly paternalistic in nature. As the Indian department's 1933 instruction booklet 'General Instructions to Indian Agents in Canada' expressed it, 'The officers of the Department are reminded of their responsibilities as guardians of the Indians entrusted to their immediate care.'[33] The department's officials were committed to paternalistic management of Aboriginal people and they expected their clients to be grateful for it. This explains much of the conflict between the two groups, which occurred not only because many Aboriginal people wished to run their own affairs, but also because of the gulf between the two cultures with respect to gratitude. First Nations cultures placed little or no emphasis on gratitude as a response to assistance, since helping others was simply the correct thing to do. They did not display gratitude in Euro-Canadian fashion, and this was one factor in the tendency of both external and internal officials to perceive their clients as 'ungrateful'. Shortly after World War II, a senior official in the Indian Affairs Branch expressed this attitude vividly:

> If there is an Indian anywhere who speaks words of appreciation about the things we are attempting to do for him . . . well, I have never met him. This mistrust and suspicion on the part of the Indian population is, to me, appalling, shocking and frankly, discouraging.[34]

It is worth noting, of course, that some of the 'ingratitude' and suspicion witnessed by DIA officials actually arose from resentment about the many negative experiences the people had had with the government and its representatives.

The meaning of paternalism for agent Daly is summarized in this book's epigraph: 'behind all the seeming indifference of the Indian for the officials of the Department, I am glad to say that in their heart, they know the Department is watching with a fatherly eye to their care and protection.'[35] Here Daly constructed his work in terms of offering fatherly protection. For Aboriginal people, this child-like state was to last throughout their lives. These remarks appeared in a letter about 73-year-old elder John Manitowaba, who was attempting to address the issue of treaty rights. Regardless of their age, First Nations people were considered to be legal minors who might never reach the stage of assuming responsibility for their own lives. Daly's next sentence framed Aboriginal people clearly as immature dependants: 'I notice this when they are sick, and in need of help, they depend as little children on the officials of the Department to see them through.'[36] After a century of guardianship over the people, department officials had come to see this relationship as open-ended, rather than as a temporary, goal-oriented process leading to Aboriginal independence.

The notion of British authorities as paternal figures had a long history in British-Aboriginal relations and had been accepted or even encouraged by the Anishinabek, but with hindsight it is clear that the two sides interpreted this metaphor quite differently. In the eighteenth and nineteenth centuries, the Ojibway and other Algonquian groups addressed British authorities as 'Father' and during the long Victorian era they referred to the Queen as their mother. But the meaning of the parent-child relationship for the British and Euro-Canadians was quite different from that of Ojibway culture. In British and Euro-Canadian culture, the most important feature of the father-child relationship was the child's duty of obedience—this was particularly pronounced in the eighteenth and nineteenth centuries, but remained true well into the twentieth century. For the Ojibway, however, children did not owe their parents obedience. The distinguishing feature of the relationship for them was the father's duty to feed and protect his child. Thus, what appeared to be a shared metaphor was actually a great misunderstanding in which the two sides drew on vastly different cultural norms. Legal scholar Paul Williams has aptly summarized the diverging meanings: 'In receiving a European sovereign as their "father," the Indian nations would believe they had someone who would care for them and protect them from their enemies. The British, on the other hand, thought they had arranged for the acquisition by the King of new subjects with a duty of absolute obedience.'[37]

In theory, the purpose of the department's paternal authority was to enable its officials to make full citizens out of its wards. Yet the state of their work was discouraging. It was long since clear that the assimilative programs were not working and that First Nations people rejected the goal of assimilation. The people had recognized the long-term assimilative aim of enfranchisement as soon as the provision was introduced, and waged effective passive resistance by simply refusing to undergo the process. Administrators adapted to this reality in two ways. On the one hand, head bureaucrat Duncan Campbell Scott worked to secure increased coercive powers through amendments to the Indian Act. On the other hand, most of his fellow officials appear to have resigned themselves to a more or less permanent state of tutelage for Aboriginal people.

This resignation contributed to a hardening of racist attitudes, in which First Nations people were perceived as having character flaws that explained both the defeat of Indian policy and Aboriginal economic difficulties. Older attitudes, which saw First Nations people as intelligent and capable of adaptation to 'civilization', persisted, but there was a parallel current of scapegoating. As Daniel Francis found in his study of the 'Imaginary Indian' created by non-Aboriginals, the frustration experienced by DIA officials led them to conclude that 'Indians were by nature lazy, intellectually backward and resistant to change.'[38] This conception served to explain the low success rate of assimilation: the administrators 'blame[d] the Indian for not becoming a White man fast enough.'[39]

Aboriginal people's rejection of assimilation and enfranchisement had serious consequences—in fact, it made Indian policy nonsensical. Indian Affairs had envisioned a gradual diminution of its client base as individuals enfranchised and received parcels of reserve land as their private property. Instead, the vast majority chose to retain their Indian status. Meanwhile, after generations of numerical decline, the Aboriginal population stabilized and then began to grow.[40] Since reserves remained fixed in size, and often even shrank due to further land surrenders, this meant that a growing population had to be sustained by diminishing resources.

Such a situation had not been foreseen, and there were no plans in place to guide Indian agents in dealing with it. The long-term planning of the Indian department had not included involvement in the economic development of the reserves. The reserves were not conceived as economically self-sufficient units, nor were they really intended to sustain even their original populations. They were training grounds, from which Canadian citizens were to emerge and disappear into the general population. Instead, the department found itself in charge of an increasingly impoverished people who clung tenaciously to their land, their cultural identity, and their Aboriginal rights.

While officials were concerned about the failure of enfranchisement, they seemed less dismayed by the problem of poverty. In part this was due to the individualistic, laissez-faire ethic of the period, which blamed poor people for their own misfortune. But racist ideas played a part as well. The accepted standard of Aboriginal subsistence was very low, as demonstrated by the exceedingly low rates of relief and other evidence in the records.[41] First Nations people were expected to integrate into Canadian society as part of the unskilled and semi-skilled working class. There was little effort to provide more than a rudimentary education for First Nations children, and programs in residential and day schools prepared the students only for farming, domestic service, and working-class occupations.

Indian Policy in the 1920s and 1930s

Deputy Superintendent General Duncan Campbell Scott was acutely aware of the lack of progress on assimilation, and he took action at the level of policy. Scott was engaged in the 1920s in a vigorous campaign to silence Aboriginal protest and enforce compliance with assimilation. He pursued the former goal in various ways, including an amendment to the Indian Act forbidding the pursuit of claims against the government without Indian department authorization.[42] Scott sought to forward assimilation primarily through a simplified enfranchisement procedure and a provision that allowed the department to enfranchise people against their will.[43] At the same time, the Indian agents and lower-ranking internal officials seemed to pay little attention to the policy of promoting enfranchisement. Rather, they were absorbed in routine tasks and confronted daily with evidence of Aboriginal cultural persistence and segregation. The agents made no visible effort to urge enfranchisement on their clients and expressed doubt about the wisdom of the procedure. Their immediate superiors in Ottawa constantly emphasized the importance of promoting self-reliance, but never explicitly linked this strategy with the long-term objective of assimilation. Thus, contradictions existed between the stated objectives of the department and the everyday behaviour of its staff.

By the 1930s, a pragmatic consensus seems to have emerged within Indian Affairs, based on an acceptance that assimilation would not occur quickly. The interim goal became 'making the Indians self-supporting on their reserves'. At a conference held in 1939, three highly placed officials from the Indian Affairs Branch expressed their views on their work. The speakers were Deputy Superintendent General Harold McGill, who succeeded Scott in 1932; T.R.L. MacInnes, long-time secretary; and D.J. Allan, in charge of reserves and trusts. Their speeches permit insights into the policy goals being pursued in the period and the attitudes informing policy.

The most common theme in the printed speeches was a paternalistic conviction that First Nations people needed to be taught, guided, and moulded according to the vision of branch officials. The work of the branch was depicted primarily in terms of its control functions. For instance, secretary T.R.L. MacInnes cited financial and resource management, service provision, and 'agricultural and industrial supervision' as the main activities. In the midst of stereotypes about Aboriginal character and inability to manage their own affairs, the theme of self-support was repeatedly stressed. For public consumption, at least, there was a unanimous disavowal of compulsion, especially with respect to assimilation. MacInnes, whose job probably entailed the most significant role in day-to-day decisions affecting First Nations people, criticized them for 'cling[ing] to tutelage' and endorsed complete enfranchisement as the long-term goal. Yet he concluded that the immediate aim was to encourage Aboriginal self-sufficiency under branch supervision.[44] D.J. Allan actually rejected the assimilation model:

not equal

> [The Indian] need be assimilated only as he wishes to be, and our object should be, and is, rather to make him a good Indian than a third- or fourth-rate imitation of a white man. This we will do if we try to force him into a stereotyped white mould for which he is not fitted, and which he may abhor.[45]

Forced assimilation, then, would lead to a highly inferior imitation of whiteness—a suggestion that speaks volumes about Allan's view of First Nations people.

The administrators' assumptions about Aboriginal economic pursuits were shaped by a set of stereotypes about 'instincts' and 'character' that normalized the existing confinement of First Nations people to low-paying forms of labour. Branch head Harold McGill claimed credit for 'directing' Aboriginal energies into primary industries—work in forests, sawmills, fishing, and agriculture—that were supposedly connected to their traditional lifestyle.[46] Perhaps understandably, then, the long-term prognosis of the administrators did not seem particularly optimistic. D.J. Allan stressed in his address that 'Indian maintenance' did not need to become a significant problem for 'a young and virile nation', especially since First Nations people were such a small proportion of the population. In other words, maintenance would remain necessary, but a 'virile' nation like Canada could withstand the expense.

As these comments demonstrate, administrators were convinced that the 'Indian problem' would persist for many years to come, perhaps indefinitely. The underlying reason was the character of 'the Indian', who was seen as essentially different from non-Aboriginal Canadians. 'Indians' were childlike, dependent individuals who were incompetent to manage their own affairs and inclined by nature to certain pursuits. The officials could see no solution to this 'Otherness' of First Nations people, which had persisted despite roughly a century of Indian administration dedicated to its erasure. Harold McGill and T.R.L. MacInnes clung to the hope that time would eventually achieve the desired transformation. D.J. Allan seems to have concluded that assimilation was unrealistic. Much of the pessimism about the Indian Affairs program centred on the officials' essentialist ideas about the nature of 'the Indian'. These ideas, which played such a significant role in both the formation of Indian policy and its application, need to be explored in greater depth.

Ideas of 'the Indian'

The term 'Indian' was associated with two interrelated sets of meanings that were embedded in Indian policy and administrative practice. First there were the racial ideas, often expressed as notions about 'Indian character', which were current in Canadian society as a whole and shared by department officials. These ideas took the form of images elaborated in art, literature, anthropology, and many kinds of popular culture. In addition, DIA officialdom had generated its own ideas about 'Indians' and the proper ways to handle them. These ideas were specific to the system of Indian administration and had a powerful, institutionalized impact on Aboriginal people that was quite distinct from the experience of generalized Canadian racism. As Noel Dyck pointed out in his study of Canada's Indian administration,

'There is an important difference between individual ethnocentrism or cultural bias supported by ignorance and the practice of state racism in the form of bureaucratized systems of discrimination and inequality.'[47]

The department was technically responsible only for those who possessed Indian status, that is, those who fitted the Indian Act's definition of an Indian. Yet in practice the attribution of Indian status was fluid and arbitrary. Decisions about an individual's eligibility for the administration's services were generally based less on the strict Indian Act definition than on prevailing notions about Indianness. Aboriginal people whose lifestyles differed from the stereotyped 'Indian mode of life' were viewed as non-Indian to some extent, regardless of their legal status or possession of band membership. By the same token, 'non-treaty Indians' who conformed to the 'Indian mode of life' were often treated very much like band members: they were permitted to live on reserves and treated like status Indians. The attribution of Indian status was like so many other elements of the Indian Affairs system: despite careful codification in law, the application of policy was characterized by a high degree of arbitrariness.

The definition of an Indian was set out quite explicitly in Canadian law. The Indian Acts of 1906 and 1927 identified two categories of First Nations people to whom the Act applied: first, a man of Aboriginal ancestry who was recognized as belonging to a particular band, along with his wife and children; and second, the 'non-treaty Indian', defined as 'any person of Indian blood who is reputed to belong to an irregular band, or who follows the Indian mode of life'.[48]

The Act did not define the term 'Indian mode of life'. Yet it was used continually in correspondence—officials clearly considered the expression self-explanatory. They applied it frequently in making judgements about an individual's right to the privileges of Indian status and also when making recommendations about applications for enfranchisement. The 'Indian mode of life' was usually placed in opposition to a 'white man's' way of earning a living. Living 'like a white man' involved living off the reserve and supporting one's family through farming or paid employment. It implied self-reliance, self-support, stability, and independence from the Indian agent.

The phrase 'Indian mode of life' was apparently adopted directly from the 1894 decision of the North-West Territories Supreme Court in *Regina v. Howson*. The court had been considering the case of a white man accused of selling liquor to an 'Indian', in contravention of the Indian Act. The defence argued that the purchaser of the alcohol was not an 'Indian' but a 'halfbreed' and therefore not subject to the Act. In its attempt to define what an Indian was, the court considered skin colour, language, and lifestyle, and concluded that reputation should be the definitive factor—that is, whether a person was reputed to be 'Indian' or not. Its actual words are worth quoting:

It is notorious that there are persons in those bands who are not full blooded Indians, who are possessed of Caucasian blood, in many of them the Caucasian blood very large [*sic*] predominates, but whose associations, habits, modes of life, and surroundings generally are essentially Indian, and the intention of the Legislature is to bring such persons within the provisions and object of the Act . . . .[49]

This judgement, then, was founded on the notion that Indianness was not merely, or even primarily, about biology or genetics, but rather was first and foremost a question of culture, associations, and lifestyle. Such a notion was strikingly similar to the attitudes of DIA personnel, who likewise considered 'mode of life' the decisive ingredient of Indianness. Shortly after the decision in *Regina v. Howson*, the Indian department amended the definition of 'Indian' in the Indian Act's clause banning the sale of liquor to Indians. The new definition extended the meaning of Indian to include 'any person, male or female, who is reputed to belong to a particular band, or who follows the Indian mode of life, or any child of such person'. As legal historian Constance Backhouse has noted, '[t]he "mode of life" phrase was lifted straight out of the *Howson* decision.'[50]

It remained necessary, of course, to infuse meaning into this nebulous phrase—but officials seemed to have no difficulty in doing so. Presumably the core ideas about the 'Indian mode of life' came from the prevailing image of how Aboriginal people lived before the advent of Europeans. But this was one stereotypical model that actually allowed for change over time—the typical mixed economy developed by many reserve residents, which retained only some elements of the 'traditional' lifestyle, was viewed as an 'Indian mode of life'. It included living either on a reserve or in the bush, and subsisting by some combination of hunting, fishing, guiding, and the sale of crafts, furs, and game. Most likely a high degree of mobility was an important component of the model. Wage labour often belonged to the picture, but, in contrast to the image of Euro-Canadian labourers, there were connotations of shiftlessness, unreliability, and/or the intermittent resort to traditional means of subsistence such as hunting. Above all, the model was predicated on an assumption of Aboriginal people living at the subsistence level. Daly, for instance, once remarked that he was considered 'rather hard' by local non-Natives for not assisting his clients more, because the sympathizers 'don't understand the Indian mode of life.'[51]

The idea that 'white' and 'Indian' economies were intrinsically different does not withstand close scrutiny. Euro-Canadian men around Georgian Bay, like many Aboriginal men, performed seasonal labour in the lumber industry and moved around from one camp or mill to another. White labourers had to be mobile in order to conform to the seasonal rhythms of work in the region. They also resorted to game and fish as a supplement to their diet, particularly during the Depression.[52] Members of both groups often maintained gardens to supply basic foods such as potatoes and vegetables. Nevertheless, officials remained convinced that there was a profound difference—perhaps not so much in the means of livelihood as in the attitudes with which those in each group were expected to approach their work.

An implicit element in the idea of the 'Indian mode of life' was the notion that First Nations people were not as industrious or work-oriented as Euro-Canadians. The image of the 'lazy Indian' is an old trope in Euro-Canadian mythology. The constant official reiteration of the need to teach Aboriginal people to be self-supporting stemmed in part from this myth. Duncan Campbell Scott once boasted that the DIA had 'made these Indians self-supporting in two generations, a remarkable transition.'[53] This statement belies the strong pre-colonial Aboriginal ethic of self-sufficiency, and seems to assume that the concept of self-reliance was lacking in their traditional cultures. In similar fashion, Daly wrote of one man in his agency, 'I have nothing personal against him, any more than he is an Indian and not very fond of work.'[54]

Industriousness in First Nations people was, of course, important from an economic standpoint because it would spare the government the expense of providing occasional relief. But there was a deeper ideological reason. Converting Aboriginal people, particularly men, to the virtues of hard work was a cultural imperative. Canadian society in this period had a strong tendency to view work as the proof of a man's morality, masculinity, and overall worth. As Angus McLaren has described this attitude, 'To be work-shy, it was understood, was unworthy of a real man. . . . A good worker was assumed to be a good man.'[55] The agents were often gratified when they saw their clients performing heavy labour such as farming, lumbering, and roadwork. Participation in these types of labour was assumed to advance the process of assimilation and to turn 'Indians' into 'honest men'.

Like 'the Indian', the 'Indian mode of life' was gender-specific, employed exclusively with reference to men. This underlines the fact that it was fundamentally an economic concept. The measures of civilization differed according to gender: men were expected to show their adaptation to Euro-Canadian standards primarily in the economic realm, while women's degree of civilization was appraised by their social and, especially, their sexual behaviour. Women were not classified as living the 'Indian mode of life' because agents viewed them in terms of Euro-Canadian norms and thus expected them to be economically dependent on men. Provided that they required no assistance from the department and satisfied the agents' notions of sexual propriety, Aboriginal women's manner of supporting themselves was of little interest. Revealingly, even those who were living with Euro-Canadian men in towns were not referred to as having adopted the 'white mode of life', nor were others ever pronounced unqualified for enfranchisement on the grounds that they still followed the Indian mode of life.

The 'mode of life' concept was applied more frequently than the other Indian Act definitions to decide who was an Indian and who was not. Those who lived off the reserve and earned their living independently could find themselves penalized for their lifestyle through loss of the department's services along with treaty and interest payments. Even those who were registered band members were liable to be placed outside the category 'Indian' when it came to dispensing the benefits of Indian status. In 1923, for instance, a registered member of Wahnapitae band appealed to R.J. Lewis when his house burned down, asking for assistance from band funds to rebuild. Lewis passed this request on to the department but advised against granting it because the man and his mother had lived in Killarney for a number of years and earned their living 'in the same manner as *other* White people', namely by farming and fishing.[56] The pair's transition, in Lewis's eyes, out of the category of 'Indian' is revealed in the linguistic slippage that made them like other 'White people'. Significantly, the agent based his position not on these people's lack of need, but on his claim that they were no longer Indians. Both their means of support and their place of residence stood against their being considered

Indians in Lewis's view, in spite of their undeniable Indian status (both were band members). The agent concluded that he could not recommend giving them assistance, '[a]s these people do not reside on any Indian reserve and *do not consider themselves Indians*, only in regard to what they receive financially, and when they rebuild it will not be on any reserve.'[57] The department concurred, and these individuals were denied help. Had they resided on a reserve they would almost certainly have been treated more generously—reserve residents who suffered losses due to fire were routinely given financial compensation from band funds.

Of the two agents investigated in this study, Robert Lewis seemed more inclined to question people's status, perhaps because more of the members of his agency were off the reserves working much of the time. Lewis distinguished between Aboriginal people strictly according to their place of residence and lifestyle, with little regard for the other legal definitions of Indian status. After conducting a census in 1926, he wrote to John Daly, 'There are many other residents at Killarney who claim they should be on the Henvey Inlet[58] pay lists, but I could not see my way clear to add them in as Indians as they do not draw annuity payments and do not follow the Indian mode of life.'[59] The confusion here between the legal category of status and the conceptual one of 'Indian' is obvious. If the Killarney residents were members of the Henvey Inlet band—which was determined by birth or marriage— they were Indians according to the Indian Act. Yet in this case Lewis was clearly judging solely by people's lifestyle, without investigating the question of their band membership. Apparently the Killarney people's choice of location and livelihood had led to an effective lapse of their Indian status.

Interestingly, considerations such as quantum of Aboriginal 'blood' or heritage were not raised in these discussions. Killarney had been populated by people of mixed Aboriginal and Euro-Canadian heritage from at least the mid-nineteenth century.[60] This factor may have influenced Lewis's judgements, but he did not mention it. Certainly the issue of the Killarney Aboriginal population was problematic for Lewis, and his tendency was to deny most of them Indian status. He wrote to a local doctor that most of the people in Killarney 'try to crawl in under the Indian Act at times.'[61] This letter again revealed the conceptual confusion in the term 'Indian': it referred to 'the Indians around Killarney' but implied that they had no right to the benefits of the Indian Act. These people, in Lewis's mind, were Indians in terms of a racial category but not in a conceptual sense (following the 'Indian mode of life') or in the legal sense that would entitle them to the privileges of Indian status.

Daly's approach to the question of status was markedly different, in fact, the two agents stood practically at opposite poles. Daly did not disqualify people based on their location or occupation, perhaps because the people of his agency generally lived on the reserves and conformed more or less to the 'Indian mode of life' category. In fact, Daly practically never used the expression 'Indian mode of life'. His tendency was to see all Aboriginal people generically as Indians and himself as their guardian. The Parry Sound agency attracted many First Nations people from other bands, as well as 'non-treaty Indians', and the agent explicitly stated that they all received the same treatment.[62] To Daly, 'Indian' was primarily a racial category.

Indeed, 'Indian' was a racial category to most officials. Aboriginal people were often seen as, literally, a breed apart, biologically different from non-Aboriginals. Deputy Superintendent General Harold McGill implied this clearly in his 1939 speech, where he also addressed the question of miscegenation. Using terms that must have passed as scientific at the time, McGill attempted to alleviate any concerns about interracial marriage, noting that '[t]here seems to be a certain blood compatibility between the Indian and white races, and we have not the evidence of biological shock exemplified in other instances of racial intermixture.'[63] It is remarkable that McGill considered such a statement necessary in a country where such 'racial intermixture' had been occurring for about three centuries, with no adverse physical effects. Yet by the 1930s the mixed societies of the fur trade era were long forgotten, and despite the hundreds of thousands of mixed-race people in Canada at the time, Aboriginal people could still be seen as a separate breed that happened to have a 'blood compatibility' with Euro-Canadians.

The sharp distinction between Indians and the rest of the population was enshrined in the Indian Act, where an 'Indian' was actually defined in contradistinction to a 'person'. The definitions in the opening section of the Act included the following: '"person" means an individual other than an Indian.'[64] This was not merely a legalistic distinction. DIA officials used language in a similar way when they wrote about Aboriginal people. The discourse employed in official correspondence carefully distinguished between Aboriginal and white people, and tended to reiterate the word 'Indian' frequently, rather than referring to Aboriginal people generically as people, as men or women. For instance, in recommending that a young man receive subsidies to continue his education, Lewis described him as 'a clever Indian boy' instead of simply 'a clever boy'.[65] This tendency is indicative of the 'Otherness' of First Nations people in the minds of officials. First Nations people were not simply people, they were 'Indians', with all the ideological connotations that the term conjured. They were all perceived in the light of racial thinking and the generally held stereotypes about the nature of 'the Indian'.

Officials approached much of their work based on stereotypes so one-dimensional they were essentially caricatures—the grumbling Indian, the improvident Indian, the manipulator, the troublemaker. Perhaps the most powerful image was that of the ungrateful Indian, alluded to above as a source of discouragement for DIA officials. All of these images reflected the relationship between agents and their clients, in which the agent held more power and his clients were forced to coax, cajole, and persuade him to gain his co-operation. Aboriginal people were not unaware of the stereotypes—as activist Howard Adams later noted, they shaped their behaviour accordingly: 'Indians and Métis . . . know that the white man communicates with them on the basis of his stereotypes, so they learn to conceal their resentment and relate to him only on the surface.'[66]

Officials also sometimes classified reserve communities or band councillors into two groups: the progressive and the unprogressive. The 'progressive' ones were those who, in official eyes, accepted federal control and the goals that Indian Affairs had set for Aboriginal communities, including agriculture and assimilation. The 'unprogressive' were those who rejected the Indian agent system, opposed assimilation, or insisted on raising issues such as treaty entitlements and griev-ances. Another theme that recurred frequently in Indian Affairs documents was the notion that First Nations people had adopted primarily the worst traits of Euro-Canadians while retaining the Aboriginal traits considered least desirable. A typical example is the remark made by Indian agent Nelson Stone of the Moravian agency in southern Ontario: 'The great trouble with a lot of these Indian Soldier Settlers, is that they have more ability than a white man to expend money, and only the capac-ity of an Indian in the matter of making repayment.'[67] All of these ideas, common to the bureaucratic culture of the DIA, not only reflected but also shaped relations with First Nations people.

Agent John McLean Daly (Parry Sound, 1922–1939)

Key figures that they were, the agents' personalities significantly influenced the tone of Aboriginal-government relations and the outcome of initiatives and con-flicts. It is therefore of some importance to sketch the backgrounds and character traits of the two agents investigated in this study. Robert John Lewis occupied the Manitowaning agency on Manitoulin Island from 1915 until 1939, a career span-ning 24 years. John McLean Daly, of the Parry Sound agency on the eastern shore of Georgian Bay, was appointed in 1922 and retired 17 years later, in 1939. The Indian department's personnel was typically stable and such lengthy careers were by no means unusual. For this study, the two men provide continuity and relative consistency for an examination of policy application in the field.

John Daly was born in the Highlands of Scotland in 1873, an only son with eight sisters.[68] In 1904 he moved to Canada, where his wife and two children joined him later. After settling initially in North Bay, he worked from 1909 to 1914 for the Transcontinental Commission, apparently in some kind of supervisory capacity.[69] When World War I broke out, Daly (aged 41) volunteered along with his eldest son and served for three years and three months as a quartermaster in the Canadian Expeditionary Force. By 1922 he was working in the Customs Department, where he was employed for only three months before being named to the position of Indian agent in Parry Sound.

There is no record that explicitly discusses how he obtained the posting, but most probably it was through standard political patronage. Given that there were no real requirements for the job beyond basic literacy, patronage was the obvi-ous way to fill the position—most government jobs were allocated this way. Daly's previous known employment in Canada was all government-related, which suggests that he was connected to the local patronage network. Daly him-self later advised an acquaintance against accepting a post as Indian agent, explaining that 'even returned soldiers' in these jobs were 'at the mercy of politi-cians' and only those who were 'very well posted' should consider accepting a position.[70] These observations strongly suggest the value of political connections in landing the agent's job and also the risk of losing it when political power changed hands.[71] Daly himself was apparently well enough connected to pre-serve his job until his retirement.

For Daly, the job as Indian agent was a livelihood, a means of feeding his substantial family and perhaps of experiencing social mobility. He was an ambitious man who aspired to attain a certain socio-economic status and had specific notions of the income he should enjoy. He once wrote to an acquaintance for help in obtaining a raise in salary to $2,000 per year, thus achieving the financial position 'to which I really belong'.[72] Although he obviously understood how to work the system, this effort was unsuccessful. Not until three years later, in 1927, did he attain the salary of $2,040 a year.

In personal character, John Daly was a man of great energy and determination, raised in the high era of British imperialism and steeped in its paternalistic and patriarchal notions. He headed a large family, having been widowed once and remarried to a younger woman at the age of 54.[73] He attached great importance to his family, which included 10 children from two different wives, the last born when Daly was 60 years old.[74] He was clearly an educated man of literary tastes, writing sentimental poetry that he shared with friends and later published privately at his own expense.[75] In his correspondence with the Department of Indian Affairs Daly revealed an intense Canadian patriotism and made frequent references to his optimism about his adopted country's future.

Daly took a proactive approach to his job. He sometimes arranged jobs for Aboriginal men, he wrote to various government departments to make requests on their behalf, and in the Depression he agitated with roadwork supervisors to obtain work quotas for the men of his agency. He visited most of the reserves under his jurisdiction regularly and closely monitored band council activities. As agent, Daly appears to have been a tangible presence in Aboriginal communities; he could be very helpful, but he could equally be very controlling. He felt that he had done a great deal for First Nations people, an assessment that was passed down in his family.[76] His motivations in this ongoing activity appear complex: in part, he was a true paternalist who was genuinely concerned for the welfare of his charges, as he defined it. His own prestige and credibility with the Indian department were increased by a low rate of unemployment in his agency. Perhaps most of all, such an approach was in keeping with his value system and enabled him to exercise an influence over the lives of others. He fully embraced the heavy responsibilities of the paternalist's role, which meant that he worked a good deal more than he needed to—in fact, he appears to have been quite tireless in his schemes and activities to bring money into the reserves.

Daly's attitude towards First Nations people was generally one of superiority, which took a patronizing but benign form towards those who appeared to accept his authority and a more abrasive form when his right to rule was questioned. Daly considered himself to be the benefactor of a people who were not capable of running their own affairs, and he expected to be acknowledged as such. Moreover, he wished to mould Aboriginal behaviour through his influence and example. In 1935, for instance, he reported to Ottawa that young men at Shawanaga had been drinking and complained, 'It hurts me very much when I am doing what I can for the Indians to have them persist in their bad conduct.'[77] Nothing made him angrier than the suggestion made by some individuals that his services were not wanted, that they did not require a white man to administer their reserves.[78] There were several other occasions on which Daly expressed annoyance about opposition to the Indian agent system, and he got into conflicts with practically every council elected on Parry Island during his tenure.

At times Daly romanticized First Nations people, as a picturesque people deprived of their formerly independent way of life. Nevertheless, far from denouncing colonialism, he felt that the solution for Aboriginal people was to embrace the new dispensation, adopt the newcomers' culture, and assimilate into mainstream Canadian society. One revealing passage of a letter is worth quoting at length, as it expresses a good deal about his approach towards Aboriginal people and his view of the solution:

> Being born and raised in the west Highlands, Argyleshire Scotland, where the history of the clans is told over the peat fires, on the long winter nights, I can understand somewhat of the thoughts that pass through John Manitowaba's head and heart, and for that reason I sympathize with him and with all the Indians who live in the past, such as he does, like the Highlanders with their traditions of past glories. I do not know of anything that can be done with this Indian except that the Indian does the same thing as the highlanders of Scotland have done, and that is get out and hustle around, accept conditions as they are, and prepare themselves to take a place in their country and its affairs.[79]

This comparison of Aboriginal people to Highland Scots suggests that Daly identified to some extent with their dilemma. He was himself proud of his Scottish heritage and apparently maintained elements of the culture in which he was raised. Yet he had no difficulty in embracing the program of assimilation for First Nations people, for he felt that this solution had worked for his own people. There is a complacent ethnocentricity in his writings, a presumption of his right to determine what was best for Aboriginal people. Because of the chatty, verbose style of his letters, these attitudes are more visible in Daly's correspondence than in that of Lewis. They were fundamentally similar to the typical attitudes of officials described above. At the same time, Daly was apparently on very good terms with a few people in his agency, and he spoke with marked respect of those whose aspirations and values matched his own. Daly considered Aboriginal people essentially intelligent and capable, and spoke contemptuously only of those who were unable to support themselves or who opposed him in his position as their overseer.

John Daly was of the type often referred to as a 'character'. He was known to appear on Parry Island Reserve dressed in cavalry pants, riding boots, and a fedora hat.[80] He composed sentimental poetry (not unlike Duncan Campbell Scott) and was not ashamed to share his work with friends. He wrote letters brimming with passion to the Department of Indian Affairs, without any of the bureaucratic stiffness and formality so characteristic of much official correspondence. He was an ebullient man who liked to claim that he was 'President of the Sunshine Club', a little joke of his that referred to 'look[ing] on the bright side of life'.[81]

Daly had a controlling nature and attempted to enforce his own conception of proper behaviour on others, particularly by ensuring that men support their families on the patriarchal model. While this could make him meddlesome and sometimes harsh in his judgements, it was the accepted model of gender relations in his time. He made outrageous statements at times, but he was also a complex individual, capable of compassion as well as cynicism. Daly was a lively, conscientious individual with strong opinions and a dramatic flair. He is one of the most interesting characters in this study.

Agent Robert John Lewis
(Manitowaning, Manitoulin Island, 1915–1939)

By contrast with the energetic Scottish immigrant, Robert John Lewis appears a quiet, moderate, more bureaucratically inclined sort of man. Lewis was born in Manitowaning in 1880 of Irish Protestant descent. He began his DIA career in 1913 as agency clerk in Manitowaning. Unlike Daly, he did not enlist in the armed forces in World War I.[82] In 1915 the incumbent agent, William McLeod, died suddenly and Lewis was chosen to succeed him. This was the start of a 24-year term in office, which ended with the amalgamation of the Gore Bay and Manitowaning agencies into a single agency covering all of Manitoulin Island.

Lewis began his work as agent at a much younger age than Daly (35, to Daly's 49), and with a good deal less life experience. Although he was a full-time Indian agent, he apparently did some farming at the same time, as suggested by his remark in 1922 that he had recently sold a bull.[83] He may, then, have been a farmer before joining the civil service. As with Daly, there is no indication in the records as to how he received the appointment as Indian agent, or as agency clerk before that. When his predecessor as agent died, Lewis may have been chosen largely because he was available and acquainted with the agency routine. It was the middle of World War I and men were becoming scarce. His correspondence, in any event, gives no indication of his personal or employment history. This is in large measure the result of his particular style. Where Daly wrote letters full of personal references and expressed his opinions freely, Lewis confined himself strictly to the issue at hand. Like Daly, he was married and had children, but other details of his life outside work practically never appeared in his official correspondence. On the whole, his letters convey the impression of a reserved, rather private individual.

Lewis's career as Indian agent was spent in the town of his birth. He developed a comfortable, familiar tone in his correspondence with the chiefs and band secretaries he came to know well. His letters on everyday matters were courteous and relatively casual, and showed a fundamental respect for their recipients. Lewis would, for example, apologize if a cheque was delayed and people had to wait for payments. He also organized a good deal of business from his office, relying on chiefs to make the preparations for such matters as constructing buildings, roads, or bridges. Despite the occasional remark about his clients being 'unreliable', this choice demonstrates that he considered Aboriginal leaders capable of assuming some responsibility for daily affairs.

Lewis expressed himself in a much more temperate tone than Daly, revealing little of his general opinions. Unlike Daly, he adopted the pedantic formalities used by the department's secretaries, employing phrases such as 'I beg to say' and 'I have the honour to report' in his correspondence with the DIA, although he rarely fell into the patronizing passive voice so typical of the secretaries, who liked to express their decisions in this manner.[84] He was careful, often non-committal, content to leave much of the decision-making to the officials in Ottawa. Particularly when addressing questions that were not clear-cut, his approach was often to summarize possible arguments on both sides of an issues and leave it entirely to headquarters to resolve the problem. Indeed, at times his depiction of matters was so ambivalent that he failed to obey the departmental injunction to give a clear recommendation.

Lewis's administrative style was also markedly different from that of his fellow agent Daly. Lewis appears less controlling, less intrusive, seemingly more trusting of the judgement of others. Where Daly generally insisted on investigating every relief request himself, Lewis often left such decisions to band representatives or even local storekeepers. Lewis relied more on the mail to keep in touch with the bands under his care, although this did not spare him from travelling extensively in the course of his work. His preference for corresponding may have been due in part to the physical extent of his agency, but the Parry Sound agency was also large, which did not prevent Daly from visiting the reserves constantly. Lewis seemed to have no love for travel. His presence was clearly felt less strongly on the reserves than Daly's presence in the Parry Sound agency. While his clients may have enjoyed a greater sense of autonomy as a result, there is some evidence that their needs were also attended to less promptly. For instance, Lewis commonly left it to chiefs and band councils to report individuals in need and request relief, even though he stated on some occasions that he had been aware of the problem.[85] In other words, if no one called attention to cases of need, Lewis might be slow to take care of them.

Lewis was much less prone than Daly to make derogatory remarks about Aboriginal people in his correspondence—there are some, but they are rare and usually refer to individuals rather than to First Nations people as an undifferentiated group. Much more than John Daly, he seemed to adopt a 'live and let live' approach. He once noted that he felt 'an Indian Agent should not have any spite at any Indian',[86] and for the most part he adhered to this maxim. With a very few exceptions, Lewis revealed no bias against particular individuals. Even when someone's actions annoyed him, this agent did not indulge in political campaigns against them, as his fellow agent Daly did. By the same token, Lewis was not faced with the kinds of opposition that occurred under Daly's administration. Whether Daly's personality was a factor here is impossible to say, although some of his adversaries challenged other agents as well.

It often appears from Lewis's correspondence that he was writing of Aboriginal people with whom he had little acquaintance. This would be true of every agent at times, thanks to the mobility of their clients and the fact that band membership was not necessarily related to place of residence. Each agent would be nominally responsible for people he had never met. Yet Daly seemed well acquainted with most people he wrote about. An important factor in Lewis's case was the sheer size of his agency, the particularly high mobility of its residents, and the large population. Lewis's agency contained roughly two and one-half times as many people as Daly's.

It is worth asking, however, if Lewis's own personality was also at play here. Since this agent shared some of the agency responsibilities with others, he was probably not as powerfully visible as his fellow agent. He visited the reserves regularly, but not as frequently as Daly. Above all, if his letter-writing style is any indication, he was probably not an intrusive presence. Lewis was not vigorously engaged in exercising his authority, did not insist on an active paternalism, and seemed to take relatively little interest in the private affairs of his clients. This might simply have meant that Lewis did not have as many confrontations with Aboriginal people, but it could mean as well that people were less likely to approach him for assistance.

Indeed, it is not clear that Lewis's more casual attitude stemmed from greater respect for First Nations people or from a desire to grant them autonomy. Since he made practically no general statements about Aboriginal people in his correspondence, Lewis's overall attitude can only be inferred. It is quite evident that he was not a true paternalist, as Daly was. He showed as much concern as his fellow agent for the welfare of elders and children, but he was not very interested in intervening in anyone else's life. His mildness of tone and non-interventionist practice make him appear, on the surface, more sympathetic to Aboriginal people than Daly. But there are moments when a different Lewis appears in the records, when the mildness gives way to a kind of sharpness. Lewis reserved this tone for only a few individuals, apparently those he considered responsible for their own difficulties, particularly when they were men seeking economic help. At these moments the reader senses a man who seems relatively lacking in compassion.

There is a noticeable pattern in Lewis's extension of compassion. He exhibited strong concern for the welfare of children and especially elders, and could even be tender-hearted in writing about them. On one occasion, for instance, he wrote feelingly to the department about his experience returning some runaway boys to a residential school. Lewis had provided one poorly clad boy with warm clothing, and for once he expressed his own feelings about the task of capturing them, calling it an 'ordeal' and a 'severe test' for him to force them from their homes while they 'sobbed bitterly' and begged to be left at home.[87] His empathy for the youngsters was readily apparent. Similarly, the agent acted swiftly when he learned that an old widow at Wikwemikong was being left untended and in 'lamentable condition' by her two adult sons. Lewis's opinions about ensuring adequate care for the helpless were vehemently expressed in his letter to the band secretary, directing the secretary to 'go to these fellows and instruct them to clean up this old lady, and look after her as any sons, who are human, should care for an aged sickly mother.' The agent threatened legal action if the men did not comply.[88] Those who were vulnerable, then, received Lewis's assistance and protection.

For able-bodied adults it was a different story. Lewis was prepared to recommend assistance for some to obtain more education, and sometimes suggested financial aid for those caught in misfortunes such as sickness or fires. But his over-all approach was to emphasize the importance of adults providing for their own needs and avoiding resort to the department for assistance. This was particularly evident in the 1930s, when able-bodied, grown men were asking for aid due to unemployment. While Daly recognized the need to extend relief in such cases, Lewis took a much harder line, refusing assistance and rebuking the men for even requesting relief. Here his non-interventionist stance revealed a different side, a reluctance to intervene when the times required it. On another occasion Lewis waged a stubborn battle to prevent a man from receiving a pension for his many years as reserve constable. Apparently outraged by the man's requests for consider-ation, the agent heaped scorn on the former constable and emphasized his respon-sibility to support himself independently. Lewis was very much wedded to the idea that men should support themselves and their families, and that any man who would not or could not do so deserved only contempt. His judgements against such individuals, even in the desperate years of the 1930s, were harsh.

Thus, while Lewis still practised a form of paternalism, it was a different form from that seen in Daly's administrative practice. Lewis was less controlling, but equally less helpful. He did not endeavour to control Aboriginal people because he did not seek responsibility for their lives; this was a responsibility he wished them to assume for themselves. Lewis avoided extra cares as much as possible and fre-quently left his clients to their own devices. Daly took the paternalist approach inherent in federal Indian policy, which meant regarding First Nations as essen-tially childlike and in need of guidance. In consequence, he dominated his clients but was also there in time of need.

Conclusion

It is symptomatic of the obstacles that confronted Aboriginal people in this period that Lewis's approach, which was often more consonant with the values of today, did not always serve Aboriginal people well in practice. Many people in Daly's agency chafed under his autocratic administration and endeavoured to assert a greater level of personal and community autonomy. Yet when the hard times of the Depression struck, Daly showed a good deal more sympathy for his clients than Lewis. Daly remained paternalistic, imperious, and controlling, and the experience cannot have been enjoyable for some of the individuals concerned. In practice, however, the people of the Parry Sound agency received more concrete help when they needed it than did those in Lewis's charge.

These two men thus complement each other well for a study of the effects of personal character on the functioning of the agent system. Each had his own approach to fulfilling his responsibilities, based on his personal character and on the values that were most important to him. Each adapted differently to the require-ments of the job and to the pressures they were subjected to from both sides—from the Department of Indian Affairs and from First Nations people. Lewis's non-inter-ventionist style left Aboriginal people freer to choose their own course and allowed band councils to exercise a good deal of authority over the community's affairs.

On the other hand, Lewis's attitude also meant that Aboriginal people had more limited access to assistance when they were in economic need. Daly's paternalistic views caused him to exercise strict control over elected band officials and to intervene in internal affairs. Although he allowed First Nations people less autonomy as a result, he was also much more active in assisting his clients, especially when the Great Depression set in. The legal disabilities and social and economic marginalization of Aboriginal people in this period meant that a paternalistic agent could play a positive role in their lives. By the same token, for many in the Manitowaning agency in the 1930s, the agent's faith in their ability to look after themselves must have seemed of dubious benefit.

① So far... admin. during the depression glossed over sure dills in aid, but what a/b the particulars?

② Need more of an idea of interactions/reactions from white neighbourly comm. unities. Relationship is not elaborated as much as I'd like.

3

'It Did Not Matter Who Was Chief':
Band Councils

'I have explained to the Band, in a nice kindly way that so far as the Parry Island Band, or any other Band in this Agency is concerned, this office is the Department of Indian Affairs to them. . . . [and that] they did not have to worry[,] that the Department of Indian Affairs would function, it did not matter who was Chief.'[1]

John Daly, 1934

'he [agent Daly] conducts his office as being a whole Dominion Government, Indian Agent, Indian Chief and Council, all into one . . . the Agent appears as taking too much advantage of his powers over the Chief and council and causing a considerable strife an [sic] animosity among the Indians of this Reserve . . . foiling the labors of the chief and members of the council, discrediting those who assist to maintain good government of the Band.'[2]

Francis Pegahmagabow, Parry Island chief, early 1920s

'you made statement to certain parties you dont give a damn to any of the member[s] of the Parry Island Band you as much to tell me this morning if the Chief and Council has no voice in the affairs of the Reserve this will have to be explained fully by the Dept.'[3]

John Manitowaba, Parry Island chief, 1934

Conflict between Indian agents and First Nations people was an inevitable outcome of the federal government's unilateral assumption of authority, to which the people had never consented. Lacking even the basic political right of the franchise,[4] First Nations people had access to only one body capable of representing their interests: the band council. Yet the band council, an entity invented by the DIA, was not intended to represent their interests. On the contrary, it was intended to displace traditional Aboriginal leadership, which had often opposed government policies, and to act as the executive that carried out the Indian administration's will. Although Native people were not slow to appreciate this reality, the council remained an obvious site from which to challenge federal authority. Particularly on Parry Island and at Shawanaga, leaders made repeated efforts to subvert the band councils and transform them into useful platforms for Aboriginal self-determination. Moreover, as the only available sites for political contention within bands, the councils also became the locus for internal conflicts. This was especially the case on Manitoulin Island, where control of the unceded territory and ownership of its resources were hotly contested.

In the interwar period, a good deal of the resistance to federal control was spear-headed by veterans of World War I—the same demographic group that became active after World War II. The veterans had been to Europe, proven their courage, experienced comradeship and equality with Euro-Canadian soldiers in the trenches, and returned home impatient with conditions on the reserves. They had seen a world much larger than their reserves and had little tolerance for the expec-tation that they would silently suffer their return to economic marginality and polit-ical exclusion. They formed a new generation of First Nations leaders who were more experienced in the ways of the dominant society and no longer willing to allow Indian agents to dictate to them. These men have been referred to as the 'returned soldier chiefs', a group particularly active in the southeastern corner of Georgian Bay. Lawyer and legal historian Paul Williams has singled out Francis Pegahmagabow of Parry Island, Henry Jackson of Christian Island, and Henry Abetung of Shawanaga as important figures in this movement.[5] These individuals fought for more independence, and in the process locked horns with agent John Daly, among others.

The presence of the 'returned soldier chiefs' goes some way towards explaining the perennial conflicts under Daly's administration, which in his correspondence seemed to take on the character of individual feuds. Daly's personal and letter-writing style often had the effect of reducing vitally important political conflicts to an appearance of triviality. His writings depict the leaders as irrational, petty, fool-ish, and self-serving—a prime technique of DIA officials to dismiss Aboriginal spokespersons. Daly portrayed the grievances they raised as mere pretexts for posturing and self-aggrandizement. Yet many of these grievances were legitimate, unresolved issues that the government had been refusing to address since the settle-ment of the reserves. The resulting battles took place both within and outside the band councils, but the agent's most determined adversaries usually ended up on the council at one time or another. A perusal of the council minutes for the period reveals constant references to dissatisfaction directed mainly against the agent per-sonally, accusing him of acting in bad faith, fostering harmful divisions within the band, disregarding the band's interests, and governing in a dictatorial manner.[6] Since Daly would have been reading these minutes, it is not hard to see why he would perceive the council members as personal antagonists. In any case, his chal-lengers made no secret of their opposition to him.

The Structure of Authority in Band Politics

The Indian agent system supplanted and largely destroyed indigenous leadership systems, since all meaningful authority over band affairs was placed in the hands of Indian agents and their superiors. Once the old systems of choosing leaders were defunct, the search began for new ways to mount a coherent response to colonialism. Men elected as band officials often attempted to fill the old roles of a chief, but they operated from a position of weakness. Among their own people, they did not enjoy universal recognition as leaders. Even though they might have some of the qualities traditionally associated with authority, they could never claim to represent the whole band.[7] More seriously, they were compromised by the perception that they were servants of the Indian department, unable to function autonomously. In a letter written to John Daly in 1931, for example, Chief Frank Judge of Parry Island expressed a widely felt dissatisfaction with the chief's powerlessness in office: 'I am sorry to write to you to day [sic] regarding that I am a chief. My Indians think that I am a dependent, So I told them that I get my instructions from the Indian agent.'[8] It is not clear if Judge meant these remarks to be sardonic, or if he was temporarily assuming a subordinate role to obtain Daly's co-operation (the note then requested assistance for another band member).

DIA officials shared the expectation of most Aboriginal people that chiefs and band councillors would serve the federal agenda, in spite of their frequent refusals to do so. John Daly even fell into the use of expressions such as 'paid officers of the Dept.' in referring to council members, and once recommended that a new council be 'appointed'—linguistic slips that reveal his presumption of federal control over the council.[9] But Daly was frequently irritated by the ambitions of nearly all the Parry Island chiefs when they were in office. For example, he wrote of Chief Judge and his council that they had explicitly rejected his right to run their affairs: 'Chief [Frank] Judge has shown over and over again, also his councillors Peter Judge and James Miller, that they do not consider it necessary to have a white man looking after the business of the Reserve, and they have stated in public that they are quite capable of looking after their own affairs.'[10] By the same token, department correspondence records the vigorous protests of many chiefs against their inability to exercise authority within the Indian Affairs system. Men who had sought election to council hoping to influence the system quickly learned how little they could accomplish. In reality, power had passed from the community into the hands of the Indian agents. This situation provoked the period's open conflict between the representatives of bands and the federal government.

The structure of authority under the Indian agent system was not complex. All administrative matters and all economic questions related to the bands were under DIA control. As the Indian Act succinctly stated, the Superintendent General had 'the control and management of the lands and property of the Indians in Canada'.[11] As already discussed, the Indian Act gave the Superintendent General a wide variety of powers over bands, which in practice were exercised by internal DIA officials and Indian agents. Minor decisions were made on the spot by the Indian agent, while more important issues were decided by internal officials on the advice and recommendation of the agent. In all of this the only real role envisioned for the band councils was to manage minor matters such as truancy and weed control, and to pass band council resolutions, when necessary, giving force to decisions made by department officials. The council was elected by the male band members aged 21 and older, and the chosen councillors then selected a chief from among themselves. The chief was to some extent a figurehead, since he had little more power than his fellow councillors, apart from the right to a deciding vote if the council's or band's vote was evenly split.

The Indian department had conceived band councils as an approximate equivalent of municipal governments and assigned them areas of jurisdiction in keeping with this intention. Band councils generally had authority only over minor local matters. Their powers included passing regulations for such things as public health, the 'repression of intemperance and profligacy', the management of animals and weeds on the reserve, and the construction and maintenance of roads, bridges, ditches, and public buildings.[12] Even in these areas, federal power was constantly in evidence. The Indian agent actually oversaw most construction and maintenance, and the Indian Act decreed that bands were required to keep roads and bridges 'in proper order'—in part because public roads, and later highways, frequently passed through reserves. The Superintendent General also had the power to enforce the performance of statute labour on roads and to determine where roads would be placed on a reserve.[13] The councils did have a few significant areas of jurisdiction—most importantly, they controlled the distribution of land in the reserves and were supposed to maintain a register of those located on land. In addition, they divided timber-cutting permits among the band members once an overall permit had been approved by the department. These latter powers were the main material sources of the councils' importance within Aboriginal communities. Concerns about larger economic and political issues, such as timber operations, often reached the council, too. Yet most of the time the band councils concerned themselves with everyday matters on the reserve. They passed regulations governing conduct on the reserve and voted band funds in small quantities for many reasons—to provide relief for the sick and aged, for small loans, to mend public fences, and so on. The majority of band council resolutions in the period dealt with these small amounts of money parcelled out to their members as a form of assistance or for local projects.

The most contentious issue between the councils and the department was the expenditure of band funds, which both wished to control. In disputes about this the department was in a far stronger position, since the funds were actually in its hands and the law gave it a veto over expenditures approved by the council. In practice, there was a certain amount of negotiation in decisions about band monies. Although officials in Ottawa did not hesitate to forbid expenditures, it was rare for them to spend funds against the will of a band. In fact, the department's general tendency was simply to hold the funds untouched as much as possible. Its approach contrasted noticeably with traditional Anishinabe principles of sharing. Moreover, it was clearly galling to many First Nations people that the government controlled their use of their own money.

We have already seen that agents had many ways to control band councils if they so wished—by deposing individual members, by delaying relief payments, by refusing loan requests, and so on. The agent's range of powers enabled him to exact petty sorts of revenge on those who crossed him. Personal influence could also be exercised at the council meetings themselves, to silence people or set a particular tone. Men like Daly, with forceful personalities and a desire to influence reserve politics, might significantly constrain the activities of a band council. In an interview, Verna Petronella Johnston, an elder of the Cape Croker (Nawash) band, recalled that Indian agents exercised strict control over council meetings. Agents are remembered on this reserve as acting very imperiously in the meetings. Mrs Johnston related that one agent arrived at a session with DIA literature, which he placed on the table. Although no one looked at the material, the agent later claimed that it had been read by all. She also stated that this official would tear up the minutes if he did not like their contents. Naturally, such conduct would be unlikely to come to the department's notice, and it would be difficult for band members to counter. Although Daly once admitted in official correspondence that he was omitting some band council resolutions because they were 'too frivolous and nonsensical to send forward', most agents would be disinclined to mention such an omission.[14] Mrs Johnston felt that the members of her band were unable to stand up to the agent until after World War II.[15] The documentary evidence supports her portrayal, given the overall power position of the agents. And council members were surely unaware that their deliberations were so casually dismissed (although some chiefs on Parry Island suspected Daly of failing to report their recommendations to the DIA).

One of the most potent weapons in the department's arsenal was the ability to depose chiefs and councillors. The Indian Act allowed the DIA to depose a chief or councillor 'on the ground of dishonesty, intemperance, immorality or incompetency', and to declare that person ineligible to stand for office for as long as three years.[16] The qualities named are vague and intangible, and it was the agent who made judgements about fitness for office. As far as the ground of intemperance was concerned, Aboriginal people were forbidden by law to drink alcohol, so in theory they could be deposed for consuming any liquor. The records suggest that repeated convictions for drinking almost automatically led to dismissal from the council. Depositions for the other named reasons were less common; in fact, decision-makers at headquarters proved reluctant to invoke the procedure. On the other hand, both Indian agents and band members proposed depositions quite frequently, most often in response to political disputes.

A case in point was that of Jonas Odjig, who was deposed as chief of the Manitoulin Island Unceded band in 1920. An initial attempt by his own council to depose him in 1917, when he was a band councillor, failed when department secretary John D. McLean decided that Odjig must first receive a warning.[17] Odjig was elected band chief on 20 August 1918, but two years later the council again voted to remove him from office on the grounds of immorality. On this occasion, as on the first, the main charge against the man was that he was having an affair with a married woman. The agent supported the deposition a second time, noting that Odjig had now been warned more than once. Perhaps more importantly, he had shown himself to be an opponent of agriculture and of the main tenet of Indian policy: assimilation. Lewis stated that the chief was 'against everything that would help the progress of the Indians'. In particular, he claimed that Odjig opposed extensive farming on the unceded territory, 'as he maintains that Indians are Indians and should live as Indians, and if the Indians wish to live as Whitemen they should leave the reserve.'[18] If Lewis's portrayal is accurate, Odjig was essentially drawing the same distinction that department officials made between 'white' and 'Indian' modes of life. He was also advocating the safeguarding of Aboriginal cultural distinctiveness through an adherence to the ancient ways and a rejection of farming. Little wonder, then, that in May 1920 Odjig was removed from office.

In Daly's agency, depositions occurred more frequently. Four council members on Parry Island were removed from office between 1918 and 1939. The *threat* of deposition occurred even more often, particularly in Parry Island politics. It was wielded by both the agent and political players within the Anishinabe community. Events here reveal that failure to attend to duties was not a strong argument in Ottawa's view. (Even the allegation of adultery had failed to effect Odjig's removal in 1917.) Two primary reasons moved officials at headquarters to dismiss a council member: intemperance and active opposition to federal policies. When faced with objections to band officials who were not caught drinking or agitating against the Indian department, Ottawa preferred to abstain from intervention. Indications in letters suggest that the main reason for this restraint was the attitude that the band council was of little importance.

In certain situations, band councils were able to exercise some power vis-à-vis the Indian agent and/or the DIA, though they needed the united support of the rest of the band to do so. This could occur when a DIA official wanted to pursue a particular project and required the council's consent. A united band and council could successfully thwart official plans, as long as they could sustain their unity. Steadfast refusal to approve a DIA proposal would bring down official displeasure, but the department was unlikely to act against the united will of a band. Nonetheless, it was often difficult to maintain the necessary unity, especially given the divisions colonialism had created or exacerbated within First Nations societies. When an agent stubbornly pursued a project, marshalling his own allies and utilizing the people's economic vulnerability, he stood an excellent chance of eventually obtaining Aboriginal consent.[19]

Parry Island Conflicts

Daly made his overall attitude towards the place of band councils abundantly clear. In his correspondence he spoke repeatedly of the importance of maintaining the Indian department's authority, and he waxed indignant about any Aboriginal attempts to show 'independence' or to circumvent him and deal directly with the department. The flavour of his approach towards band officials is nicely captured in his remarks following an unsuccessful effort to have a fractious chief deposed: 'This was an opportunity for the Department to show that the Department rules the Band and not the Chief.'[20] In interactions with his Aboriginal clients, Daly stressed the insignificance of band officials and his own centrality as the DIA's representative: 'I have always explained [to those dissatisfied with a chief or councillor] . . . that the Department of Indian Affairs would function, it did not matter who was Chief.'[21] Several chiefs who held office during Daly's tenure made efforts to have him investigated by the department with a view to his being dismissed or at least reined in.[22]

Daly made a point of belittling anyone who challenged his authority, especially when they attempted to bypass him and approach the Indian department directly. In part, his ad hominem attacks on the character of his challengers reflected his need to discredit them in the eyes of his superiors. In disparaging Aboriginal men, the agent made use of prevailing class and racial stereotypes. In 1931, for instance, two members of the Parry Island band, one of them a band councillor, travelled to Ottawa to complain about non-Natives hunting and trapping on Parry Island Reserve.[23] These two men were ongoing adversaries of the agent: the band councillor was James Miller, an opponent of the Indian agent system, and the other man was John Manitowaba, whose battles with Daly are analyzed in more detail below. Daly began his dismissal of the two men's visit to Ottawa by denying that they had any authority to speak for the band. He then proceeded to construct images of each man designed to ensure that their views would not carry weight with the Indian department.

In John Manitowaba's case, the agent painted a picture of an aging, economically dependent old man who did not understand or appreciate the benefits bestowed on him by the benevolent Indian administration—the classic picture of the 'grumbling Indian'. Daly noted that Manitowaba received a pension as well as relief during the winter, implying that one who received money had no right to voice grievances or address historical injustice. He also made sarcastic reference to the elder's concerns about the implementation of the Robinson Treaty, including the long-standing complaint of the Parry Island people that they had never surrendered the islands in Georgian Bay. As for Miller, the agent used innuendo and the stereotype of the 'improvident Indian' to discredit this opponent. Daly wrote slightingly, 'The Department I presume, heard as well as saw him.' He claimed that Miller had asked for credit on his fall interest payment to purchase a second-hand car, in spite of the fact that he also had other debts.[24] These were, of course, all matters that had nothing to do with the allegations the two men had made, which related to illegal poaching on the reserve. Miller was presented as a frivolous, irresponsible character who wanted to buy a car rather than pay his debts. Manitowaba appeared as a troublemaker, who dared to question the validity of treaty implementation, and an ingrate, who proverbially 'bit the hand that fed him.' Daly could not offer any particularly damning information about either of them, obviously, but he relied on classic racist stereotypes of Aboriginal people to delegitimize their protests.

No doubt Daly's controlling personality and patronizing attitudes played a role in calling forth protest against his administration. At the same time, his resort to racial stereotypes might also have been a sign of his powerlessness to resolve the ancient grievances and simmering resentment that predated his own arrival. Daly's tenure as agent coincided with the period of dissidence that followed the return of

Aboriginal war veterans to the reserves. Many of the issues raised by Daly's challengers were already several generations old when Daly arrived in Parry Sound, and their persistence was a predictable outcome of the Indian administration's refusal to address any treaty grievances. When Daly raised one of the old grievances early in his term (an issue relating to fishing rights, discussed in Chapter 4), he quickly encountered the standard set of denials with which the department responded to long-standing problems. The agent was not in a position to resolve these issues on his own, and he thus learned to wield the standard disclaimers in his turn.

The two most persistent and active dissenters in Daly's agency were Francis Pegahmagabow and John Manitowaba, both of whom became band chiefs during Daly's administration. The agent participated actively in an attempt to have Pegahmagabow deposed as chief, and made strenuous efforts to have Manitowaba removed from office as well. He also had serious conflicts with John Manitowaba's son Stanley, who succeeded Pegahmagabow as chief until he was deposed himself. All three men were a source of vexation for Daly because of their conviction that band officials should have the power to run band affairs.

Francis Pegahmagabow

Francis Pegahmagabow was a lively and dynamic character, a decorated war hero, and a sort of lone crusader personality. Born in 1891, he had been orphaned at an early age and raised at Shawanaga Reserve, although a member of the Parry Island band. He returned to Parry Island in 1911, at 20 years of age, to attend school in nearby Parry Sound.[25] A highly determined man who seemed to enjoy controversy, he engaged in active campaigns against Indian agents, the Indian department, and both the federal and provincial governments. He also fought with other members of the Parry Island Reserve community. Pegahmagabow has been described as a 'rugged individualist', a character trait that made it difficult for him to work in cooperation with either his own people or government officials.[26] He attempted in various ways to address both long-standing treaty grievances and disenchantment with the department's handling of the band's natural resources. He believed that the chief and council should have considerably more power than the Indian agent system allotted to them.

Pegahmagabow had quickly enlisted in the armed forces when World War I broke out and was shipped to the front in September 1914.[27] He hoped to continue a family tradition of military prowess such as his grandfather had displayed in the War of 1812, and he certainly succeeded. He was a superb soldier, demonstrating exceptional skill and daring as a sniper and scout, and received a Military Medal with two bars as well as three other medals for his wartime exploits.[28] Only 38 other members of the Canadian Expeditionary Force could claim to have won the honour of a Military Medal with two bars. Of the 4,000 or so Aboriginal men who fought in the Great War, he was the most highly decorated.[29] He was reputed to have been one of the best sharpshooters in the Allied armies and reportedly killed 378 of the enemy as a sniper. He also led his company almost unscathed through a battle at Passchendaele and captured 300 Germans at Mount Sorrel.[30] Even among

Corporal Francis Pegahmagabow, c. 1919, shown in his military uniform with numerous medals for bravery adorning his chest, including the extremely prestigious Military Medal and two bars. Photo courtesy Fred Gaffen, *Forgotten Soldiers* (Penticton, BC: Theytus Books, 1985).

local Euro-Canadians he was something of a hero, at least in the first years after the war.[31] He joined the militia later, serving in the Algonquin Regiment and drilling other young soldiers. Not surprisingly, he placed enormous value on his impressive military accomplishments. His feats in World War I also enhanced his claim to leader status on the reserve, since courage and success in war were seen in Anishinabe culture as markers of the potential leader. In addition to this, he came from a family that traditionally provided chiefs: his father and grandfather had also been chiefs at Parry Island.[32]

Pegahmagabow's rebellion against the department was not solely a response to Daly himself, for other agents of the period expressed annoyance about Pegahmagabow as well. Daly's predecessor and successor agents were entirely unsympathetic to Pegahmagabow. The previous agent, Alexander Logan, remarked, 'This man is very hard to handle as he suffers from dementia and takes very strange notions.'[33] Daly's successor, Samuel Devlin, was equally intolerant of Pegahmagabow's battle with the DIA. At the end of the dissident's term as chief in the 1940s, Devlin wrote that he was pleased Pegahmagabow was not continuing in office, since 'during his term of office, his time was largely taken up with quarrels and a succession of ridiculous charges against the Indian administration.'[34] Officials at headquarters eventually decided that Pegahmagabow was 'a mental case' and wrote him off entirely—a convenient conclusion about a tireless campaigner against the department.[35]

Pegahmagabow's own writings show a highly independent spirit and a strong sense of being called to help his people. More than once he expressed the belief that he had been chosen to free his people from what he called 'white slavery'.[36] He attempted to organize resistance to the DIA on a regional level, making several efforts to unite like-minded individuals from the area in a larger campaign for Aboriginal rights. He also raised local issues, many of which were old band grievances. Pegahmagabow fought against the department's control of band resources such as timber, complained about violations of the band's timber contract with a local lumber company, and raised treaty issues such as the ownership of nearby islands, which the First Nation always believed had not been surrendered in the Robinson Treaty. Daly, unlike the other agents, was much more inclined to see this challenger as a troublemaker rather than a lunatic. The truth was that the two men had a good deal in common. Reading between the lines, it is clear that Daly, for all his exasperation with Pegahmagabow, also respected and liked the man. They were well-matched opponents, both proud veterans of World War I, and they waged their verbal and ideological warfare with gusto.

Pegahmagabow was elected chief of the Parry Island band in February 1921, a year and a half before Daly took over the Parry Sound agency. By the time Daly arrived in 1922, Pegahmagabow had already alienated part of the Parry Island community by writing a letter to the DIA in which he suggested that certain individuals be removed from the reserve (Pegahmagabow at times attempted to eject non-band members, and also objected to the presence of 'halfbreeds' on the reserve). The Parry Islanders were never solidly behind Pegahmagabow, even though he was re-elected chief in February 1924 and again in the 1940s. The disagreements in the community reflected its fragmentation along lines of religion, band affiliation, and treaty status, as well as Pegahmagabow's own tendency to make personal enemies. In addition to his battles with government officials, this activist also sparred with his own people, particularly certain individuals.

Pegahmagabow quickly made it clear to Daly that he expected to exercise authority as chief, and that he rejected the veto power of the Indian department. At the beginning of their acquaintance Daly wrote a letter that gives a good sense of the issues and the relationship between the two men: 'This young man is a problem . . . . I try to explain to him that he must get in line. He is of the opinion, that if the Council passes a resolution, it should be carried out by the Department. To mention the Department to him, is like tossing a red rag to a bull.' The agent went so far as to intimate that if he had not had experience with 'the disgruntled returned men' he would be 'nervous' around the chief.[37] Clearly, both men were working to establish their authority. Daly wished Pegahmagabow to 'get in line' and assume the subordinate position expected of a band official. Pegahmagabow wanted the Indian department to respect the will of the band council.

Pegahmagabow was a thorn in Daly's side from the beginning. In September 1922, two weeks before Daly was appointed agent, the band council had passed a resolution that Chief Pegahmagabow was to visit other Robinson Treaty reserves to discuss co-operation in fighting for treaty rights. The intent apparently was to send documents to British authorities citing the grievances of all the Robinson Treaty bands in an attempt to regain lost rights.[38] This campaign continued into 1923. In a July letter to Chief Samuel Noganosh of the Magnetawan band, Pegahmagabow stated that he was planning to travel to England himself to 'press our claims and complaints'.[39] The following year this letter made its way into Daly's possession, and he wrote the department to inform them of the chief's activities, suggesting that measures be adopted to stop his 'seditious campaigning'.[40] The letter to Noganosh, according to Daly, revealed Pegahmagabow's insubordinate way of thinking, and worse, 'his actions and talk show that he spurns the authority of the Dept. of Indian Affairs.'

The department advised Daly to warn Pegahmagabow that his political organizing might lead to his dismissal. The agent had requested that an official letter be sent to the chief with this threat, but department secretary J.D. McLean responded, with striking condescension, that a direct communication 'might convey to him an exaggerated conception of the importance of his activities.'[41] This belittling phrase was a clear expression of McLean's low estimation of First Nations people and of his determination to downplay the threat posed by Aboriginal organizers. The DIA's primary strategy in this period was to ignore Aboriginal political organizers in the hope of discouraging them.[42] At the same time, officials watched them closely and took more active measures when their activities seemed likely to bear fruit. It was clear from this point on that Pegahmagabow would be closely watched.

Pegahmagabow was also concerned about how the band's timber was being exploited. The Canadian National Lumber and Tie Company had been granted a licence in 1921 to cut timber on the reserve, and both chief and council were unhappy with various elements of its operations. In a resolution addressed to the

DIA they claimed that some of the timber was wasted by being left to rot, that it was not properly scaled (measured), that the company was exceeding the area assigned to it, and that Aboriginal men were being refused work by the company while whites were given preference. Overall the council felt that the band did not receive any benefit from the timber concession and wanted to have the company's licence cancelled. Evidence of the power struggle between the council and the agent is clearly marked in the resolution, which specifically mentioned that the agent had already been approached on the matter but had done nothing about it. Across the top of the document, in Pegahmagabow's hand, is written the word 'Ignored'.[43] The timber operations on Parry Island continued to be a source of friction between agent and council for some years to come, until the company itself halted operations because all the valuable timber had been removed.

Pegahmagabow himself was thoroughly frustrated with the agent's power to thwart his aims and ignore his concerns. A band council document from the early 1920s listed a series of complaints about Daly, including that he 'would not listen to the Chief half of the time' and that he would not recommend the council's resolutions, but either rejected them or 'retained' them (i.e., never even sent them to Ottawa). Moreover, the agent was seen as favouring the opponents of the current council and causing conflict within the band by taking sides. The document was unfinished and presumably never sent to Ottawa, but it conveys a vivid sense of the antagonism between agent and council.[44] Another document, headed 'Declaration Against the Agent', voiced similar complaints, castigating Daly for 'taking too much advantage of his powers over the Chief and council and causing a considerable strife an [sic] animosity among the Indians of this Reserve, . . . foiling the labors of the chief and members of the council.'[45]

In response to his disputes with Daly, Pegahmagabow tried other avenues to effect change. In 1925 he was working with lawyer Wallace Nesbitt to make complaints to the DIA about Daly. He also engaged Nesbitt to help assert Aboriginal fishing rights in Georgian Bay. Nesbitt promised Pegahmagabow that he would write to the provincial Department of Game and Fisheries asking them 'to warn all persons who obtain a license to fish with nets in Georgian Bay that their license does not give them the right to fish in waters, the fishing rights in respect of which are reserved by the Crown for the use of the Indians.'[46] This may have been a reference to rights the Shawanaga band argued had been secured to them in the nineteenth century, reserving a sizable area of Georgian Bay for their use. Pegahmagabow had spent his childhood at Shawanaga and retained ties there later.

Finally, the chief took action on the issue of Georgian Bay islands. In 1925, just before he resigned as chief, Pegahmagabow was apparently involved in an interband organizing effort to reopen the question of these islands. The islands were being used for cottage sites, and Pegahmagabow, John Manitowaba, and others felt that the Parry Island band should at least receive rent for these properties. Daly reported to the DIA that he had gleaned some information about this campaign from Chief Wesley Jacobs of Shawanaga, a former president of the Grand General Council of Indians of Ontario who had been advocating Aboriginal rights for years.[47] Jacobs stated that a delegation was preparing to go to Ottawa to discuss the islands in Georgian Bay. They were also approaching the local member of Parliament, Colonel J. Arthurs, to secure his support. Daly attempted to dissuade Jacobs from his course, explaining that the department would not like the organizers 'stepping over the head of the Dept. to go to Parliament'.[48] Jacobs was unmoved and stated that the delegation would go ahead.[49] Daly was convinced that bands 'all over Georgian Bay' had been approached about the unsurrendered islands, citing a letter he had received from a Native man at Collins Inlet,[50] who asked 'if it was so that the Indian lands are being taken from them'.[51] Obviously, Pegahmagabow and his colleagues were having some success in spreading the word, a fact that was alarming to the agent.

Clearly, then, this chief took a proactive role not only in attempting to protect the rights of the Parry Island band, but also in addressing larger issues related to treaty rights and land grievances. His activities explain why Daly considered Pegahmagabow an agitator. It is likely that Daly would have taken action against the chief himself, but somewhat ironically the first initiative was taken by the band. After Pegahmagabow's re-election in February 1924, a group of Parry Islanders decided to get rid of him, and they managed to have a motion to depose him passed at a band council meeting on 2 April 1925.[52] Daly supported the resolution, not surprisingly, and internal department officials were also initially quite keen on deposing the chief. An internal department memorandum recommended his removal on the grounds of incompetence, noting that he had already been warned of dismissal 'if his conduct did not improve'.[53] The foremost issue was Pegahmagabow's political agitation, described as 'causing trouble on the reserve by agitating an uprising of the Indians against the Department's method of running the reserve'.[54] But the process was halted shortly after this, when a petition from 17 band members was sent to the department opposing the chief's removal.[55]

In the end the impasse was resolved by Pegahmagabow's decision to resign of his own accord. In August 1925, Daly reported that the band council had passed a resolution to approve Pegahmagabow's resignation, moved by Pegahmagabow himself.[56] Ottawa demanded a written resignation from the chief's hand, which it duly received. Pegahmagabow later claimed that Daly had given him 'continued trouble till I had to resign.'[57] He also felt that the agent had tried to influence other band members not to associate with him, at least for political purposes. Apparently he resigned because he felt his position as chief had become untenable.

Although Daly was no doubt gratified by this victory, Pegahmagabow's political campaigns were far from over. He was not re-elected chief under Daly's administration, but he served as band councillor for a term in the 1930s and was as active as ever in his opposition to the DIA bureaucracy. He continued to agitate about the unsurrendered islands, an issue that other band members also took up. In 1932, Daly again noted that Pegahmagabow had been 'trying to stir up trouble about the Indians owning all the Islands in the Georgian Bay'.[58] The incumbent Parry Island chief, Frank Judge, also began to pursue the matter, though apparently not in concert with Pegahmagabow, who refused to hand over his copy of the Robinson Treaty to Judge.[59] Daly at first tried to help Judge acquire the various papers that

Pegahmagabow held, but soon concluded that the best course was to leave them in his possession. The agent mistrusted Judge and considered him a potential agitator as well, so he reasoned that it was better to keep important documents out of his hands. As Daly wrote, 'in the past Pegahmagabow tried to make trouble with his knowledge of these Treaties, and according to the recent actions of Chief Judge, he seems to me to be of the same ilk as Pegahmagabow.'[60] Similarly, the agent linked the political action of Henry Abetung, another returned soldier chief and tireless campaigner, with his inconvenient knowledge of the treaties. Clearly, given the 'great unrest' that these men had stirred in their people, it was important to prevent Aboriginal people from obtaining detailed information about the treaties.

It was, in any case, not an opportune moment for political activism against the department. By 1932 economic depression had struck the Parry Sound area in earnest, and Aboriginal people in the region were hit even harder than non-Natives. Daly's position as dispenser of relief meant that few First Nations people could afford to challenge him. This may have been the cause of Daly's confidence in reas-suring the department: 'I have to state that so far as the Band is concerned, that is, all the Band, they do not give a hoot for these treaties, it is just this contemptible sneaking representative . . . of the Parry Island Band, who would like to make trouble.'[61] This portrayal clearly understated the extent of Parry Islanders' interest in the ownership of the nearby islands, an issue that has resurfaced regularly right up to the present time.

Francis Pegahmagabow was never able to create a lasting political alliance with other Aboriginal activists, but he never gave up the struggle. His relationship with Daly remained a complex combination of antagonism, patronage, and occasional collusion. In 1930 Daly helped Pegahmagabow obtain a pension for his wartime service, the one common experience that fostered a certain bond between the two men. Pegahmagabow seemed to have mixed feelings about Daly's help, claiming that the agent had afterwards extorted a gift for his wife in return for his assis-tance.[62] Only a year later Pegahmagabow wrote to M.H. Ludwig, a Toronto lawyer, that he was 'still after' Daly and that Daly was 'the most unpopular Indian agent we ever had'.[63] He was also convinced that he had been denied land on the reserve as a result of Daly's machinations. The relationship between the two men wors-ened in the Depression, when Pegahmagabow along with the other two council members wrote a letter to the local newspaper complaining about Daly's forcing men of the reserve to do roadwork for relief. The agent was outraged and wrote the department that he was considering intervening to deprive Pegahmagabow of the pension he had helped him secure. Daly commented to the department that Pegahmagabow was 'the most ungrateful piece of humanity that I have ever run across' and that he was contemplating approaching the Pension Commission to have Pegahmagabow 'examined mentally'.[64] The economic woes of the period, and particularly Daly's strengthened power position and promotion of roadwork, eroded the two men's relationship. In spite of their intermittent feuds, however, the two collaborated at times, notably in the effort to depose another activist, Chief John Manitowaba.

John Manitowaba

John Manitowaba became band chief in February of 1933, apparently because he had convinced his voters that he could obtain the long-sought compensation for the Georgian Bay islands. Daly later quoted Francis Pegahmagabow as declaring that 'some of the young men believed John Manitowaba when he told them he would make the Department pay back a large sum of money to the Band funds for the islands and other land around Parry Sound, which has been sold to the tourists.'[65]

Daly had very little sympathy with the movement to regain the islands in Georgian Bay, and even less sympathy with Manitowaba himself. The agent adopted an exceedingly patronizing attitude towards this rival, to whom he referred in terms such as 'a blathering old Indian'.[66] Daly had nothing in common with Manitowaba, held no shared experiences as he did with Pegahmagabow, and also at one point disparaged the man for being 'a General or admiral or some of these grand things in the Salvation Army', a Christian sect the agent probably considered vulgar, unseemly, and lower class.[67] Manitowaba was about 70 years old when his political conflicts with Daly began,[68] and he clearly perceived himself as an elder whose opinion ought to be respected. When attempting to limit the exploitation of timber on Parry Island, for example, Manitowaba cited his seniority: 'I am the oldest people on Parry Island and I want this to be settled right!'[69] Daly made a point of mentioning his challenger's age, too, but used it as a means to dismiss him: 'He is an old man and [is] not taken very seriously by any of the members of the Band, but I have found him to be quite a trouble maker and his wife is a good second to him in this respect.'[70]

These two divergent views of Manitowaba's status largely reflect a cultural clash. Daly employed his own society's stereotype of the hidebound, backward-looking, senile old man to discredit his challenger. John Manitowaba seemingly adhered to the traditional Anishinabe view of elders as important community members and sources of wisdom. Each man believed that the other owed him deference due to his position in the community. Yet Daly relegated John Manitowaba to the category of the dependent, ungrateful Indian. Due to his age, he was not expected to alter his views, so he was simply written off. He would be kept from starving, but that was all the department felt it owed him. Daly's conception of the lifestyle for which Manitowaba was fitted was based on a class-consciousness in which the 'dependent Indian' was placed at the very bottom of the hierarchy. When Manitowaba wrote to Ottawa to complain of the unsatisfactory condition of his house, for instance, Daly retorted, 'John Manitowaba's house is nothing to be proud of, but owing to circumstances and taking into consideration what John Manitowaba is, his house is good enough for him.'[71] In any case, the agent claimed that nothing would satisfy the man: 'He is one of those Indians, who although he is old and deserving of sympathy, if you [gave] him a handful of stars he would want a chip off the moon.'[72] This tactic dovetailed neatly with a well-established DIA belief that the frequency of Aboriginal complaints merely reflected their inability to be content with their lot.

The rivalry between Daly and Manitowaba predated Manitowaba's election to the Parry Island council. It may have started when Manitowaba's son Stanley, who was elected band chief in 1925, was removed from office in 1926 on the grounds of being intoxicated.[73] In any event, direct rivalry between the father and Daly first appears in the records in 1927, when the two men clashed over the use of resources on Parry Island. Daly learned that Manitowaba had been cutting firewood on the property of Mrs Joseph Partridge, which had been surrendered to Mrs Partridge's father, Reverend Allan Salt, and thus no longer belonged to the band.[74] The agent took Manitowaba to task publicly for this transgression, thus violating Aboriginal principles for handling conflict, which prescribed tact, avoidance of criticism, and above all the maintenance of harmony. Daly's account suggests that Manitowaba was deliberately flouting the agent's authority, for the man did not deny taking the wood and simply stated that he needed it for fuel. Daly threatened Manitowaba with jail, and the battle lines were drawn.[75] Manitowaba persisted in cutting wood on the same property off and on for the next four years, causing repeated complaints from the land's owner. The agent reported in 1931 that he had warned Manitowaba and others 'over and over again' to stay off this lot. In 1931 he finally implemented his threat of legal action, writing the department that he was about to haul John Manitowaba and two of his boarders before the magistrate for trespassing on Mrs Partridge's lot.[76] Manitowaba may have received a small fine in consequence, but it is worth noting that Daly had hesitated for four years before taking legal action—a fact that was presumably not lost on his opponents.

Manitowaba's private activities were only a part of his challenge to Daly's authority. In addition, he attempted to intervene more generally in the exploitation of natural resources on Parry Island. In 1930 he wrote to the King of England protesting the timber-cutting operation on the island, which he felt was excessive and would rob future generations of this resource. Predictably, the letter was forwarded to the DIA to be dealt with, which immediately turned to Daly for an explanation. The agent made prompt use of this opportunity to discredit his opponent and neutralize his potential future influence. He resorted to the usual tropes for the purpose, claiming that Manitowaba knew nothing about timber operations. Just as importantly, Manitowaba's receipt of relief from the DIA disqualified him, once again, from criticizing the department—as Aboriginal people have long complained, any assistance from government was expected to result in total acquiescence to its authority: 'He has every reason to be grateful to the Department of Indian Affairs for their kindness and consideration in granting him relief all winter.'[77] The agent promised, however, that he would speak to Manitowaba and report further on his views.

It turned out that the elder's grievances were mostly objections to specific forestry practices and the resulting depletion of forest. In addition, he was concerned about land in general and made what amounted to land claims against the government. He had a detailed conception of which land and islands around Parry Island had belonged to his own family and maintained that his family had never sold these areas. Some of the land was now occupied by non-Natives as cottage sites, and no rent was paid for it. The use of the concept of rent clearly suggested that the Aboriginal people retained title to the lands. Manitowaba also added his voice to the old agitation about the unsurrendered islands around Parry Island.[78]

Daly's response to Manitowaba's grievances revealed much about the agent's solutions for Aboriginal dissatisfaction and his attitudes towards treaties, as well as his vision of Aboriginal people's place in the new order. The agent claimed to sympathize with the elder and with all the others who 'live in the past', comparing their supposedly romanticized vision of an earlier era with that cherished by the Highlanders of Scotland. But he advocated that the people should forget the past, 'get out and hustle around', and 'prepare themselves to take a place in their country and its affairs.' The solution for this problem, in Daly's eyes, was the education of the young—in other words, assimilation.[79] The treaties, as far as Daly was concerned, were part of the past and no longer had any relevance. A stark display of his condescending attitude towards Aboriginal people occurs in a letter written at this time:

> As I sit and listen to John Manitowaba telling his story I can see the tragedy of it all, from his point of view, and his point of view, is this, that the white man is taking advantage of him and will always take advantage of him, taking away his land and giving him nothing in return. I feel very sorry for him . . . because there is no living man able to explain to him the meaning of the treaties that were passed, the reason for this is that he does not wish it to be explained to him. He does not want to know, and in his heart he wishes to have a complaint.[80]

Daly had a few proposals for silencing Manitowaba, reconciling him to his fate as a ward of government, and ending his political interventions. The agent felt that the elder should be reminded of the department's benevolence and of the supposed advantages he received from federal wardship. One of these advantages was the relief Manitowaba received due to his advanced age. Daly's comments clearly implied that these relief payments contradicted Manitowaba's view that First Nations had received nothing in return for their land and resources. The agent also pacified his critic with meaningless assurances. Daly promised Manitowaba that he would send a letter to the DIA outlining his protests and that the department would 'put it on file and keep it there for all time.'[81] Daly even demonstrated how the letter would be filed, and related that Manitowaba had been pleased. How was Manitowaba to know the meaning of a filing cabinet and the forgetfulness it facilitates? In truth, Daly was unwittingly making an ironic comment on bureaucratic inaction—a filing cabinet was a place to store the records of grievances that were never pursued. He also suggested that the DIA send Manitowaba a letter acknowledging receipt of his protests, which would 'cause a little thrill to John Manitowaba knowing . . . that he was in personal touch with the Department.'[82] The elder could then believe that he had accomplished something, although the officials fully intended to ignore his opinions.

With that the episode ended. The agent had dutifully transmitted Manitowaba's concerns to the department, and they had been duly noted, acknowledged, and filed—which in effect was nearly the same as consigning them to oblivion. Such was the fate of virtually all concerns expressed by Aboriginal people in this period, no matter how well-grounded their fears and claims.[83] Half a century later hundreds of such complaints were rediscovered in Indian Affairs files and served to bolster many a land claims case—but until then they were simply forgotten.

By the time Manitowaba was elected chief in 1933 he had had his object lesson in the futility of raising legitimate concerns with the Indian agent, never having heard anything more about the issues he had raised in 1930. He clearly had little faith left in Daly's usefulness as a conduit to the Indian department and was determined to find another way to draw attention to his claims. By this time he was taking an overtly adversarial position vis-à-vis the agent. While the elder continued to voice his concerns, Daly easily convinced the department to disregard the Parry Island chief.

Daly and Manitowaba had widely diverging views on the nature of the chief's office, the powers it conferred, and the reciprocal duties of chief and agent. Chief Manitowaba quickly became disillusioned with the delays involved in bureaucratic procedure. In May 1933, three months after his election, he wrote the department to convey his frustrations. He began by asserting that he had 'always done all I am supposed to do' but that he was not receiving replies from the department, and questioned the agent's claim that resolutions were being submitted to Ottawa. Moreover, he was suspicious that 'communications' were being sent to the department without his knowledge—it is not clear who was the object of his suspicions here.[84] Clearly, however, the chief expected a certain level of reciprocity in his interactions with the agent, and also the maintenance of regular contact with Ottawa. These expectations were not met by the Indian agent system.

The first outbreak of serious conflict between Daly and Manitowaba occurred when Stanley Manitowaba, the chief's son and a band councillor, was deposed for drunkenness, having been convicted more than once of being intoxicated. Stanley had been deposed as chief in 1926 for the same reason. John Manitowaba was angry at his removal and probably perceived it as politically motivated, which it may well have been—Stanley had a strong record of combatting Daly and clearly believed that band councils should wield decisive authority. This man's convictions for drinking made it easy to remove him from office, for the department took a strict view of this issue. Daly's comments in recommending his second removal are worth noting, though. The agent objected to Manitowaba's political approach much more than to his drinking patterns, presumably because he was another representative of the view that band councils should exercise significant power: 'Stanley Manitowaba is an apparently intelligent fellow, until you get talking to him, and when acting as a councilman he has peculiar ideas as to his powers.' Because of this the agent claimed that he was 'not fit' to be a band councillor.[85] Daly also claimed that several deputations from the band had come to request that he remove Stanley Manitowaba, but there is no way of knowing if this statement was true.

John Manitowaba himself was in some ways a less than ideal representative from the band's point of view: he spoke little English, could not read, and required help from others to write letters.[86] He was already on bad terms with the agent before his election. These characteristics placed him in a poor position to negotiate with non-Natives in general, and particularly with the DIA. For these reasons, and probably due to internal divisions as well, a group of Parry Islanders wrote the department immediately after his election in an unsuccessful attempt to have him deposed at once.[87] A year later, at the council meeting where Stanley's removal was announced, John Manitowaba apparently displayed his anger at the decision. Only Daly's side of the story has been recorded, and he portrayed the chief's behaviour in strong and demeaning language as an undignified outburst of temper.[88] This council meeting culminated in the first open attempt to remove Manitowaba as chief. The attempt was clearly in part a reflection of internal band politics. Francis Pegahmagabow was one of the main advocates of deposition, and he had his own scores to settle with Manitowaba, including the latter's active role in the effort to depose Pegahmagabow himself in 1925. Joseph Partridge, the band secretary, also supported the resolution to remove the chief. Partridge was a favourite of Daly's, whom the agent later selected as the foreman for roadwork on the reserve.[89] Perhaps Partridge also resented Manitowaba's former habit of cutting wood on property owned by Partridge's wife. The resolution to depose John Manitowaba was carried unanimously, although Daly did not state how many band members were actually present at the time.[90]

Daly was keen to see Manitowaba deposed and did his best to persuade his superiors to invoke the procedure. He stressed that a number of deputations had approached him from the beginning of Manitowaba's term in office, seeking to dismiss this chief. He detailed Pegahmagabow's charges against Manitowaba, including that he 'did not know how to run the council meeting, did not know how to put a resolution to the Band, never tried to do anything for the welfare of the council, all he was interested in was himself.'[91] Above all, Daly stressed the chief's character, as he saw it: 'He is an old man, stupid, vindictive, and abusive, in his treatment of an official of the Government.'[92] (The agent claimed that Manitowaba had pounded him on the shoulder and called him a drunkard during the heated council meeting.) Daly concluded by recommending that Manitowaba be deposed 'for the good government and welfare of the band'.[93]

The department, however, saw fit to veto the resolution, and stated that Manitowaba would be allowed to remain in office.[94] Although the band passed another resolution asking the Ottawa officials to reconsider, and Daly 'strongly recommended' deposition this time, the DIA stood firm. The internal officials apparently felt that Manitowaba posed no threat to the administration and was only an annoyance to Daly. Where Francis Pegahmagabow had been seen as an agitator who opposed federal policy and was attempting to instigate widespread resistance to it, Manitowaba was not involved in organizing. Daly himself had asserted that he could function regardless of Manitowaba's activities, and apparently the department felt that he should do just this.

For the remainder of the chief's three-year term, Daly persisted in his campaign to have John Manitowaba deposed, and the two men continued to clash over the powers associated with the chiefship. They had an altercation in the fall of 1934 about the visit to Parry Island of a certain Henry Jackson, a known political activist. The agent had the band constable expel Jackson over the strenuous objections of the chief, who felt that the agent had no right to ban anyone from the reserve. Manitowaba countered with a letter to the Indian department in which he not only defended his own prerogative in the matter, but also attempted to get rid of Daly. He wrote that 'the Chief and council are the proper body to say who is and who is not desirable on this Island.' Moreover, he promised to send evidence about the agent's activities that would 'necessitate an enquiry on Daly [*sic*] entire stewardship as your agent', and stated that he would be asking for Daly's dismissal.[95] Of course, Manitowaba had no real hope of dislodging Daly. The chief wrote to the agent at the same time expressing his indignation about the expulsion of Henry Jackson and particularly about remarks Daly had made regarding the chief's powers: 'you as much to tell me this morning if the Chief and Council has no voice in the affairs of the Reserve this will have to be explained fully by the Dept.'[96] This comment gives some indication of Daly's open flaunting of his own power position.

But the DIA steadfastly refused to dismiss Manitowaba as chief, taking the view that Manitowaba's actions were harmful only to the band and that leaving him in office would teach the community a lesson. Daly implied as much in one of his letters from this period: 'as the Department has suggested let the Band stew in their own fat, they have elected him, let him stay.'[97] Daly could do nothing to alter his superiors' position on the matter, and his failure to rid himself of the chief must have been noted by the people as a kind of defeat. Perhaps the most revealing point here is the contemptuous and punitive attitude of the officials at headquarters, who used the dispute over Manitowaba's chiefship merely to discipline a fractious band and remind them of the department's power. Daly's sentiment that 'it did not matter who was chief' was obviously shared by his bosses.

Wikwemikong Conflicts

The power dynamics in Lewis's agency were markedly different from those we have just discussed. Lewis rarely interfered with the band councils under his jurisdiction and frequently missed their meetings, although he was supposed to be present. He tended to establish co-operative relationships with band councils and let them take charge of most of the everyday matters on their reserves. Lewis's authority was not questioned to the same extent as Daly's, and it seems that one of the reasons was his more easygoing management style. Witness, for example, the removal of Jonas Odjig from office, discussed above. The agent did not approve of Odjig's perspective on farming and his opposition to assimilation, and the chief's outlook would certainly have been conducive to clashes between him and Lewis. Yet there is no record of actual conflict between the two. When Odjig was removed from office the initiative came from within the band and Lewis merely approved its resolution. While Lewis did not shrink from conflict when it became necessary, he also did not engage as actively as Daly in internal band politics. In part, this was a function of his own non-interventionist personality and a less vigilant attitude towards the maintenance of federal authority. In turn, Lewis inspired few direct challengers and thus was seldom forced to battle for supremacy with the people.

Different internal band politics were also a significant factor in the more peaceable character of the Manitowaning agency. To a large extent, the politics on Manitoulin Island, particularly on the unceded portion, were shaped by the inequities stemming from the 1836 and 1862 treaties. The unceded territory was home to a large population of members from other bands who shared the land and resources of the unceded territory while also benefiting from the resources of their own bands, such as annuities and interest payments from their band funds. By contrast, members of the MIU band did not receive any regular distributions of money: they had no treaty annuities and no band fund to speak of, which meant they did not receive interest payments. The unceded band had only its land and the resources that remained on it.

The main conflicts during Lewis's administration revolved around these issues. Even though DIA policies had created the problem, the disputes occurred between bands instead of being focused on Indian Affairs and the Indian agent system. Tensions over economic disparities had already led to a decision in 1912 to exclude non-members of the MIU band from council elections at Wikwemikong, in which they had previously participated.[98] At this time the threat was also made that non-band members would be forced either to leave the unceded territory or to add their revenues to the common fund of the MIU band in order to equalize economic resources.[99] The threat of expulsion was never implemented, but the resentment continued to simmer.[100]

In 1921 there was a fresh wave of agitation about the issue and a major conflict broke out. Jesuit historian Reverend Julien Paquin has described this series of events as 'The Great Trouble', which he depicted as a clash between the MIU band council and 44 families of Ojibways originally from Robinson Treaty bands on the north shore of Lake Huron.[101] In an attempt to fold all the territory's residents into a single band, the MIU band council passed a resolution that everyone who lived on their territory ought to transfer their membership to the MIU band and merge their funds. Those who were unwilling to change bands were threatened with exclusion from the use of timber, the main natural resource on the territory. The unceded band did its own lumbering,[102] and wintertime woodcutting on the reserve was an important source of work and income, allowing men to stay close to home instead of travelling to distant lumber camps to earn cash. For this reason, the timber became a tool with which the MIU band council tried to pressure resident non-members.

According to the diary of the Jesuit Superior at Wikwemikong, Father Gaston Artus, the conflict was chiefly with the South Bay band. On 3 January 1921 there was a council meeting at Wikwemikong, of which Father Artus wrote, 'Many people from South Bay are here. [The council] is discussing their right to be a separate band and to have funds of their own.'[103] The council concluded that the South Bay people should transfer to the MIU and add their funds to its band fund. If they did not comply, they would be excluded from use of the unceded territory's wood resources, even for personal use.[104] The South Bay people responded by engaging Father Artus to intercede on their behalf with the DIA so they could regain their timber rights.[105] The MIU band, meanwhile, sent a delegation to Ottawa in June 1921 and won the DIA to their side.[106] The department approved the MIU band council's resolution and confirmed its right to determine the use of the timber. Despite further protests from the members of other bands, the decision was upheld by both the MIU band and the department.[107] The department's approach to the problem was not surprising—DIA officials had always found it administratively inconvenient when reserves were occupied by groups of non-band members, and hoped to restrict people to the reserves to which they 'belonged' by band membership. This dispensation resulted in continuing inter-band tensions and attempts on the part of non-MIU members to regain access to the timber.

Initially, Lewis was sympathetic to the plight of the excluded bands and individuals,[108] since many, including the South Bay band, had long occupied the unceded territory. Lewis therefore sought in 1921 to reinstate the timber privileges of Michel Trudeau, a member of the Spanish River band. But the DIA refused this request because the MIU band was opposed to it.[109] From this point on, the agent maintained the position that he could not authorize any but MIU band members to cut timber. The result was that the bands and individuals involved were left to fight it out among themselves. It was a matter of deciding the distribution of scarce resources, and there was no obviously fair and just means of settling it. The rigid structure of the band system exacerbated the problem, since it made older Aboriginal methods of settling disputes harder to apply. In the pre-treaty era, the composition of bands had been very fluid, allowing for frequent shifts of individuals from one band and its territory to another. When conflicts over resources or other issues arose, people could solve them by simply going somewhere else. But once the government controlled band membership and confined the people to the small areas designated for reserves, these traditional solutions became difficult and sometimes impossible to implement. Transferring band membership was a complicated process and requests were often refused by the band concerned or by the DIA.[110]

Lewis chose to minimize the issue's importance in his correspondence with Ottawa, blaming the conflict on a few agitators and the interference of the Jesuit priest, Father Artus, in band politics. In 1921, after Father Artus had written to the DIA about the conflict, Lewis acknowledged that the different bands could not agree, but added that trouble was being caused only by 'a few members' of Spanish River Band No. 3, who he felt should be transferred to the MIU band. He portrayed the MIU approach in favourable terms, stating that their only wish was 'for all the Indians now occupying the reserve in question to unite into one band and all work together and develop their reserve'.[111] Tensions between the agent and the priest were obviously high—the agent belittled Artus's concerns and remarked sarcastically that there was 'not any danger of effusion of blood' among the people, as the priest had suggested. As far as Lewis was concerned, the priest was a key factor in the difficulties: 'if he would be satisfied in looking after the mission spiritually instead of trying to dominate the Chief of the Manitoulin Island Unceded Band there would not be much trouble between the Indians of the Spanish River Band and the Manitoulin Island Unceded Band.'[112]

Although Father Artus clearly was deeply involved in the conflict, Lewis's depiction was still an oversimplification of the matter. The trouble in 1921 had begun between the MIU band and members of the South Bay band, not the Spanish River band. The South Bay band was in a particularly difficult position because, unlike some of the others involved, this group had no other reserve to return to. They had lived on the unceded territory since the mid-nineteenth century and had nowhere else to go. These people continued their attempts to participate in the exploitation of the timber resource. They also attempted, with some others, to regain voting rights in the MIU band, but the agent summarily refused the request.[113]

The timber issue led to one of the few disputes into which Lewis was drawn during these years. Michel Trudeau was the most prominent protestor concerning the issue, and he waged a two-year campaign to regain his woodcutting rights. Trudeau had his brother Dominic (an MIU band member) hire him to cut timber. It appears that others followed suit, leading to more friction. In 1923 Lewis ordered Dominic Trudeau to cease employing outsiders, threatening to seize the timber if it was cut by anyone but band members. This was in part a disciplinary action, as the agent had decided that Michel Trudeau was a troublemaker and needed to be taught the error of his ways: 'Michel Tredeau [sic] is the most troublesome Indian I have to contend with in this agency. He maintains that the Spanish River Indians #3 are the rightful owners of the unceded portion of Manitoulin and he has the right to cut timber as he is a member of that Band.'[114] But Lewis had overstepped his authority by threatening to seize the wood, and complaints to the department resulted in his being brought to heel.

The only further development in the issue at this time was the voluntary transfer of some members of the South Bay band to the MIU band in 1926. Judging from population statistics published in the department's annual report, roughly 30 people were involved in the move.[115] Their decision to transfer was bitterly opposed by another faction within the band, and the South Bay band remained in existence, still deprived of timber privileges. This was a problem created largely by DIA regulations, the economic inequality between bands, and the anomalies in the treaty-making process on Manitoulin Island. Lewis dealt with these issues on an ad hoc basis, and after an abortive attempt to intervene he adopted a neutral position that left the conflict unresolved. In fact, for many years after, the people continued to disagree over the most equitable settlement of the problem, until a major amalgamation finally occurred in 1968.[116]

The most significant difference between this situation and the issues on Parry Island was that the troubles on the unceded territory caused problems only for the residents of the territory. Neither the department nor local Euro-Canadians were affected, nor were there any resulting challenges to federal authority. Rather, the people here carried out their disagreements internally, on an individual basis and through the band councils. Neither the agent nor officials in Ottawa had to worry about a challenge to their right to administer affairs on the reserves. Vigorous struggles between agent and band councillors thus had no reason to develop, and Lewis's relations with band officials remained much more harmonious than was the case in Daly's jurisdiction.

Conclusion

While Aboriginal protest became much more publicly visible after World War II, Indian agents faced significant challenges to their authority in the 1920s and 1930s. Conflict was, after all, inherent in the system, since federal control had been imposed without First Nations consent. Aboriginal dissidents in the 1920s and

1930s were working in an unsympathetic climate and the department was able to stifle their discontent quite effectively. It was powerfully assisted by the poverty and marginalization of First Nations people, the general indifference of the Canadian public, and a 1927 amendment to the Indian Act that prevented the engagement of lawyers to battle Indian Affairs. Nevertheless, the dissenters were a tenacious and ever-present force.

The conflicts discussed in this chapter show the determination of many First Nations people to assert their right to run their own affairs. Band councils were a kind of affront: they provided the appearance of self-government, but were in fact strictly subordinated to the Indian agent. Most agents, like Daly, insisted on enforcing this subordination of band officials to DIA bureaucrats.[117] They also ensured that the councils had very limited usefulness as platforms for raising grievances. The grievances created during the treaty-making process thus remained unresolved in the period, for the simple reason that Ottawa refused to consider any adjustments to existing arrangements or to discuss the possibility that errors had been made. In both agencies, the struggles over issues of resource exploitation and land loss were based on arrangements that had been made long before these agents assumed office. Lewis's response to the trouble on the unceded territory was to hold aloof from the issue as much as possible, although to some extent he took the part of the Manitoulin Island Unceded band against the others. In his bureaucratic, non-interventionist style, Lewis was content to enforce the decision of headquarters. Daly faced a different kind of opposition, one that at times seemed to be aimed at him personally. His aggressive approach was in part a response to this factor. It is not, however, the only explanation for the disparity between the two agents' administrations. Daly's impulse to assert authority was also a character trait, which was revealed clearly in his relations with band councillors.

The handling of these issues shows the extent of the control that Indian agents exercised over band councils, and more generally over Aboriginal communities. A number of individuals contested the agent's position, especially his right to thwart the will of the elected council. They also disputed Ottawa's authority over the use of band funds and resources. The outcome varied little from one situation to the next. Aboriginal people's wardship status and the provisions of the Indian Act ensured that authority over band councils and band affairs remained firmly in Ottawa's hands. The agents were primarily Ottawa's instruments, but the ways in which they constructed events and personalities in their correspondence played a significant role in determining the official position. Band councillors who sought to implement greater self-determination were bound to feel the weight of the department's heavy hand returning them to their place. When they were dealing with a paternalistic and controlling agent as well, their disempowerment had a visible symbol in their everyday lives. It is little wonder, then, that Daly experienced such a long series of altercations and power contests with elected officials of the Parry Island band.

4

'Easy to Trick People by Putting Words on Paper': Treaties and Aboriginal Rights

'My father and his father and my great grandfather were all very intelligent men but they weren't lawyers and the older generation did not receive much schooling—it wasn't important in those days. It was easy to trick people by putting words on paper.'[1]

'They said they would never have given up the hunting and fishing rights because that's like saying you're not an Indian any more.'[2]

'Hunting and fishing is part of the Indian identity. . . . You take the hunting and fishing away and you've taken away part of who we are. It doesn't make any sense. They never would have given that up. And besides, everyone around here has always hunted and fished and people could never understand why the Game Wardens would chase us.'[3]

In 1926, Joseph Traunch of Collins Inlet wrote a letter to the Department of Indian Affairs.[4] It was the sort of Aboriginal protest letter that department officials found easy to ignore. Traunch's command of the English language was poor, and he had no authority to speak on behalf of anyone but himself. Moreover, instead of raising complaints about specific instances, he assailed the system in general: the department's perceived indifference to Aboriginal welfare, its failure to uphold treaty rights, and the game conservation regime that imposed licences on the Anishinabek. In spite of his difficulties with the English language, Traunch's central grievances were quite clear. He felt that Aboriginal people received no assistance from the Indian department, and he objected to the imposition of licences for harvesting activities. He particularly protested the fact that, as he believed, the people could not even fish on their own reserves without a licence. He felt that Aboriginal people had been unjustly robbed of their resources, especially their fish, and tried to provide an analogy to make officials understand his point of view. Traunch asked rhetorically how the department would respond if it had a pond full of fish and Native people stole the fish and also killed the cattle in the department's yard: 'he wolden like it and us Indian we ar the same.' Furthermore, he was concerned that the department was going to attempt to deprive the people even of their reserves: 'the Department try to take the reserve from [us] the same [as] he don with the Island . . . and the same with the fishing.' In short, Traunch was suspicious of government intentions, and he perceived the DIA as failing to protect Aboriginal interests.[5]

Traunch's effort to address the violation of Aboriginal rights had no impact. DIA secretary J.D. McLean simply sent a brief response instructing him to contact the Department of Game and Fisheries about fishing.[6] In part, the letter could be ignored because it did not conform to Euro-Canadian conventions—it did not cite specific instances in which his rights had been violated, nor did it propose measures the department should take. In any case, the department very rarely took Aboriginal views into account. But more importantly, government officials had no intention of altering the existing game and fish regime, regardless of the fact that it violated several treaties. The Canadian government would not deal with Aboriginal hunting and fishing rights until forced to do so by litigation in the late twentieth century.

In Ontario, treaties are a critically important part of the historical relationship between First Nations peoples and government. Aboriginal people often insisted on negotiating treaties against the government's will, particularly when non-Natives were moving to seize resources in unsurrendered territories. As we have seen, for example, the Robinson treaties of 1850, which involved most of the First Nations around Georgian Bay, were forced on a reluctant Canadian government when mining prospectors began to encroach on Aboriginal lands.[7] On Manitoulin Island, by contrast, the 1862 treaty was virtually forced on the island peoples, leading to the Wikwemikong group's refusal to take part. Once the treaties were signed, however, Aboriginal people perceived them as binding and eternal compacts governing their relations with government and their rights over lands and resources. Aboriginal leaders in the post-treaty period expended considerable energy trying to enforce provisions relating to harvesting rights in an attempt to maintain an independent economy.

First Nations people had never intended to surrender control of their lives to the government or any other outsiders—on the contrary, by signing the treaties they had sought to retain a measure of self-determination. By negotiating treaty provisions, leaders had sought to create an enduring relationship in which the parameters were agreed on in advance. This was a way of exercising some control when they knew that their people's power would decline in direct proportion to the number of Euro-Canadians who settled on their lands. One of the ways in which the government violated the treaties, from the Aboriginal viewpoint, was in imposing a whole new set of conditions and restraints on the First Nations to which they had never consented. In fact, the entire framework of the Indian Affairs system was imposed unilaterally well after the region's treaties were signed. Indian agents, elected band councils, the endless series of provisions in the Indian Act that ensured DIA control—all of these were decreed by legislation without reference to Aboriginal communities. In the Aboriginal view, then, First Nations people had fulfilled their part of the bargain by relinquishing their lands, while the government had only fulfilled part of its own obligations. Since the treaties were supposed to be in force in perpetuity, they expected to be able to hold the government to its undertakings.

The government view of the treaties was in many ways diametrically opposed to that of First Nations people. By the 1920s and 1930s, government officials essentially regarded the treaties as simple real estate deals, whose provisions had long since been fulfilled. They had been a convenient way of obtaining agreement from First Nations people to the loss of their lands and (in the government's view) their sovereignty. As such, they had already served their purpose. In John Daly's words, the treaties were 'past and done with', an archaic relic of times past.[8] He and other agents were impatient with Aboriginal people who raised grievances about how treaty provisions and promises had been implemented, and about lands they believed they had never surrendered. The Indian agents viewed such discussions as irrelevant, and saw their proponents as troublemakers. Officials of all types vigorously resisted the notion that Aboriginal people had their own valid interpretations of what had been agreed to in the treaties. Rather, they considered that the DIA was the sole arbiter of its own duties and responsibilities. Daly actually tried to prevent the people from obtaining information about the exact contents of their treaties. DIA responsibilities were defined largely in terms of the Indian Act's provisions, not the details of specific treaties. What this meant, in practice, was that government determined its own obligations, since the Indian department was always the source of Indian Act provisions and amendments. In fact, in everyday affairs the Indian Act superseded the treaties as far as DIA officials were concerned.

These attitudes were profoundly frustrating for First Nations people. The significance of the issue is nicely highlighted by this observation made in the Hawthorn Report of 1966: 'The discrepancy between the relative unimportance of treaties as determinants of government policy and Indian perception of the treaties as *basic items in self-identity* constitutes an important complicating factor in Indian-government relations.'[9] The fundamental incompatibility of Aboriginal and government views was highly visible in the period of this study.

Treaty harvesting rights, in particular, held twofold significance for Aboriginal people. Most obviously, they were of crucial economic importance. If upheld, they would have improved the people's ability to make a decent living and simultaneously eased their adaptation to the industrial economy. But hunting and fishing were also important for reasons of principle and for their cultural significance. Aboriginal people viewed the fish and animals as resources that the Creator had placed on the land for their benefit and sustenance. They had never authorized the newcomers to make use of these resources, much less to take possession of them and then dictate when and how Aboriginal people could access them. Moreover, activities such as pursuing game and spearing and netting fish were deeply ingrained in Aboriginal culture, so much so that these practices were seen as part of a distinct Aboriginal identity. The quotations from contemporary elders at the beginning of this chapter suggest the enduring attachment to these ancient occupations, and their predecessors in the interwar period undoubtedly shared their views. It must have been an additional insult that the conservation measures adopted by governments were so poorly enforced and ineffective, especially for certain species of fish.[10] While conservation measures were often strictly enforced against Aboriginal people, for a long time they received few benefits from the planned preservation of

Aboriginal men around Georgian Bay and Lake Huron continued to trap and sell furs throughout the interwar period and beyond, although competition from non-Aboriginal trappers was increasingly damaging. This photo from the 1940s shows the bargaining and appraising process between Mammattawa trappers and a fur buyer. Archives of Ontario, RG 1-448-1, Box 37, #8.

game because competition from non-Aboriginals continued to deplete stocks. Especially in the region north of Parry Sound, local and visiting non-Aboriginal people participated avidly in hunting from the early 1900s on and bagged large numbers of animals.[11] While tourism declined drastically during the 1930s, reducing competition with outsiders for game, the Depression forced many local people to supplement their meagre incomes with game and fish.

As for the Indian agents, they were continually faced with their clients' demands to deal with long-standing problems related to non-fulfillment of treaties. The grievances that emerged in this period were many, but they centred on issues of resources, land, and economic strategies. The violation of harvesting rights was only one of the important issues. On Parry Island there were also outstanding problems with land surrenders, such as the alienation of land and islands that the Anishinabek believed had not been included in the surrender. At Shawanaga an old agreement about fishing grounds had been unilaterally abrogated by a later fisheries overseer. Chief Odjig at Wikwemikong resented the introduction of Euro-Canadian farming and advocated a return to the old hunting ways. In all of these concerns, economic questions were prominent. Given the economic stresses of the 1920s and the severe depression of the 1930s, the agents could not ignore the importance of preserving some access to food animals for First Nations people. Nor were they allowed to forget the general Aboriginal perception that Euro-Canadian rule had resulted in a regime that chronically violated their interests.

Government Disregard of Treaty Harvesting Rights

The early twentieth century witnessed increasing disregard of treaty provisions, as Ontario legislation concerning hunting and fishing encroached ever more directly on treaty rights. After a brief struggle with the province, DIA officials concluded that they had no power to enforce treaty rights and largely abandoned the attempt. The federal government had consistently garnered court defeats when it sought to fight the expansion of provincial rights, and there was no will to risk another costly defeat over an issue of concern only to Aboriginal people. By the second decade of the twentieth century, DIA officials actively defended the provincial government's policy of restricting Aboriginal hunting and fishing, even though this policy contravened treaty provisions. The Ontario government historically has a record of denying the existence of Aboriginal title and treaty rights, and this tendency has been clearly evident in its approach to conservation legislation and enforcement.

As we saw in Chapter 1, the treaties had varying provisions concerning hunting and fishing rights. The Robinson Huron Treaty (covering 10 of the bands of this study) guaranteed to its Aboriginal signatories 'the full and free privilege . . . to fish in the waters [of the surrendered territory] as they have heretofore been in the habit of doing.'[12] The only restriction was that they could not fish or hunt on lands occupied by newcomers. The Bond Head Treaty of 1836 made no written reference to harvesting rights. Still, the agreement was supposed to establish Great Manitoulin and its surrounding islands as an Aboriginal refuge, whose resources would thus be reserved for the people. Bond Head chose the island in large part for its fisheries, which formed a major part of Aboriginal sustenance, and no Europeans had yet begun to appropriate this resource.[13] Certainly no statement was made suggesting that First Nations people would cease to control the fishing industry around the islands. It is difficult, then, to see how this treaty can be interpreted as a surrender of hunting and fishing rights. By 1862, when the second Manitoulin treaty was signed, officials had become more cautious about their promises, and the 1862 treaty's written provisions stated only that First Nations people would have the same harvesting rights as anyone else. It is doubtful that the full meaning of this clause was clear to the Aboriginal signatories, however, given the centrality of fishing in their economy. Moreover, the people of Wikwemikong did not sign this treaty and the 1836 agreement was still in force as far as their portion of the island was concerned. They argued vehemently that they had never ceded their fisheries, which were the mainstay of their diet and their most important trade item.

The First Nations around Georgian Bay had all drawn a considerable part of their food supply from the rich fisheries in the lakes and rivers. Most of the Robinson Treaty signatories selected their reserves in locations close to their best fishing stations, and Wikwemikong on Manitoulin Island was also located by an abundant fishery. As far as they were concerned, treaty guarantees secured to them an exclusive right to this resource.[14] For a decade or so after 1850, they faced little competition from Euro-Canadians, but soon large commercial interests from Canada and the United States began to exploit the Great Lakes fisheries intensively. Although First Nations people attempted to defend their rights, they were easily defeated by the powerful commercial and sport fishing interests.

At an early stage, government officials established a definition of Aboriginal fishing rights that restricted their exercise to personal consumption, as opposed to fishing for trade or 'commercial' use. This definition was established as early as 1859, when the Province of Canada passed its second Fisheries Act.[15] At this time an agreement was reached between the DIA and the Department of Crown Lands, which was responsible for fisheries in Canada West and Canada East. The agreement, designed for 'the Protection of the interest of native tribes', exempted Aboriginal people in Canada West (Upper Canada) from paying fees for fishing leases.[16] In effect, this meant that the Fisheries Act was presumed to apply to First Nations people, but they would not be made to pay for fishing. Moreover, while the agreement provided for granting them exclusive rights to certain fisheries, the fee exemption applied only when fishing was done for 'bona fide domestic consumption'.[17] This principle was sustained for years and remains an important concept in contemporary court judgements about Aboriginal fishing rights, now often couched in terms of 'subsistence' use. Its significance is that it has restricted treaty rights by introducing a novel distinction between 'subsistence' and 'commercial' use of fish. Such a distinction was meaningless when applied to an Aboriginal economy that for centuries had depended on fish not only for food but also as a trade item. Trading had always been part of their subsistence, and when they signed the treaties they expected to continue fishing and trading as they always had. Aboriginal people had exchanged fish with other nations before contact with Europeans, and they quickly began to sell this item to Europeans after their arrival. Particularly at Shawanaga and on Manitoulin Island, the fish trade was an important economic resource in the nineteenth century. Thus, in limiting treaty fishing rights to 'domestic consumption', the government interpretation drastically reduced their value.

Governments handled treaty hunting and trapping rights in much the same manner as fishing. The Robinson Treaty made no provision for government regulation of Aboriginal hunting. Nevertheless, Aboriginal hunters were subjected to increasingly intensive policing by game wardens, who confiscated their take and their equipment, including boats and canoes. Aboriginal hunters were often fined and in some cases even imprisoned.[18] Again, the artificial distinction was drawn between subsistence and commercial harvesting of game animals. As in the case of fishing, the violation of treaty obligations was justified in part by the overriding goal of conservation. The failure to uphold the treaties was rationalized on the grounds that conservation was of particular benefit to First Nations people.[19] As DIA secretary J.D. McLean wrote patronizingly to an Aboriginal hunter fined for killing a moose, 'you must remember that there is no class or community who will ultimately benefit more from proper protection of the game than Indians.'[20] Moreover,

A uniformed man, possibly an official from the Ministry of Natural Resources, examines a Mammattawa trapper's pelts (1948). Archives of Ontario, RG 1-448-1, Box 37, #7.

it was commonly believed that Aboriginal people were a major factor in the deple-tion of game, since they were accused of disregarding conservation needs.[21]

The erosion of hunting rights in Ontario was a gradual process in which the provincial government progressively tightened its conservation regime and ability to enforce game laws. As Frank Tough has outlined the process, the federal govern-ment was slowly outflanked by its provincial counterpart: 'As provincial game pro-tection laws evolved, both in terms of the technical ability to manage the exploitation of wildlife and in terms of the provisions which affected Indians, the capacity of the federal government to protect treaty rights slipped away.'[22] Early Ontario game protection legislation (beginning in 1892) specifically mentioned treaty rights, which were not to be affected by anything contained in the legislation. The legislation also did not apply to Aboriginal people hunting in unsurrendered territory.[23] Yet these exemptions were ignored in practice and dropped entirely by 1914. Game wardens frequently harassed Aboriginal hunters. Numerous arrests, convictions, confiscations, fines, and prison sentences were the result. Aboriginal people persistently sought recognition of their rights, primarily through appeals to the Indian department and also by fighting their convictions whenever they could. The department faced pressure from individuals, lawyers, chiefs, and band coun-cils, as well as from Aboriginal political organizations such as the Grand General

Indian Council of Ontario, asking that officials act to protect treaty rights.[24] Robinson Treaty people were prominent in correspondence with the DIA on the subject. Unfortunately for them, department officials had ceased to feel an obligation to defend treaty harvesting rights, having convinced themselves that they were powerless to do so, and that, in any event, game conservation was in the best interests of First Nations people. In the absence of federal intervention, the Ontario government effectively criminalized Aboriginal hunting.

The Impact of Conservation Regulations

On Manitoulin Island, the transfer of resources occurred early, as pressure from commercial fishing operations ensured that Aboriginal fisheries were effectively expropriated. Beginning in the late 1850s, the Province of Canada instituted a system of fishing leases that was quickly used to exclude Aboriginal fishers from the commercial fish trade. In the first round of lease distributions, only 12 of 97 leases were accorded to 'Indian bands'.[25] By the early 1860s, the number of Aboriginal fishing leases had been reduced almost to zero. The people of Wikwemikong took decisive action to defend their fisheries, but they were fighting a losing battle.[26] Governments were determined to enforce the English common-law principle that the fish resource was open to all and publicly owned, and organized its exploitation in the interest of Euro-Canadian society. Although Aboriginal people did not own any fishing leases in the interwar period, the Manitoulin Island First Nations remained involved in fishing—agent Lewis reported incomes of $4,000 to $10,000 annually from fishing in the 1920s, and reduced amounts throughout the 1930s (see Table 3, Chapter 1). This figure is surprising considering the restriction of Aboriginal fishing rights, and the most likely explanation is that it reflects the earnings of First Nations men hired by non-Aboriginal fishing concerns. Certainly it is clear that commercial fishing was governed by non-Aboriginal people and organized to exclude Aboriginal rights.

In the same period, the people of eastern Georgian Bay also attempted to preserve their fisheries. The Parry Island and Shawanaga bands both sustained themselves largely on fish in the mid-nineteenth century, and both reserves had been selected for their proximity to excellent fisheries. Between 1852 and the turn of the century the Parry Island band made repeated efforts to have the waters by the island reserved for their exclusive use. But their requests were not heeded, although the nearby Christian Island band received a licence in 1883 for the sole use of their fishing grounds.[27] By the late nineteenth century, the Parry Island fishery was largely destroyed thanks to the sawdust from nearby sawmills, which severely depleted fish stocks.[28] The Shawanaga and Henvey Inlet bands had some success in commercial deep-net fishing towards the end of the nineteenth century.[29] By the early twentieth century, however, all these groups confronted the depletion of fish stocks and, more seriously, government licensing requirements and restriction of their access to the resource.

The ability to hunt was equally negatively affected by government regulations. As early as 1884, game wardens were destroying traps and harassing hunters from

Parry Island. Although Indian superintendent Walton attempted to protect the hunters, he found no support at the Department of Indian Affairs and was powerless to effect change on his own.[30] D.F. Macdonald, Parry Sound Indian superintendent in the early twentieth century, felt that game wardens were particularly ardent in their pursuit of Native hunters and fishermen (he was himself a sportsman and often hunted in company with Aboriginal men).[31] Again, this agent could not engage the DIA in their defence, nor did his assessment match the perceptions of other Euro-Canadians. As we have noted, the general Euro-Canadian public commonly perceived First Nations people as recklessly destroying animal stocks and being largely responsible for their depletion.

In the 1920s and 1930s, First Nations people continued to face harassment from wardens for fishing, trapping, and hunting. This meant, for some, that their access to traditional sources of food and trade items was curtailed. At the same time, many flouted the regulations and were punished with equipment seizures, fines, and jail terms. The DIA proclaimed that it had a policy of attempting to

Ontario Department of Game and Fisheries District Supervisors in 1932. Minister George Challies is seated in the front row, second from the left. Local officials are standing in the back row—the Sault Ste Marie official is on the far left, while those responsible for Orillia and North Bay, respectively, stand at the far right. Archives of Ontario, RG 1-448-1, Box 106, #485.

secure 'special privileges' for Native people in regard to hunting and trapping regulations, but this merely meant that it would intervene occasionally to request short-term leniency.[32] DIA officials also endeavoured to ensure subsistence access to fish, without questioning the validity of the licensing regime. The department's policy was designed to balance two competing goals: the wish to avoid any appearance of interfering in provincial matters, and the desire to facilitate some Aboriginal access to animal resources so that the people could support themselves. DIA officials were willing to intervene with the Department of Game and Fisheries to ensure that small-scale fishing was allowed, but there was no question of encouraging fishing on a commercial scale. In fact, the records show no indication of its being discussed as a potentially lucrative industry for First Nations. Rather, the Indian department entirely accepted the principle that Aboriginal people should be allowed to harvest fish as a 'subsistence' activity only.[33] The exclusion of commercial fishing from treaty rights had a severe impact, although many people continued to trade fish for other goods despite the laws.[34]

When it came to harvesting rights, the viewpoints of internal DIA officials and First Nations people were usually diametrically opposed. As often happened, Indian agents fell somewhere in between since they faced conflicting demands from both sides. These men witnessed the impact of fish and game regulations on their clients and tended to object to the application of the laws. At times they attempted to shield their clients from wardens, or at least from more drastic actions such as impounding boats, nets, guns, pelts, and so on. Parry Sound agent D.F. Macdonald paid fines imposed by fish and game wardens out of band funds so as to minimize their impact.[35] The agents' appeals to the Indian department, however, were usually without effect, and on their own they could not protect the people.

The Struggle for Treaty Rights

Given all of the above, it is not surprising that political conflicts between Aboriginal people and governments in the interwar period frequently focused on issues related to treaties, especially unfulfilled promises, the use of resources, and land questions. The enforcement of government regulations regarding fishing and guiding permits surfaced repeatedly in the agents' correspondence. Like much of the Canadian legal regime, the permit system was not well understood in the Native community. In particular, Aboriginal people did not understand why fish and game wardens interfered with them and demanded that they produce licences or permits. The wardens' activities were bitterly resented because they stood in opposition to the community's own view of its fishing and hunting rights. Long before the existence of Aboriginal political organizations that could publicly assert these rights, the First Nations people in these two agencies held a coherent understanding of their rights that differs little from that which their descendants claim today. They felt that their prior occupation of the territory endowed them with special rights to harvest the land's resources. Further, they believed that the treaties they had made with the Canadian government had enshrined these rights in law—or if not, that justice had not been served and their natural rights were being violated.

But officials of the provincial Department of Game and Fisheries interfered frequently enough with Aboriginal hunting and fishing to convince the people that government did not share their views. In response, Aboriginal people called on the agents to intervene to help retain these sources of nourishment and income for the Native economy. Here the agents tended to share First Nations people's calculation of their own interests and to intercede with the Department of Game and Fisheries on their behalf. DIA officials in Ottawa, on the other hand, were less concerned with this question than the agents and did not always co-operate with such efforts.

We have already seen that Joseph Traunch wrote to the Indian department about the injustice of requiring licences for Aboriginal harvesting and about the general disregard of Aboriginal rights. Daly and Lewis also heard frequent complaints about these issues. In January 1923 the Shawanaga band approached Daly about their grievances with respect to fishing. The band had an oral tradition that in 1853 government surveyor John Staughton Dennis had secured them exclusive fishing rights to a sizable area of Georgian Bay off the shore of their reserve. Captain T.G. Anderson, Indian superintendent at the time, had told the leading men to ensure that no one encroached on the territory without their permission.[36] Band spokespersons further stated that French fishermen from Penetanguishene had paid the band a fee for using its fishing grounds, and that former band chief Solomon James had been fishery officer for all of Georgian Bay and had observed the band's right to the designated fishery. The band wanted to know if the department had any information on file that would help them regain their rights.

Daly, who had only recently been appointed agent, took this oral tradition seriously and explained the situation to his superiors. It is clear from his first letters on the subject that the agent was disposed to believe his clients and prepared to defend the rights they asserted. But he was quickly taught the department's stock method of dealing with these kinds of claims, namely, to disregard oral traditions and accept the provincial government's position (which was to deny Aboriginal rights altogether). Department officials informed Daly that this same issue had been raised with his predecessor, Alexander Logan, in 1917 and 1918. Logan recorded that the chiefs and councillors of Shawanaga, Parry Island, and Henvey Inlet all wished to have fishing grounds set apart for their sole use. He wrote derisively that the areas they desired were 'ridiculous' in size and that 'they just about want all the Georgian Bay.'[37] Since these groups had formerly shared the entire bay's resources among themselves and other First Nations, it is not inconceivable that they were, in fact, attempting to reclaim their old fishing grounds, which they had never agreed to share with the newcomers. Having received a new agent who was initially more sympathetic than Logan, the Shawanaga council had decided to air their grievance again in the hope of a more positive resolution.

Unfortunately for the band, department officials had no intention of revisiting the question. Since there was no record on file of Dennis's action in reserving the waters, the band's historical claim was assumed to be untrue, even though it was strengthened by the information that Penetanguishene fishermen had paid them for access to the grounds and it was consistent with the fact that Dennis had laid out their reserve at the time they named. The provincial Department of Game and Fisheries was unwilling even to grant a fishing licence at a 'reasonable rental' since its officials claimed the area requested was 'beyond reason', and 'at any rate they would not set apart those waters.'[38] These were rich fisheries and many Euro-Canadians were earning their living from them. The band's question was thus treated not as a claim to resources once legitimately reserved for them, but as an unreasonable application for a fishing territory to which they had no right. Logan sealed the matter by stating that hardly any of the people of Shawanaga currently fished, as if this were proof that the territory would not be put to any use instead of being evidence of their prior exclusion.[39]

Faced with the intransigence of both DIA and Game and Fisheries officials, Daly dropped the matter. By 1936 the Shawanaga people had definitively lost the rights they believed were confirmed to them in 1853, and Daly had ceased to support them on the issue. The band council passed a resolution to purchase a fishing licence for the whole band, to be paid from band funds. The agent opposed this move on the grounds that the members should be responsible for their own licences.[40] The original agreement remembered by the elders of the Shawanaga band was thus no longer honoured once First Nations people were outnumbered by the newcomers.

Parry Island people, who had close links with Shawanaga, were undoubtedly informed of the outcome of their negotiations in 1923. Francis Pegahmagabow concluded that Daly would be of no help, and consequently made an effort to work through a sympathetic non-Aboriginal lawyer, Wallace Nesbitt, who took on a number of cases related to Aboriginal issues. The issues he raised included the problem of fishing rights. Unfortunately for Pegahmagabow, the time had not yet arrived when lawyers and litigation would force the government to the bargaining table. Nesbitt informed his client that he had written to the Ontario Department of Game and Fisheries about harvesting issues. The strategy, not unlike that of the Shawanaga spokespersons, was to assert Aboriginal rights over certain fishing areas: Nesbitt asked Game and Fisheries to 'warn all persons who obtain a licence to fish with nets in Georgian Bay that their licence does not give them the right to fish in waters, the fishing rights in respect of which are reserved by the Crown for the use of the Indians.'[41] No response from the department was in the file, but it is clear that the Ontario government would not entertain such a proposal.

Efforts to regain fishing rights occurred in the same period on Manitoulin Island. Here the people did not have a history of having areas reserved for them by government officials—on the contrary, they had been among the first Aboriginal groups to be shoundered aside in the interests of Euro-Canadian commercial fishing operations. But until this time there had been a certain room for manoeuvre, since local game and fisheries overseers had tolerated small-scale fishing—indeed, they had apparently given a limited recognition to treaty rights. Lewis wrote in 1923, 'Other Game and Fisheries Overseer's [*sic*] in this district did not interfere with the Indians catching a few fish for food as they considered it was within the Indian treaty rights.'[42] But now a new Game and Fisheries overseer had been appointed and had threatened to seize the nets of anyone caught fishing without a licence.

Thus, 61 years after the treaty, a new official was trying to change the rules unilaterally—and he had the power to do so. Therefore, in 1923, the Sucker Creek band addressed the problem by passing a resolution to purchase individual fishing licences for each of its members, charging the cost to band funds.

Once again, the fact that the people had previously been excluded from large-scale fishing, and therefore allegedly did not fish much, was used as a rationale for refusing their attempt to revive their fishing business. Lewis did not take a position on the question of treaty rights, but characteristically argued on pragmatic grounds. He was opposed to the purchase of licences 'as the Indians at Sucker Creek do not catch enough fish to warrant it.'[43] He did wish, however, to ensure the people's small-scale access to fishing as a supplement to their diet. The DIA responded by contacting the Department of Game and Fisheries to resolve the issue as an executive decision between governments. The mandarins decided that they were willing to tolerate subsistence fishing. As Lewis wrote afterwards to the band chief, Ottawa had instructed him that 'the Indians of the Sucker Creek Band . . . may continue to take fish for their own use from the waters of the Georgian Bay . . . providing that they do not operate any Seine Nets.'[44] The members of the Sucker Creek band were thus spared the expense of paying for licences, but their catch was to be strictly limited and the issue of their treaty rights was not raised. Their exemption from fishing licences was presented as a matter of grace and was linked specifically with the fact that they harvested fish in limited numbers and only for their own consumption. Large-scale, commercial fishing was a business for non-Natives, who could easily cover the cost of licences through their profits.

In October of the same year Lewis wrote directly to the district warden, appealing to him to allow Aboriginal people to catch fish in small numbers. He was apparently responding to concern about the likelihood of nets being seized, for he noted that some of the people had had their boats, nets, and all their equipment seized by an overseer in 1917 when they were fishing for their own use. The agent presented his case on the basis of need and made it clear that the people wished to fish for personal use only, to catch food for the coming winter. Lewis stated that the people were poor: 'This is the third hard dry year we have had in this district and now the Indians are feeling the effects of it.'[45] The records do not show the district warden's response, but given the arrangement worked out with the DIA only a few months before, it is likely that he agreed to overlook Aboriginal fishing in this case, ensuring that they could obtain fish for food without paying for licences. But the premise was always that the people were engaging in subsistence fishing. By protecting this source of food the DIA was also acting out of self-interest, since it wished First Nations people to feed themselves.

Lewis was also unsympathetic to complaints about Euro-Canadian trappers who encroached on traditional Aboriginal trapping grounds. One trapper who belonged to the Whitefish River band wrote an eloquent protest letter in 1930, objecting to the fact that non-Aboriginal people easily obtained trapping licences and offered fierce competition to First Nations men. Edward Paibomsai wrote from the Timmins area, in northern Ontario, that there had been 'too many white men trapping around here in the last few years and has cleaned us up on everything.'[46] When he took care to leave some breeding animals in an area to preserve the stock, white trappers came along and took them all. As a result Paibomsai had been experiencing real privation, and he remonstrated that 'it is no good for an Indian around here any more.'[47] The solution he proposed was that trapping licences should be available only to treaty Indians. Lewis clearly was not willing to contemplate any such proposal. In response to Paibomsai's comments, made in explanation of an application for enfranchisement, the agent observed dryly, 'The Department can ascertain from the tone of this Indian's letter whether, or not, he should be granted his enfranchisement.'[48] The internal officials saw things the same way, and punished Paibomsai by refusing to grant his request for enfranchisement.

John Daly at first made little objection to government regulation of trapping, although he tended to be more proactive than his contemporary Lewis. Daly kept the people informed about existing game regulations and did not protest against the application of game laws to First Nations people. In 1925, for example, he reported to the DIA that he had instructed everyone in his agency about a new set of regulations established by the Department of Game and Fisheries.[49] He had also taken the opportunity to point out that the government had reserved the hunting of beaver and otter for First Nations people, and he urged the people to make the most of this provision. He clearly viewed the monopoly as an act of generosity on the part of the government, stating that the people 'seemed to understand and appreciate the special priviledge [*sic*] given to them.'[50] Here Daly's approach was practical and oriented simply towards encouraging the people to obtain the greatest possible benefit from existing conditions. On the other hand, when the regulations proved too restrictive, he took action in an attempt to bend the rules in their favour.

Daly's Advocacy of Special Rights

To a limited extent, Daly argued for special harvesting rights for First Nations people based on their long-standing occupation of Canada. He sometimes fought for the extension of trapping seasons, and he argued against the imposition of guiding licences on the grounds that the people had fished and hunted in their lands from time immemorial. In part these efforts were simply integral to his paternalistic mission to protect the people and ensure that they were able to support themselves. His approach remained in keeping with the DIA policy of 'endeavour[ing] to secure special privileges for the Indians with regard to hunting and trapping.'[51] But where the DIA explained this policy with reference merely to the fact that 'hunting is their natural means of livelihood',[52] Daly went beyond this rationale, highlighting the people's prior occupation of the territory as the source of their claim to special treatment. It is important to distinguish here between legal (or treaty) rights, which carry government obligations, and special treatment, which does not convey any enforceable right and can be withdrawn at any time. Daly did not argue on the basis of treaties. Nevertheless, the position Daly took downplayed the element of charity and poverty stressed by Lewis, and instead emphasized special rights linked to Aboriginality.

In 1926, for instance, Daly fought to have the trapping season extended after a long winter had prevented muskrat trapping until the season was nearly over. Daly wrote to the Deputy Minister of Game and Fisheries, emphasizing the importance of the fur industry to the local Aboriginal economy and the deprivation that would result if the regulations were enforced without regard to climatic conditions: the people depended on the muskrat hunt for a living between their winter logging and the summer tourist season.[53] He made a similar intervention two years later, again in response to a late spring breakup. Daly approached the DIA, the Department of Game and Fisheries, and the local member of Parliament, lawyer Wallace Nesbitt, for support.[54] His letter to Nesbitt stressed the economic need of Aboriginal trappers, but also made reference to their traditional way of life in terms that implied this tradition was worth preserving. Daly spoke of ensuring 'that the Indians get special consideration so that they may make a livelihood in their native way.'[55] This was a different approach from Lewis's emphasis strictly on need. Both positions appealed essentially to charitable sentiments and implied that bending the rules for Aboriginal people would be an act of grace on the government's part. Yet, unlike his contemporary, Daly constructed Aboriginal heritage as a factor that justified special, more favourable treatment.

Daly concluded his letter with an appeal for Nesbitt's help in getting an Order-in-Council annulled 'so far as the Indians are concerned'. Did he mean the Order-in-Council that had proclaimed the existing trapping season? This would, in fact, amount to exempting First Nations people from the application of the laws regarding trapping seasons. Daly wrote that these laws might be necessary 'as regards the white men of this section of the country', but they would cause suffering among First Nations people.[56] When it came to the fur industry, Daly wished to establish different laws for non-Natives and First Nations people. In this he did not have the support of the Department of Indian Affairs.

With regard to guiding licences, Daly took a stand that came even closer to advocating the recognition of a limited form of Aboriginal rights. As we have seen, guiding tourists who wanted to hunt and fish in their homeland was a good source of cash income for Aboriginal people on the east shore of Georgian Bay. Access to Aboriginal guides was also of value to the tourist outfitters, as a way of satisfying the desires of their wealthy clients: in the bush or out on the lakes, Aboriginal skills were of paramount importance and garnered the respect and admiration of tourists. Even here, however, the government interfered to regulate the men's participation and to demand a small share of their income. The provincial government imposed a licensing system under which guides had to acquire a licence and pay two dollars for the privilege. Not surprisingly, there was some resistance, which may have been heightened by the fact that the persecuting game warden was also the official responsible for collecting these fees. Elijah Tabobondung of Parry Island, for example, wrote to Daly in 1923 on the subject, relating that the game warden had visited him the previous Saturday stating that he had to pay for a guiding licence. Tabobondung had refused: 'I was thinking I have no right pay guide licence that I am non citizen have no vote for Dominion election also Provincial vote and have no voice government.'[57] This amounted to a clear and rather sophisticated argument that, since First Nations people were ruled without their consent, they should not have to pay government levies or abide by the decisions of imposed governments.

Tabobondung asked Daly to look into the matter and find out whether the licence system applied to First Nations people.

Daly did intervene on behalf of the people, hoping to have First Nations men exempted from paying the annual guiding fee. In opposing the imposition of this fee, Daly argued that it violated Aboriginal people's rights. In 1924 Daly took it upon himself to write directly to the Deputy Minister of Game and Fisheries on the subject. He explained that his clients objected to the idea of licences and particularly to the fees connected with them. He also relayed to the Deputy Minister the people's conviction that they deserved special status: 'They, the Indians, maintain that they, being natives, should be exempt from paying any fee.' The agent asked if the fee could be waived for First Nations people, and attempted to strengthen his appeal by adding that he thought the DIA 'would appreciate anything that you could do in that line for the Indians on the Georgian Bay.'[58] The records do not show how the Deputy Minister responded on this occasion, but the guiding fee remained in place.

Daly tried again in a letter written to the DIA in 1929. Restating his objection to the guiding fee, the agent spoke of 'the injustice of the Indians having to pay a fee of $2.00 for the privelege [sic] of guiding in the waters that their forefathers knew and paddled in a thousand years before the white men saw them. . . . he is an Indian and should not be taxed in any way, and particularly so, for guiding in the waters of his native land.'[59] This was a statement of principle rather than pragmatism. Perhaps practical issues motivated Daly, too, if he feared that the fee might prevent some of the men from taking on guiding jobs. But the issue was basically not one of subsistence; rather, it was one of declaring that First Nations people should be exempt *because* they were Aboriginal. The agent argued against guiding fees on ideological grounds: the fees were not simply an onerous burden or an obstacle to Aboriginal people earning their livelihood; they were an injustice. Although he did not use the modern language of Aboriginal rights, Daly made it clear that he felt the first inhabitants of the land had prior claim to it and a special right to its resources. It would be a gross exaggeration to portray him as an advocate of Aboriginal rights generally: as we have seen, Daly fought Aboriginal leaders who sought to organize resistance to the DIA or engage in a discussion of treaty provisions. But, unlike other federal officials, Daly did advocate something approaching the principle of distinct Aboriginal rights in the use of natural resources.

Treaties and Land Rights

Although harvesting rights were highly significant, they were not the only major grievance put forward in the period. Landownership was equally important. At Parry Island, a number of unresolved issues related to the implementation of the Robinson Treaty, and leaders in every generation attempted to open discussions about these matters. For one thing, the people who became the Parry Island band had been deprived of the mainland site they had originally reserved for themselves across from Parry Island, right where the town of Parry Sound was later built. In 1853, they informed surveyor John Staughton Dennis that they were establishing a settlement on Parry Island, which they intended as an additional reserve, not a replacement for the mainland reserve. Instead, Dennis and DIA representative John Keating decided to exchange the mainland site for the island, leaving them with just the island reserve. Only some years later did the Parry Islanders learn of their loss, and they tried for years to regain the land or at least receive compensation, but without success.[60] All the Robinson Treaty signatories, as we have seen, also disputed the government's contention that they had agreed to surrender the islands in Georgian Bay. The government had written the islands into the treaty as part of the surrendered territory, but it is clear from the immediate response of several chiefs that the First Nations had not intended to allow this.[61] Some of the islands near Parry Island had afterwards been sold or leased to cottagers, and many band members believed that they should have received payment for them. Finally, there were other specific issues—for example, John Manitowaba had a family tradition that the government had promised to build his father a house on Parry Island. This promise had never been honoured.

All of the twentieth-century agents in Parry Sound grumbled about the agitation concerning treaty and land rights. D.F. Macdonald, who served as agent in the first decade of the twentieth century, wrote that Chief Peter Megis had been 'harping' about 'Indian rights and imaginary wrongs'. Typically, Macdonald attributed the dissatisfaction to the influence of 'some busy body' who was urging them on, and complained that such questions should not be 'introduced every time it suits the whims of some childish agitator.'[62] Daly's successor, Samuel Devlin, was also confronted with the old, unresolved grievances.

We have already seen that both Francis Pegahmagabow and John Manitowaba tried to reopen the question of the Georgian Bay islands. They were not the only chiefs to do so. There was agitation about this same issue in 1932, involving then-chief of the Parry Island band, Frank Judge. In this year there was correspondence between Daly and the department about how to retrieve a number of documents held by Francis Pegahmagabow, including a copy of the Robinson Treaty itself. Chief Judge had been trying to obtain these papers from Pegahmagabow, who refused to return them (they apparently belonged to the band). Daly had already tried to secure them from his rival, but had then decided that they were better where they were. His reasons were entirely political and show his calculation that it suited his purposes to keep band officials in ignorance:

> I have come to the conclusion that it is a good thing for him to have these books, for in the past Pegahmagabow tried to make trouble with his knowledge of these Treaties, and according to the recent actions of Chief Judge, he seems to me to be of the same ilk as Pegahmagabow. I cannot see that it would do the Chief any good to have these papers. . . . I have advised him not to bother about the papers, and have told them that any information they want to get, can be obtained at this office.[63]

In fact, there had apparently been a good deal of recent agitation over the treaties from Parry Islanders and at least one member of the Shawanaga band, Henry Abetung (another returned soldier chief). The latter had become involved with a group Daly called the 'Union Council of Ontario Indians'. The agent again linked this political activism with Native people obtaining the treaty documents, which he claimed had caused 'a great unrest'. Daly settled on a strategy of containment, explaining to the people that 'these treaties are past and done with.'[64] He also decided to let Pegahmagabow keep his treaty documents so the new chief was not armed with this useful information in his attempt to address questions about lands and treaties.

Not all of the agitation about land and land use was directly related to treaties. For instance, John Manitowaba's complaints about lumbering on Parry Island were primarily about the change in land use on the island. With lumbering becoming a major industry, the island's ecology was being dramatically altered and the bush was disappearing. Manitowaba protested that their children would have no bush left—perhaps in part hoping to preserve the habitat that had formerly sustained both humans and animals on the island. Pegahmagabow had also raised issues about the timber contract. Jonas Odjig, chief of the Manitoulin Island Unceded band from 1918 to 1920, raised another set of questions when he objected to the adoption of agriculture by some of the reserve's residents. His position, as we saw in the previous chapter, was that this occupation was foreign to Anishinabe culture and should not be practised on reserve lands—those who wanted to pursue agriculture should leave the reserve and go live among non-Aboriginal people. In essence, this, too, was an argument about culture and land use. Agriculture, like the timber industry, required a massive alteration in the environment that destroyed much of the flora and fauna on which earlier Aboriginal societies had depended. The treaties had no impact on these kinds of internal debates, but the voicing of such concerns demonstrates again the central importance of land and its protection.

John Daly took a characteristically skeptical approach when confronted with John Manitowaba's concerns about the implementation of the Robinson Treaty. For instance, he waxed sarcastic about Manitowaba's previous declarations that the treaty had been improperly conducted and implemented, reducing the elder's grievances to a simple assertion that his lands had been 'given away without his consent'. He remarked flippantly that he hoped Manitowaba had 'had everything cleared up', since it had been 'an awful worry to him'.[65] The agent could safely assume that the officials at headquarters would appreciate his wit and share his view that Manitowaba's claims were not only inaccurate, but also evidence of his insubordination and ingratitude for the department's benevolence.

Daly further recorded an exchange with Manitowaba about a promise he claimed had been made by a government official to build a house for his father on Parry Island as part of the payment for the people's land. Daly recorded that he had asked Manitowaba when this promise was made and received the answer, 'Oh, before I was born.'[66] This passage is revealing, because the agent clearly considered the antiquity of the promise to be proof of its irrelevance. Events that had taken place in the previous generation were implicitly deemed to be not binding on the current generation of officials. Such a view was contrary to Aboriginal practice, in which a promise remained binding regardless of the passage of time. In the world of DIA officials, however, promises effectively came with an expiry date:

if not fulfilled within a decade or so, they became null and void. If they were oral promises never committed to paper, their period of validity was even shorter. Of course, Daly was operating partly on the premise that Manitowaba's word was unreliable. But his attitude also confirms the truth of a charge made by a critic of the Indian Affairs system in 1911: 'The government seems to think that an obligation entered into with an Indian may be implemented as it pleases.'[67]

As we have seen in our examination of Daly's conflicts with Manitowaba and with Francis Pegahmagabow, the islands in Georgian Bay continued to be a sore point with the Parry Islanders and other Robinson Treaty groups. Several leaders made repeated efforts to initiate a revisiting of this issue—Manitowaba was elected as chief partly on the basis of a promise to make the government pay for the islands at last. Pegahmagabow had also raised the point, as did Joseph Traunch in his protest letter quoted at the beginning of this chapter. Some of Daly's remarks suggest that other chiefs had joined their voices to the chorus. It was all in vain. Throughout the era we are examining, the government was firmly committed to enforcing the surrender provisions of the treaties, as written down by the government negotiators. When it came to the islands, probably all of the Robinson Treaty signatories had been 'tricked by putting words on paper'. The economic importance of the islands, along with the swift response of several chiefs to the news of their appropriation by non-Aboriginals, strongly suggests that the First Nations had intended to retain the islands for their own use. But not until the late twentieth century, with the beginnings of successful litigation, would this sort of testimony affect the federal government's position on the real contents of treaty agreements.

Conclusion

Land was of central importance to First Nations people, both for its economic benefits and for the preservation of Aboriginal cultures. Hunting and fishing, central pursuits of the older generations, were particularly important as elements of Aboriginal identity. In treaty negotiations, these concerns had been clearly displayed and efforts had been made to preserve access to these resources. The treaty signatories had never intended to give up hunting and fishing rights. Yet in the 1920s and 1930s they were losing access partly because of resource depletion and partly because of the implementation of provincial game conservation regimes. Within government, the only officials who pleaded on behalf of the First Nations people were the Indian agents—and even they did not appeal to the treaties. Rather, they appealed for special, often temporary, measures to facilitate Aboriginal people's subsistence use of fish and fur-bearing animals. Lewis argued on the basis of simple need, not entitlement, and portrayed fishing as a minor occupation for the Manitoulin Island people, despite their long history in the fishing business. Daly, on the other hand, tried to make a case for a limited form of rights, which he suggested arose out of First Nations people's prior occupation of the land. Yet the government officials responsible for making such decisions acted only under extraordinary circumstances, and as a matter of grace rather than entitlement. When it came to game and fish provisions, the treaties were a dead letter in these years.

5

'Economy Must Be Observed': Assistance and Mediation

'The Department relies on me to act with discretion in this matter [providing relief], and has instructed me to guard against pauperizing Indians who can provide for themselves as economy must be observed.'[1]

'. . . our philanthropy, like our friendship, has failed in its professions.'[2]

As the previous chapter has indicated, Aboriginal people had to rely on Indian Affairs officials in their attempts to maintain some access to the resources of their ancestral territories. This was only one of a great variety of areas in which they hoped for backup from these officials, especially from their local agent. Many factors compelled Aboriginal people to call on their Indian agent for help, particularly their poverty, social subordination, cultural and linguistic difference, low levels of education, and legal disabilities under the Indian Act. First Nations people were also positioned within Canadian society as 'wards of the state', a group legally placed under the authority and tutelage of the federal government. In response, they assumed that the DIA's primary role was to help them. Many of their complaints about the department and its agents reveal this persistent belief, which they shared with missionaries and probably many other Canadians as well. Robert Lewis of the Manitowaning agency once wrote, for instance, 'Both Indians and Missionary believe that the Department should look after all Indians who cannot care for themselves.'[3] In general, most Canadians assumed that any matter related to an Aboriginal person should be dealt with by the DIA, and they quickly delegated any problems to the Indian agent.

First Nations people expected the agent to provide a wide variety of assistance, including financial aid, advice, mediation with the dominant society and its rules, intercession in conflicts with outsiders, and internal dispute mediation. One source of ongoing problems for the people was the need to deal with the rules, laws, officials, and institutions of the dominant society. The resulting problems frequently led the people to invoke the agent's help. We have seen that the provincial regime for controlling hunting and fishing enforced certain kinds of interactions, such as the payment of licences and the effort to avoid or respond to punishment by local game wardens. The performance of wage labour also involved interacting with Euro-Canadians. For First Nations people, difficulties with the English language (a second language for almost all of them at this time) made it harder to solve a variety of problems with the dominant society. The linguistic and cultural gap also meant that Aboriginal people had trouble understanding laws that affected them, such as closed seasons and licences for hunting. Few, if any, had much knowledge of the provisions of the Indian Act, although it decisively shaped their lives. It is also quite likely that some of the people, resenting the endless restrictions and complications imposed on them by Canadian governments and institutions, felt that the Indian agent should take care of these matters.

Engaging outsiders to help with these sorts of issues was probably unavoidable, but it served to heighten the general perception that the people could not manage their own affairs. Being in the position of requiring assistance can be demoralizing, and those providing the aid can quickly adopt an attitude of condescension and disdain. Consider the following remarks made in 1939 by a white fur trader about his interactions with his Aboriginal clients:

> I have to read most of their letters, write most of their letters, give them their licences, look after their interests, write for them for relief, work, fishing licences, wolf bounty and even sign their time certificates for work done. If they work on a fire [firefighting], I get their time and payment slip. If they work on the road or other work they never bother about what they have [earned], but the lists are sent to me. With their cheques they often tell me they don't know anything about it and I do, so they leave it to me. When they commit an offence, as J.P. [justice of the peace] I try [them] and fine them and then I pay their fine. When they have to go to hospital, if I tell them they have to go they go, and I see that they get there. . . . When they vote, they vote for whom I tell them. If they have a fight with their wives I settle the argument and reinstate the wife, and very often decide to whom the child belongs. If they don't get their cheques when they should they blame me, and if they want something from the government and they don't get it then they blame me. If their child dies while in hospital they blame me.[4]

Allowing for a degree of exaggeration and self-aggrandizement, this portrayal nevertheless shows parallels with agents' comments about their role. Agents acted as brokers and arbitrators in many of the areas the trader mentioned, including personal, financial, and marital issues. Aboriginal people certainly did not vote according to the wish of the Indian agent, but they often did blame him for late cheques and an unresponsive government. Many Native people were able to run their affairs themselves without an outsider's help, and the people of this study were not nearly as dependent as the trader has represented his clients to be. But many did turn, out of necessity, to the local representative of Euro-Canadian society. Unfortunately, mediators such as fur traders and Indian agents were men who were already in a position to exercise power over them. The words of the fur trader quoted above convey a distinct impression of disrespect, clearly stemming from the position of

Did FNS really see IA as another chief? Skeptical [handwritten annotation]

tutelage in which the Aboriginal people found themselves. Agents, too, were subject to this sense of superiority after years of maintaining a hierarchical relationship with the people. A superior attitude, combined with the powers attached to their position, could create an unhealthy climate for the interaction of agents with First Nations people. It only became worse as the period wore on.

This chapter examines the interactions between Aboriginal people and Indian agents that revolved around the agents' provision of various kinds of assistance. A careful reading of the sources reveals a consistent strategy on the part of the Anishinabek around Georgian Bay: the people sought to turn the Indian agent system to their benefit by using it to acquire the social services that chiefs could no longer supply. This reflected Anishinabe values, which required the wealthy and those in positions of authority to demonstrate generosity and concern towards those less fortunate. Since Indian agents clearly had access to resources and were granted authority over them by the Indian department, the Anishinabek believed that the agents had an obligation to offer aid. It is unlikely that the Anishinabek pursued these goals in a fully conscious way; rather, the demands they made on Indian agents were consonant with the responsibilities traditionally placed on chiefs, and thus emerged from a deeply held understanding of reciprocity in personal relationships.

This understanding was not entirely foreign to Indian Affairs officials: indeed, the paternalistic values they embraced contained some of the same core ideas. They shared the belief, for instance, that they had a duty to protect their clients and to provide relief when they were in dire need. But European paternalism was based on a strictly hierarchical social order that was foreign to Anishinabe and other Great Lakes societies. The paternalistic emphasis within Indian policy also conflicted with its other central aims, particularly with the goal of enforcing self-sufficiency. The latter goal clearly took precedence. In privileging self-sufficiency as the foremost objective, DIA officials often violated the Aboriginal principle that the powerful were duty-bound to help the poor and needy. In fact, the officials were convinced of the need to refuse all but the most necessary aid. In the area of financial and social assistance, then, Aboriginal people and government officials were engaged in a contest of cultures, each side trying to impose its cultural norms on the other. Aboriginal people were interested in invoking the traditional obligation on leaders of providing service, while government officials were intent on enforcing self-sufficiency.

The Anishinabe Agenda

From the Aboriginal point of view, there was really only one benefit to having an Indian agent running their affairs, and that was the ability to obtain assistance from him. The power to distribute financial and other aid was one of the primary buttresses of the agent's authority, allowing him to outrank the chiefs. George Manuel has expressed this reality pointedly: 'what really made the agent more powerful than the chiefs was that he was now empowered to dispense welfare to anyone who could not make a living while their neck was within this noose woven by foreign laws [i.e., the fish and game regime].'⁵ Faced with the DIA's insistence on ruling them through the Indian agent, the people tried to make the system work for them.

Before they were subjugated by colonial governments, First Nations people had never permitted anyone to exercise the kind of authority among them that an Indian agent expected to wield. The closest equivalent to the agent in Anishinabe culture was a chief or *ogima*. We have seen that the authority of chiefs was founded on the strength of their personalities and the respect they inspired by their actions. It was also based on the extent to which they were perceived to have fulfilled their duty towards those for whom they were responsible, since responsibility was arguably the most dominant feature of the role. By the 1920s and 1930s, the elected chiefs put in place by the DIA were unable to perform many of the *ogima*'s former roles. They had no access to surplus wealth to distribute, and it was obvious that the main power on the reserve was wielded by the Indian agent. Therefore, the roles of mediating disputes and caring for those in need were transferred to the Indian agent.⁶ Many agents complained about the frequent expectation that they settle family and other interpersonal quarrels, an aspect of their role that was imposed on them by the people themselves. In other ways, too, Aboriginal people imposed certain additional responsibilities on the agents.

Working within their own cultural framework, the Anishinabek of the Georgian Bay area worked to subvert the Indian Affairs system so that it functioned to replace the traditional leaders' provision of social services and aid. The federal government was a large, powerful institution with access to considerable resources, including the people's own band funds. Within the Anishinabe frame of reference, it was only legitimate to expect that federal officials should use their power and resources to help people who needed it. One of the leadership roles that Francis Pegahmagabow assumed was the attempt to intercede with government on behalf of other Parry Islanders—his letter-writing activities, which so annoyed Daly, were primarily oriented towards gaining assistance for others. The expectation of assistance also echoes in Joseph Traunch's complaint, 'your not trying to help [an] Indian a tall.'⁷ For the Anishinabek, it was not a matter of abdicating responsibility for their lives or abandoning the effort to provide for themselves. Like their fellows across the country, the Anishinabek had always worked hard to support themselves, and they continued to do so. But they felt that the wealthy, powerful government officials had a moral obligation to prevent suffering among their people and help them out in moments of need. Within their world view, this ethic of sharing and mutual aid was paramount.

The Anishinabe goals concerning assistance involved them in a contest of values with Indian department officials, for the latter were operating according to a radically different cultural framework. The officials were certainly aware of the expectation of assistance, but they interpreted it within a Euro-Canadian frame of reference as demonstrating a dependent attitude. On the one hand, the deeply ingrained paternalism of the Indian Affairs system worked in the Anishinabek's favour. Both the officials in Ottawa and Indian agents shared the notion that they bore some paternalistic responsibility for the people. On the other hand, Euro-

Canadian culture differed significantly from Anishinabe culture on the issue of aid to those in need. While dire situations called for assistance, the officials were intensely concerned with observing economy in their administration. In addition, they were convinced that assistance was potentially disastrous, because it could lead to the expectation of ongoing aid, a situation they defined as dependence. DIA employees did not share the Anishinabe value system in which entitlement to authority was contingent on generosity. On the contrary, in their eyes a government should never routinely dispense aid. They considered it their responsibility to withhold aid whenever possible, in the interest of enforcing self-reliance.

The economic hardships of the 1930s intensified the cultural gulf. Far greater numbers of First Nations people were now placed in a situation in which they desperately needed help. Moreover, if Daly can be believed, some of them blamed the Euro-Canadian population for the economic collapse. Daly recorded the prevailing local opinion on this matter in 1935, writing to an official of the Dominion Bureau of Statistics: 'It might interest you to know that the Indians state that they were not the cause of the Depression and they cannot see why their funds held in trust by the Government should be used to give them relief, when the white man, who was the cause of the Depression is being helped by the Dominion Government.'[8] The capitalist economy that was in such serious trouble had been deliberately established in Canada by the newcomers and had forcibly supplanted the Aboriginal economy. Why should they be refused help or assistance with their own money (band funds) when the whites who were responsible for the troubles were receiving direct government aid, and at more generous rates than they? Under these circumstances, refusal to help seemed particularly reprehensible. Indian agents took a relatively individual approach towards the crisis, depending on their personalities and the conditions of their own areas. In the cases of Lewis and Daly, both took a course that raised objections, Lewis supplying only the most minimal aid, and Daly taking the opportunity to impose a rigid work ethic.

For the Anishinabek, there were limitations to the strategy of enlisting aid through the DIA system. In the minds of DIA officials, this strategy was misconstrued as an attempt to avoid responsibility for their own lives. The officials were unaware of the cultural gulf represented by differing attitudes towards assistance. And while they had certainly intended to undermine traditional leadership, they had never meant their own program to replace the chiefs as providers of social services. A further serious drawback for the people was that the need for assistance heightened the Indian agent's power. Unfortunately, there was really nowhere else to turn. In the context of the times, with few other options for coping with their socio-economic plight, the Anishinabek had come up with a workable strategy they were able to implement with considerable success. This was particularly the case in the Parry Sound agency, where Daly's strongly paternalistic value system inclined him to co-operate, albeit with a good deal of grumbling. Applying their own value system, and within a social and economic context that offered them very little, the Anishinabek sought to derive what benefit they could from the government administration that had been imposed on them.

The DIA Agenda

Indian Affairs officials regarded the matter of material aid from an entirely different angle. Assisting Aboriginal people was one of the pre-eminent responsibilities of the Indian department, but officials approached this responsibility with wariness. Of all possible forms of assistance, financial aid alarmed them the most. A 'first principle' of policy, as stated in 1933 instructions to Indian agents, was 'to promote self-support among the Indians and not to provide gratuitous assistance to those Indians who can provide for themselves'.[9] One of the great fears was fostering 'dependence' on band funds or, worse yet, government money. Department officials believed that dependence was virtually a hereditary predisposition for First Nations people, and official correspondence is replete with remarks about the need to counter it. Thus the people's requests for aid were viewed with intense skepticism, under the preconceived notion that some of the assistance they claimed they required was really 'gratuitous', i.e., not needed. Any assistance was potentially harmful to the recipient, but none more than 'gratuitous aid', which would only encourage the idleness and improvidence believed to be inherent in 'the Indian character'.

Discouraging 'dependence' was very much in keeping with the liberal individualist attitudes of the time, which placed a premium on self-reliance. There was also a widely shared conviction that no one should 'get something for nothing', a phrase that occurs repeatedly in the agents' correspondence. John Daly summarized it well, writing in the midst of the Depression of the 1930s: 'In my opinion it is the worst thing that ever happened to the Indian, getting relief without having to work for it, in fact I think it is a bad thing for any person to get something for nothing, either whites or Indians.'[10] Particularly in the case of impoverished and racialized groups like First Nations people, there was a corresponding fear of 'pauperization', that is, the development of long-term dependence on financial assistance. Many Canadians believed that providing assistance to those in need could quickly lead them to abandon their own efforts to provide for themselves. Stern discipline was required to check this tendency, to train the people to the much-vaunted 'habits of industry'. The endeavour was fraught with difficulty for two reasons: first, the Indian department considered itself bound to supply assistance in cases of severe need (an obligation entrenched in the Indian Act and also in some treaties); and second, the social and economic marginalization of First Nations people had led, for many, to chronic poverty. In consequence of all these factors, concern about the issue of dependence was a constant theme in official correspondence throughout the early twentieth century and beyond.

Financial relations between government and First Nations people had become considerably more complicated, and also more interventionist, with the development of the band fund system. Under this system, the government established accounts of communally owned monies for each band. The band funds were held in trust by the government and controlled by the DIA. Being collectively owned by the band, they represented a jarring contradiction to the individualism the department wished to inculcate in Aboriginal people. This provided an additional reason to exercise strict supervision over their use. Once elected band councils were established, these bodies could vote to use funds for certain types of expenditures, but as we have seen, the Indian department had a veto power over council decisions. Not surprisingly, many First Nations people found this arrangement frustrating. Fed from sources such as land sales, timber sales and dues, and leases of land, the funds of some bands grew to contain sizable amounts of money. They represented a tangible resource, but one that could only be accessed with the approval of government officials. The system thus placed limits on the people's ability to use their own money to help themselves. During the 1930s, the Indian department's use of the funds to provide relief also sparked resentment among some of the people, who argued that they should have been supported out of government money, as the non-Aboriginal unemployed in the area were.

Assistance Strategies

We have seen that the DIA faced competing paradigms when it came to the issue of assisting First Nations people. The paternalist paradigm suggested that the department take an interventionist tack, training and guiding the people in ways that would involve some assistance. This paradigm had been more dominant in the early to mid-nineteenth century, when the department was charged with helping First Nations people in the transition to Euro-Canadian society. The liberal individualist paradigm, on the other hand, promoted the avoidance of assistance on the grounds that it would foster dependence. Liberal individualism was a strong cultural force in Canadian society in the early twentieth century. Since department officials typically subscribed to both paradigms at once, they were hard-pressed to devise policies relating to assistance. This may explain why assistance strategies were not articulated at the level of policy. Instead, ad hoc decisions were made on a case-by-case basis.

In regard to aid, the practice of individual officials illustrated the ideological split created by the conflicting paradigms. Some officials, such as Robert Lewis, were firm liberal individualists and eschewed most assistance to the able-bodied, except for occasional help with further education. Others, including John Daly, were more paternalistic and therefore willing to take a larger role. Interventionist approaches varied according to local conditions and individual personalities. Daly, for instance, quite often attempted to act as a broker in obtaining work for individuals and also applied for military pensions for Aboriginal war veterans. One enterprising agent in Port Arthur, J.G. Burk, went so far as to establish a small business to create employment for the men of his agency. He was able to employ a small number of men in his agency for several years by having them make canoes, snowshoes, skis, snowmobiles, and camp stoves.[11] Unfortunately, in the end the venture failed.[12] In any case, Burk was an exception. For the most part, Indian agents took much less active roles in the people's work lives.

One of the central dilemmas of Indian policy, which was heightened in the context of the Depression, was the lack of strategies for preventing dependence. Official policy stated that First Nations people were to be made self-sufficient, but the DIA had no larger economic vision or program for turning its 'wards' into prosperous, self-supporting citizens. Department policy stated that deserving individuals would be helped to gain a higher education, but in practice such aid was denied much more often than it was granted. As a result, very few First Nations people gained an education that would help to move them out of the unskilled or semiskilled working class. Although officials publicly claimed to be 'guiding' the people into certain kinds of work, this was a fallacy. They had no means of doing so, nor did they make the attempt. The one area in which the DIA offered some support was farming, the most approved occupation—the department hired experienced farmers as Indian agents for some reserves, expecting them to teach and encourage farming. But relatively few reserves offered good conditions for intensive agriculture. Instead, the vast majority of the people located their own niches in local economies—successfully enough, it may be added, until the Depression struck.

In effect, the department really had only two basic tactics for combatting dependence: refusing aid whenever possible, and urging people to support themselves. The kinds of assistance the department would consider supplying were small-scale, individual, and fell essentially into the category of charity, as opposed to the more recent concept of development. The most common kind of aid was 'relief', a type of handout that usually came in the form of food or clothing. Relief was granted on an emergency basis when family heads were ill, or on a more continuous basis to the elderly, the disabled, older widows, and sometimes to single mothers. Otherwise, the liberal individualist approach applied, under which the provision of 'gratuitous' assistance was to be avoided at all cost.

The handling of assistance was highly gendered. Since Euro-Canadian masculinity was premised on the primary importance of hard work and the breadwinner role, officials were particularly loath to provide relief to able-bodied men. Men who were temporarily unable to support their families were often viewed in very negative terms. On the other hand, certain forms of assistance, such as loans, were extended only to men. The DIA supplied small loans to some Aboriginal men, mainly from band funds, for various purposes: to buy seed or equipment, for example, or to build houses or other needed structures. Women did not have access to this sort of help for any economic activities in which they might wish to engage. In the Euro-Canadian gender system, women were not defined by their economic pursuits and were expected to attend primarily to domestic affairs. Nevertheless, women who received relief, whether they were elderly women or single mothers, were normally expected to support themselves in the summertime. Women were granted relief only during the cold months and were cut off when the availability of berries and markets for handicrafts made it possible to earn a little through sales of these items.

Aboriginal Efforts To Control Relief

During the 1920s and 1930s, several bands made an effort to institute automatic use of band funds to assist those in need. The clear intent was to circumvent the discretionary authority of the Indian agent, who always made the decisions about who received help and who did not. These decisions involved subjective judgements, and undoubtedly often seemed unfair and arbitrary—as indeed they often were. What made the process more offensive was that such choices were made by a government-appointed outsider who wielded power over community members in countless other ways. Primarily, then, these efforts were designed to standardize and simplify the approval of relief, ensure that the community as a whole was provided for, and above all transfer decision-making power to First Nations people. Both the Indian agents and internal department officials staunchly refused to allow such a transfer of authority, recognizing the significant shift in power this would entail.

Efforts to ensure relief for all those in need were made by at least two bands, one in each agency. On Manitoulin Island, the Sheguiandah band tried twice, in 1921 and again in 1923, to alter relief procedures so as to reduce the discretionary powers of the agent. The early 1920s were years of recession, as the Canadian economy adjusted to peacetime. In 1921, the Anglican missionary at Sheguiandah wrote to Lewis, requesting on the band's behalf that any sick band member receive $5 per week out of band funds, and also that band funds be used to buy 50 bags of flour for the band.[13] Five dollars a week, incidentally, was about four times the usual relief payment, and much closer to the amount that would be required for subsistence. The agent, however, rejected the band's proposals.[14] In 1923 the Sheguiandah band made another attempt, this time through a band council resolution. In this instance they asked that the department grant from the band's funds enough money to cover half of any loss sustained by a band member.[15] Lewis again opposed this effort, insisting that all decisions about relief and compensation should rest with him. He also claimed that Aboriginal people were often the authors of their own misfortune, implying that their mistakes might disqualify them from compensation out of their own funds.[16] Lewis wrote, 'I know that you are aware of the fact, as well as I am myself, that a great number of the Indians who endure misery and hardship is [*sic*] brought on themselves by their own misbehaviour. . . . If F. [a sick man from Wikwemikong] would lead a clean Christian life there is not one doubt but he would be healthy and prosperous.' The agent's response to these proposals foreshadowed his unsympathetic stance during the much harder years of the 1930s. Even in the worst of the Depression, Lewis remained virtually unbending as far as the able-bodied were concerned. In the meantime, the band's desire to establish a *right* to help from band funds came to naught.

Efforts to standardize relief were evident in the Parry Sound area as well. In 1926, for example, the Parry Island band council passed a resolution that would grant $5 worth of relief to every family head in case of need. The chief, Stanley Manitowaba, wrote to Daly to inform him of the council's decision, and Daly pencilled his response on the bottom of Manitowaba's note: 'rushing the agent nothing doing.'[17] It is not clear whether Daly even submitted this resolution to Ottawa. In any event, the internal officials would never have agreed to any proposal that would pre-authorize expenditures from band funds. For Daly, who was typically much more generous than Lewis in the area of relief, the issue here was clearly one of power. He was often willing to help (largely, but not only, by using band funds), but he wished to control relief provision in the agency.

The Parry Island band made two more attempts, in 1932 and 1934, to ensure relief for all in need. Their persistence was a clear response to the dire economic conditions they confronted in these years, and also to the fact that Daly was threatening to cut men off relief if they refused to perform roadwork. In 1932 the council passed a resolution to the effect that every unemployed band member should receive relief.[18] In a letter to Ottawa, Daly placed the council's action in context, explaining it as a reaction to the fact that much of the local non-Aboriginal population was receiving relief without working, and some of the people felt they should be treated in the same way. Daly, of course, recommended against the resolution and confirmed that he would continue to identify those individuals worthy of relief.[19] The resolution was vetoed.

Correspondence regarding the band's third attempt, in 1934, highlights the unyielding attitude of the officials in Ottawa, whose attitudes were frequently harsher than those of the agents on the spot. The resolution this time stated that the council found it 'necessary' to demand that relief be given to those who could not support their families.[20] By this time Daly had begun to insist that men do roadwork instead of receiving relief, and some Parry Islanders resented his use of this work to punish his adversaries. Moreover, the country was deep in crisis and, like other sectors of government, the DIA was swamped with requests for help. Band funds had been severely depleted, and the costs of assistance on some reserves were now being covered wholly or in part by public funds. This further increased the reluctance of the Ottawa officials to aid Aboriginal people. Their response to the Parry Island band's resolution was a strongly worded condemnation of the people, which stated among other things that the department had 'no intention of allowing the Indians to sit down at home to be fed by public charity'.[21] Rather, they should cultivate their lands, cut fuel from their bush lands, and fish for a living (an ironic suggestion, given that these people had for years been restricted in their treaty right to fish without a licence). Needless to say, the Parry Island band had no success on this occasion either.

There were also individual efforts to deal with the inadequate relief levels. People wrote to their agents to protest, and some fought repeatedly to induce the DIA to raise its relief rates. One such individual was Julia K., a Christian Island band member who lived on Parry Island reserve and was raising several children without her husband's support. In 1933, the Indian agent for Christian Island, H.J. Eade, wrote to Daly about Mrs K's agitation for improved relief issues. Eade insisted that she was 'getting more than her share now in comparsion [sic] with other Indian women'. Eade's letter suggests his intolerance of this kind of political activity on Mrs K.'s part. He added, 'further I hear she is doing some running around with other men' and that if this were true, Daly should cut her off relief altogether.[22] Because of her place of residence, Daly took responsibility for her relief issues, but as agent for her own band, Eade had a say as well. The inquiry into the woman's personal life seems to have been motivated primarily by the desire to discipline her. Eade wrote that he was 'getting tired of this woman's constant complaints', and he clearly wanted to teach her a lesson about the risks of doing battle with the DIA. If Eade could link this agitator with sexual immorality, he could impose a serious financial consequence—loss of her monthly relief rations. Daly, who basically shared Mrs K.'s views on the subject of relief, almost certainly did not withdraw her rations. But he also shared Eade's dislike of any assertiveness on the part of his clients, especially if they were seeking more financial support.

In dealing with chronic poverty, the sole strategy of government officials for preventing dependence was the refusal of help in all but the direst cases. Officials sought to ensure that band funds were used as little as possible and that band members had strictly limited access to them. There was no attempt, even in the 1920s, to deal with the structural problems that Aboriginal people faced—their exclusion from the dominant society, the insufficient resources on their reserves, the provincial campaign to criminalize their hunting and fishing, their growing population and shrinking land base, their inadequate preparation for an Anglo-Canadian style work life. It was a daunting conglomeration of problems, and government made no systematic effort to address any of them. In the 1930s, of course, there was little that could be done, given the extent of unemployment. The Indian department retreated with the rest of the federal government into the siege mentality of the time, denying the extent of the desperation and pleading its own want of funds to stave off fresh requests for aid.

Relief in the Great Depression

The collapse of the Georgian Bay wage labour market in the Great Depression of the 1930s greatly aggravated all the tensions concerning relief. Where formerly no able-bodied men had requested or received relief, now hundreds were forced to turn to the Indian department for lack of any means of self-support. The federal government considered itself under an obligation to provide relief for Native people who could not provide for themselves, effectively functioning as an equivalent of municipal relief for the indigent. This was part of its paternalistic approach towards First Nations people, although it is important to note that, whenever possible, relief was provided from band funds—that is, from their own money. Like municipal charities, the DIA provided relief at a minimal level. The guiding principle was that levels of relief had to be kept below the lowest wage in the area to avoid encouraging dependence by making relief more lucrative than the worst-paid kinds of labour. Relief recipients had to be kept desperate enough to accept any type of work, however poorly paid. In 1933, a department circular noted that assistance to those in need would provide 'the actual necessaries of life', which essentially meant no more than was necessary to sustain life. In most cases, relief took the form not of cash payments, but of food items supplied by the agent or local merchants.

Relief provision to First Nations people followed the pattern for the non-Aboriginal population: before the 1930s, only the elderly, single mothers with young children, and the very ill were helped. Even when women had been deserted and were raising children without the father's support, it was not uncommon for Indian agents to refuse to help them on the grounds that the father should be contributing. Stepping in and fulfilling the father's role would encourage men to neglect their paramount duty to provide for their wives and children. In all these ways, the

Indian department's handling of the relief issue was in keeping with practices for the non-Aboriginal population. But officials also operated on the principle that First Nations people did not need as much money to survive as their non-Aboriginal neighbours. Around Georgian Bay, their relief issues were drastically lower than those for the surrounding population during the bitter years of the 1930s.

First Nations people in the Georgian Bay area witnessed the same phenomena as local non-Natives at the commencement of the Great Depression: a precipitous decline in the amount of wage labour available and sudden, rapid rise in unemployment levels. Both on Manitoulin Island and in the Parry Sound area, a high proportion of Aboriginal men had supported themselves partly or primarily through wage labour, so the crisis hit them and their families hard. Now, men who had never asked for relief were forced to turn to their local Indian agent for help because none was available from any other quarter—municipalities and other government bodies refused to provide relief to Aboriginal people. One of the most important results was a greatly increased dependence on government, which both parties found painful and distasteful.

In dealing with the crisis, the DIA was forced to balance its responsibility to help with its principle of avoiding 'gratuitous aid'. Avoiding the encouragement of idleness through gratuitous aid involved a precarious balance, given the poverty of the people. As J.E. Chamberlin noted in his study of Euro-Canadian attitudes towards First Nations people, 'the line between encouraging idleness and allowing starvation and utter destitution was a fine one.'[23] On the whole, the records from the 1930s suggest that the balance was not always struck. It would appear that the people of Manitoulin Island, especially, must have been hard-pressed to feed themselves. Their agent approved very little assistance, apart from limited distributions of food. The tone of discussions about need was often hard-hearted even in the relatively good times of the 1920s, but by the 1930s some officials had adopted a harsh, unrelenting attitude in response to the desperation of the times.

Yet the Depression also provided the government with a great opportunity to strengthen its control over First Nations, using material aid as a tool. Providing assistance was really the only inducement wielded by officials, especially Indian agents, to convince Aboriginal people that there were benefits to accepting government domination. By the same token, withholding assistance was a significant penalty to impose on those who fought the agents. This became particularly evident in the 1930s in the Parry Sound agency. Daly now found his opportunity to punish and outflank his political opponents by enforcing road-building work on relief recipients. Those who refused the work were cut off from assistance—a punishment few could afford. Moreover, the relief dispenser could now exercise greatly enhanced social control, particularly by compelling people to perform physical labour but also by controlling people's use of their funds.

Agents Lewis and Daly in the Great Depression

The Depression heightened the power of the local Indian agent and exacerbated pre-existing discrepancies in the treatment of First Nations people by their agents.

Agents Lewis and Daly took nearly opposite tacks in their efforts to cope with the unemployment crisis. One factor contributing to the dissimilarity may have been disparities in the relative wealth of the bands in their agencies: Parry Island, in particular, had a relatively large band fund at its disposal, which made it easier for Daly to extend relief. In the Manitowaning agency, by contrast, the Manitoulin Island Unceded band had a very small band fund, and moreover its members did not receive any treaty money. Any extensive expenditures for this band, the largest in the agency, might have had to come not from their own money but from the public purse. In addition, it appears that the collapse of wage labour around Parry Sound occurred more rapidly and was more absolute than on Manitoulin Island: the people in Manitowaning agency reportedly still earned $14,000 in wages in 1932, when the figures for the Parry Sound agency show no wage income at all.[24] But these realities are only part of the picture. The two agents' personal belief systems were also critical in determining their responses to the crisis. While Daly leaned much more towards the paternalist paradigm, Lewis was a strong believer in the liberal individualist notion that all able-bodied persons were responsible for their own support. The two agents thus parted ways in their choice of measures, but the Depression brought out the harsher traits in both their characters, especially as the crisis wore on and everyone's nerves began to fray.

Both agents had begun by taking a rather casual approach towards relief, particularly Robert Lewis. In the early part of their careers, the provision of rations and relief was limited to those groups always considered fit recipients: the elderly, the incapacitated, and women raising children alone. Lewis often approved relief for such individuals without investigating their circumstances himself and even reimbursed storekeepers for supplies they had issued on their own initiative. It was common practice to extend relief to members of these groups during the cold months, leaving them to their own devices during the summer. Summer opportunities for the sale of berries, baskets, and other handicrafts made it possible to eke out a living in the warm months. The two men took a certain pride in their ability to take care of these people. Daly stated categorically, 'the widows, orphans and old and maimed shall always be looked after, so long as I am here.'[25] Lewis took a similar attitude, noting for example in 1929 that all widows and old persons on the Whitefish Lake Reserve received relief issues during the winter.[26]

But everything changed in the 1930s. It appears from Lewis's correspondence that the economy in his area was in serious crisis by the autumn of 1932. DIA statistics show that the earnings of Aboriginal people here had been steadily decreasing since 1929. Where the wages earned in the whole agency in 1929 totalled about $93,000, they fell to less than $65,000 in 1930, a decrease of 30 per cent. The following year they were more than halved, reaching less than $26,000, and by 1932 they had plummeted to $14,000 (only 15 per cent of the 1929 total).[27] By the late summer and early fall of 1932, Lewis was receiving letters from healthy young men who stated that they needed assistance, a phenomenon that had not occurred before. Lewis was still taking a hard line, writing back to reproach the men that they were not trying hard enough to support themselves and suggesting that they grow their own food. In September 1932, for example, Stanley E. sent Lewis a

I wonder what they're whispering / laughing about.

First Nations women secured cash incomes from selling crafts, especially baskets and bark work, but the market for such items was considerably reduced by the Great Depression. These Native people, probably Parry Islanders, were photographed selling baskets in Parry Sound in July 1931. Archives of Ontario, F 1075, H 2320.

letter asking for a supply of food and was informed that no one else in the district had asked for relief. He, like others, was also told that he should be growing a garden, especially if he owned land on the reserve.[28]

Lewis had always been conscientious about assisting children and the elderly, but he had an unbending commitment to a man's duty to make his own livelihood and, when married, to provide for his wife and family. Even in the depth of the Depression, Lewis refused aid to some able-bodied men, regardless of the impossibility of finding work. It appears that the only able-bodied men who did receive aid from this agent were those who lived on the three reserves where Lewis finally agreed to distribute mass relief. By contrast, men who lived off Manitoulin Island (most of them on the north shore of Georgian Bay) received only lectures in response to their requests for help. Perhaps it was the physical distance between them that permitted Lewis to ignore their plight. The agent even claimed on one occasion not to comprehend why a young man would need help. To a man living in Sault Ste Marie he wrote curtly, 'I cannot understand why a young able bodied single man of your age should ask the Department to support you.' Lewis declared that 'not one healthy male Indian living on a Reserve in this agency' was on relief and demanded that the man 'kindly explain the reason why you should be supported by the Department.'[29] Another man was told in the fall of 1932 that the Whitefish River people were 'getting along pretty well picking pine cones' and had not asked for aid. Lewis was still convinced that anyone who made a sincere effort could get by without assistance and suggested that if the man couldn't make a living where he was, he should simply 'try some place else.'[30]

Conditions continued to worsen, however. In the fall of 1932, Lewis recommended that food relief be distributed to the people at Wikwemikong because there was no work of any kind.[31] By January 1933, Lewis had decided he had no choice but to offer general relief to at least three bands in his agency: Sheguiandah, Manitoulin Island Unceded, and Whitefish River. The people here were clearly facing real destitution. He informed the department that there was no source of income for the Sheguiandah people and that they were now 'in poor circumstances'.[32] For the Manitoulin Island Unceded band, Lewis reported that there were about 500 able-bodied, unemployed men on the reserve who were willing to take any job but unable to find work. Although Lewis had previously spoken as though growing food would solve the difficulty, he now acknowledged that matters were not so simple—even the farmers were hard hit by the collapse in prices for farm produce. The majority of the band would need assistance, although a few farmers might be able to get by on their own. Lewis now recommended large-scale distributions of food.[33]

His first proposal was for the Sheguiandah band, which passed a resolution to spend $100 a month from band funds on food rations. Lewis confirmed that this amount would be necessary to meet 'only the actual necessaries of life' and that the people would have to supplement the rations with fishing and trapping. The assistance would be required for the rest of the winter, at a level of $100 from band funds each month.[34] For Manitoulin Island Unceded band, with more than 10 times as many members as Sheguiandah, Lewis recommended a monthly expenditure of $1,200 for 'the necessaries of life, only'. He also suggested that the department supply an extensive list of items of clothing if possible, since many people were 'completely out of clothing and footwear'.[35] The Whitefish River people were somewhat less fortunate than the other two bands. As Lewis informed the band's chief, the officials in Ottawa had decided to allow a small sum to be spent each month on provisions for the Whitefish River band, but had vetoed a large-scale distribution of food. The agent had been told to use his discretion, however, and he agreed to meet the chief at Little Current so that the two could buy supplies for members who needed them.[36]

While figures are not available for the number of individuals outside these three bands who were on relief, clearly many were. By 1933, Wahnapitae's band fund had been reduced to one-third its former value because of extensive relief issues.[37] In the same year, Lewis's journal of daily activities began to record numerous journeys to the various reserves arranging for relief.[38] Lewis wrote to one woman that there were hundreds of people on relief in the agency (the total population was 2,113 in 1934). This woman had written to say that she could not make ends meet on $5 per month and would need additional help. It is perhaps significant that this woman was living at Shawanaga, where she was probably acquainted with people who had received higher amounts from Daly. According to Lewis, however, no one in the Manitowaning agency received any more than $5 per month in supplies, and many lived on less. There was no question of increasing this sum.[39] If true, this statement would indicate that Lewis never extended more than $5 in relief even for larger families. Such frugality was approved by the department, but not strictly necessary, for even before the standardized scheme of 1934 (see below), there was some room to extend greater amounts of relief in case of need.

Lewis was forced to continue issuing relief into the summer of 1933, contrary to the old routine of cutting off relief in the spring. He remarked to a fellow agent in June that he had had to give out relief for May and June, since there was still no work and no other way for the people to obtain food. His tone was resigned: 'what else can a fellow do but give them some assistance.' In closing this letter, the agent expressed a sentiment that contrasts nicely with Daly's approach at the same time: 'I am waiting patiently for something to turn up that will relieve the situation.'[40] In contrast to Daly's energetic efforts to drum up relief work through tapping into government works projects, Lewis did not take such a proactive course.

Daly's approach was radically different in several ways. As a dedicated paternalist, he considered it his duty to look after those in need. He adopted a series of tactics to fulfill this responsibility, including dispensing as much relief as he could, seeking ways to acquire needed goods to distribute among the people, and searching actively for a share of government relief work. Although Daly felt that relief to the able-bodied was undesirable in principle, he quickly recognized the magnitude of the economic distress descending on Canada. In January 1931 he wrote that he was facing a new problem resulting from the disappearance of wage labour: 'Young, married men, who never thought of coming to me for help before, are asking to get a line of credit on their spring payment.' Obviously expecting his superiors to be skeptical about the scale of the economic slump, Daly added that they could contact the local member of Parliament, who would 'explain how all the mills are closed down and nothing in sight.'[41] Although the mandarins in Ottawa criticized Daly for his 'gloomy attitude', his assessment proved to be all too accurate.[42]

One simple strategy that Daly pursued was to search for sources of clothing and footwear to augment the dwindling supply on the reserves. Daly had always had the occasional shipment of second-hand clothing from charitable groups to distribute among the people—a useful support to impoverished people, though one that some may have found difficult to accept. In 1933 he attempted to use Indian department funds to acquire extra underwear and footwear for people in his agency. He appealed to the medical superintendent for support, arguing that this would help to keep down medical expenses.[43] Although this appeal was probably unsuccessful, it is likely that Daly continued to acquire some needed goods through his connections to charitable groups.

The issue of actual relief (usually in the form of rations or vouchers) caused Daly a good deal of ambivalence, especially as the group receiving relief expanded beyond the traditional recipients. On the one hand, he shared the prevailing conviction that it was harmful to hand out charity to those who could help themselves. In some cases (especially when dealing with 'troublemakers' and political opponents), Daly delayed providing aid and left people uncertain about their chances of getting relief. Like Lewis, he also lectured some of his clients or demanded that they see him in person before he would issue relief. On the other hand, he hated to see people suffer, and he had a good deal of sympathy for the people, many of whom he had always known to work hard for their living. In 1933, after two years of serious economic depression in his area, the agent described the emotional predicament he had faced in balancing the conflicting demands of the people and the Indian department: 'I can assure the Dept. that there has been a terrible time of anxiety on my part to do what I thought was conscientiously right to the Indians, and what the wishes of the Dept. are concerning relief.'[44]

Before the Depression, Daly handed out rations and relief on a relatively liberal scale, to the point where the officials in Ottawa suspected him of excessive generosity. Daly's superiors took him to task several times for providing more relief than they believed was necessary. In the 1920s, relief amounts were still discretionary, and this agent made a practice of giving $10 a month to elders who were too old to work—twice the amount that became standard in the 1930s. In 1927, for instance, Daly recommended winter relief for four older women of $10 each per month. The department objected, and the agent was required to justify the amount of relief he proposed—and, by implication, his own attitude towards providing help. In response, the agent noted that, far from appearing to others as a fount of benevolence, he was perceived even by the local non-Aboriginal population to be harsh and unyielding with his clients.[45] In 1929, Daly mentioned that he gave some assistance out of his own pocket, remarking that things were 'pretty hard on the poorer people'. In fact, he suggested that 'if some of the officials were here they would give more relief than I do to the Indians.'[46] Judging by the stern tone of their letters, it is not certain that Daly was right in this case. His point was well taken, though: it was easier to refuse aid to faceless strangers than to turn down personal acquaintances, as the agents were expected to do.

Maintaining the relatively generous scale of relief in his agency became more difficult for Daly after the Depression set in. In the 1930s the DIA began to institute changes in the relief system in an effort to reduce and standardize assistance. In 1930, a ration system was implemented that prescribed the amount of $5 in foodstuffs per month. Four years later a more elaborate schedule was drawn up, establishing the following amounts: a minimum of $4 per month; $6 for a family with two or three persons; $7 for four to six persons; $9 for seven to eight; and $10 for nine to ten persons. The last figure was the maximum relief issue.[47] Even for the time these were paltry amounts of money, and overall they were probably lower than the amounts most agents had given out previously. The increments allowed for extra family members were tiny—at the maximum, they allowed only $1 per person per month, compared to $4 for one person. The schedule compares unfavourably with relief allowed by other agencies in this era. In the 1920s, for instance, the Mothers' Allowance Commission granted $35 a month to a single woman with three children. This allowance was calculated to ensure thrift and supply only basic necessities. In 1936, using similar criteria, the nearby city of North Bay provided a maximum monthly relief allowance of $21.66 for a family of five, three times the amount the Indian department permitted for an Aboriginal family of the same size. This amount was for food only, additional sums being allowed for fuel and rent.[48] Daly mentioned in his correspondence that the relief paid to the non-Aboriginal unemployed around Parry Sound was significantly greater than what he was allowed to dispense.[49] Small wonder that some of Daly's clients complained about the inadequacy of relief.

Daly did make an effort to adhere to the department's austerity policy. He did so by instructing the people to 'get out and hustle' and by talking as though relief would not be forthcoming, even when he was aware that he could not withhold it.[50] Another of Daly's tactics was to stall for time, forcing those in need to come to his office more than once to make their appeal. Daly made repeated reference to this technique in his correspondence, but one example from 1935 will suffice: 'There are a number of Indian women who are living alone who are in need of relief, but on general principals [sic] I am staving them off as long as I can.'[51] If this assertion was true, there must have been some hungry people in Daly's agency (and undoubtedly in many other agencies) who experienced a great deal of extra distress through this sort of delaying tactic.

Despite these measures, Daly also showed compassion. For instance, he tried at least twice in the 1930s to convince his superiors to raise the relief rates. In 1930 Parry Island elder John Manitowaba wrote to the department complaining that he could not subsist on the relief payment. On inquiry, the department learned that Manitowaba and his wife were receiving two rations—that is, $10 per month in supplies. Daly took the opportunity of stating tactfully that he thought the ration too small and inquired if the department was considering an increase. He noted cautiously, 'I find that $5.00 worth of foodstuffs is hardly sufficient for the individual Indian in this section of the country according to the Indian mode of living here.'[52] Shortly thereafter the department instituted its official $5 per month ration, thus reducing the usual rations in Daly's agency by half. The Parry Island band attempted to restore former levels through a band council resolution to double pensions for elders and to increase the monthly relief ration to $10 per month. Daly supported this move, noting that the changes would 'solve the problem of relief' on the island, but found himself overruled by the officials in Ottawa.[53]

In spite of the department's clear position, Daly made one more attempt three months later to have the ration raised. He tried to convince his superiors that the increases were necessary in his region, and stated that he sympathized very much with the people of his agency, who were facing serious difficulties for the coming winter.[54] Moreover, his words indicated a certain resentment that the new regulations, which he was compelled to carry out, made him appear hard-hearted to the people. This agent understood the real economic problems that had set in and would clearly have liked to be more generous. This was not to be permitted by the officials in Ottawa, who could make regulations without having to live side by side with the people affected.

In addition to relief rations, Daly also sought government relief work on behalf of the people in his agency. Public roadwork projects in fact became one of Daly's primary strategies for handling the unemployment problem. It took some time before relief projects were established since the federal government was loath to assume the expense. In the first years of the Depression, therefore, until the road projects began in 1933, Daly had no choice but to provide relief on an unprecedented scale. From 1931 to 1933 there was massive unemployment, and the roster of people on relief issues grew proportionately. From 17 people with 14 dependants (a total of 31) in 1929–30, the number more than tripled to 57 people with 54 dependants in 1930–1 (a total of 111). The following year it almost quadrupled again, rising to 163 people with 268 dependants (total: 431). In the peak year, 1932–3, there were 183 relief recipients who supported another 329 dependants (total: 512).[55] This constituted nearly three-quarters of the agency's population, which was 712 in 1934. Largely through roadwork, Daly achieved a 30 per cent reduction in the relief rolls in 1933–4 and a further 20 per cent reduction the next year.[56] This aspect of Daly's response to the Depression had both positive and negative implications for the Anishinabek. On the one hand, the work was considerably more lucrative than relief and it allowed men the self-respect gained by earning money instead of receiving charity. On the other hand, Daly's position as sole dispenser of relief had already enormously heightened his influence and power—dispensing jobs as well made him a force to be reckoned with.

Assistance and Control

The link between assistance and control was highly visible in Daly's practice. In part, this was a reflection of long-standing British and Euro-Canadian attitudes towards charity, which rested on the notion that only the 'deserving' should receive aid. There were many ways of making oneself 'undeserving', including failing to show gratitude, failure to use all of one's resources purely for survival, perceived reluctance to work, and various kinds of immoral behaviour. Moreover, any use of funds for what might be deemed luxury (entertainment, for example) indicated that charity was not really required. All of these could justify the withdrawal of relief. After all, those who were living on public funds should be held to public standards. Anxiety about the unprecedented level of relief expenditures during the Great Depression increased the likelihood of surveillance being maintained over relief recipients.

Indian agents exercised a good deal of surveillance even before the 1930s, but it was predictable that the new crisis would increase supervision levels. The stakes became higher as well, since those on relief might face the loss of their only income if an agent disapproved of their lifestyles or actions. For example, Daly mentioned on one occasion that he had patrolled the local poolroom to discover which men spent time there and was much gratified by the rapid exits that resulted. He then informed the men 'that if they can pay for playing pool, they can pay for something to eat, and they need not come to me for relief I would not give it to them.'[57] The men's efforts to escape before Daly saw them clearly indicate their consciousness of being under surveillance.

The early years of the 1930s took their toll on Daly's relations with First Nations people in several ways. In the first place, Daly's position as the sole source of relief greatly heightened his ability to exercise power. The attempts of the Parry Island band to gain more control over relief were a response to this predicament, and these attempts also created additional friction between the agent and those agitating for more autonomy. Daly seemed to have more opponents in this period, and his relationships with former proteges deteriorated in some cases. It was probably no coincidence that John Manitowaba, a man with a history of standing up to Daly, was elected chief in 1933. Finally, the agent himself began to feel beleaguered with all the requests for help and the seemingly endless downward spiral in the economy. He wrote the department in 1933: 'I am swamped with letters from the outlying Reserves, and the Parry Islanders are on the treck [*sic*] here all the time.'[58] Daly now seemed more inclined than ever to the belief that people were manipulating him in their appeals for help. Phrases such as 'a very plausible Indian' and 'a very s[ua]ve Indian' appeared more frequently in his letters, marking his heightened distrust of his clients.[59] All of this served to foster higher levels of tension and often a more combative attitude on the part of the agent and of some of the Anishinabek.

The tensions became particularly obvious in Daly's handling of the roadwork jobs beginning in 1933. The agent could take some credit for his tireless efforts to find replacement sources of income for the men. Having lobbied government officials for road-building from 1931 on, he had already established a rapport with the local supervisor. Thus, when the work actually began he had a good deal of success in securing work for unemployed men. The effect was to reduce the strain on band funds for relief, to transfer some of the unemployment cost to public funds, and to ensure that men who wished to work for their income were able to do so some of the time (most men were hired for short stints, a few weeks at a stretch). Earnings from roadwork were dramatically higher than relief issues: in 1935, a month of work on the road brought in $26.[60]

But it was not all good for the men concerned. Roadwork gave the agent a new option, an alternative to simply giving relief. When there was no work available, Daly had felt unable to withhold rations—but now he could offer temporary employment, and those who refused it could be denied aid on the grounds that they had chosen not to work. Daly initially tried to spread roadwork evenly among the unemployed men, particularly those with families to support. As time went on, however, he grew more interested in seeing that those who were reluctant were forced to take part in this labour. As Daly had suggested earlier to the department, the availability of roadwork would permit the agent to 'liven up all the Indians . . . and give them the opportunity of working or grubbing along without any relief from the Department.'[61] He used this occasion to distinguish between those who were willing to work and those who supposedly were not. When any man declined a job on the roads, whatever his reasons, Daly considered this a refusal to work and grounds for denying relief. In 1935, for instance, Daly wrote a fellow agent about one man, Galna K., for whom Daly had arranged a job on the road crew. Galna K. had allegedly refused the work, and Daly reported that he had then thrown K. out of his office and told him to stay away. He concluded triumphantly that there would be no further work or relief for this individual in Daly's agency, and that he would have to 'hustle and get himself a job'[62]—an unlikely proposition given the state of the job market.

Daly also used roadwork as an opportunity to settle some scores with old adversaries. The case of Alexander K. is a good illustration. Although Daly's letters give little detail about Alexander K.'s activities, he had clearly challenged the agent on occasion, convincing Daly that he was a 'bush lawyer type' (a DIA term for those who spoke about their rights).[63] Daly decided that Alexander K. should be working, even though he had tuberculosis. K. had been receiving relief for almost two years, and his medical condition had apparently enabled him to escape the arduous labour on the roads. Now the agent claimed he could do 'light' work (hardly a description that could be applied to roadwork). Daly wrote to the department asserting that the man was simply using tuberculosis as an excuse not to work. The agent's complaint was vague but damning: 'I am under the impression that this man would try to take advantage of his physical disabilities and I do not think he is very willing to work anyway.' He made this statement despite his own acknowledgement that the man did not look well and that a doctor had confirmed his poor health.[64] As the agent himself expressed it, Daly was now 'keeping at his heels like an irritated Scotch terrier'.[65] With the authorization of the department, Daly wasted little time in cutting K. off relief and forcing him to do roadwork. He wrote the Christian Island agent some months later to inform him that he had cut off K.'s rations. Daly concluded, 'He has played this sick game to a finish. I have him working now and will keep him that way.'[66] Thus, a man with a serious and debilitating medical condition— one that normally required rest for any hope of recovery—found himself compelled to swing a hammer on the roads to remind him who was boss.

Others felt the agent's wrath in similar ways. Daly commanded Joseph Partridge, the Aboriginal foreman responsible for the road crew, to get a doctor's note from Stanley Manitowaba, who was also pleading illness. Stanley Manitowaba, as we have seen, was a long-standing political opponent of Daly's, as well as the son of John Manitowaba. 'He particularly, cannot substitute without sending a note that he is sick.' Manitowaba was to be 'cut off' if he did not attend to his work.[67] Likewise, two returned soldiers aroused the agent's distrust, for he declared that both the men were 'supposed to have ruptures which would not keep them from working, but they are malingering . . . and I will not stand for it if I can get work for them.'[68] The provision of relief work was becoming a campaign to enforce a rigid work ethic that left little room for acknowledgement of the health problems that continued to plague First Nations people or of the injuries that former soldiers had suffered in war.

By the mid-winter of 1934, the agent felt that there was a change in his clients as a result of his ability to impose roadwork on them. This was just what he had hoped. According to the agent, the people now felt compelled to defer to Daly, at least in his presence. He had succeeded in instilling a sense of uncertainty about assistance and imposing a strict regime of heavy labour on all but the elderly and very sick. Daly observed in a satisfied tone to fellow agent Eade, 'In the beginning of the winter the Indians were very autocratic here telling me what they wanted. Now, they come in a respectful manner asking if they can get some relief.'[69] Daly made no secret of his relish for his newfound power, describing to his superiors his pride at watching the men 'sweating and working on the road' on a blistering hot day. He was especially pleased about observing those who had tried to refuse the work. Daly asserted that the officials of the department would see an improvement in the men and youths, who were thus 'being broken to do an honest man's work'.[70] It was a moment of exceptional opportunity for imposing a regime of forced labour on the men who had fought department control, and Daly made the most of it.

Medical Care

Medical care was one area in which, technically, the federal government had obligations to First Nations people that it did not have to other Canadians. Although Ontario treaties did not mention health care, the Indian Act stated that Aboriginal people were to receive it, and so did DIA policy.[71] This, then, was a special form of assistance. But the means by which it was put into practice varied from one place to the next. Moreover, where possible the services were paid not out of public money but out of band funds or an individual's treaty money. The agents had to ensure that medical services were accessible to their clients and that doctors were paid, but the issue of where the money came from was somewhat contentious. There were also questions concerning eligibility in individual cases and what kinds of health problems merited medical attention. In his 1933 instructions to Indian agents, Deputy Superintendent General McGill began by stating plainly, 'The Department requires that sick and injured Indians receive prompt and skilled attention.' Yet such a sweeping obligation had to be narrowed in some way, especially given the need for economy and the notion that Aboriginal people habitually sought help they did not really require. Thus, the instructions included a caveat about preventing expenditure on those who were not 'really' ill: the agents were to ensure that doctors provided 'adequate treatment' but also were advised to 'prevent doctors and the Department being imposed upon by Indians who demand attention for trivial ailments.'[72] The distinction was characteristic: there was a clearly defined duty, but agents were also to place limits on the people's demands. For their part, the people sought to maximize the benefits they obtained from the department's health-care policies.

Since the implementation of medical care was open to interpretation in a number of ways, agents developed their own policies. The instructions cited above could be read to imply that medical care would be paid by the department, but in fact a variety of systems prevailed. In many places a local doctor was paid an annual salary, on the premise that he or she would attend to any medical needs among the First Nations concerned. The salary was normally paid out of band funds. This was undoubtedly the least expensive system, but it had obvious drawbacks. The most prevalent problem was that doctors were reluctant to make special trips to the reserves because these trips did not result in extra income. Particularly where reserves were remote or difficult to access, such reluctance had a major impact on the care received. Aboriginal complaints about doctors failing to respond to calls were extremely common. As the instructions quoted above clearly suggest, the usual explanation for the doctors' reluctance to attend Aboriginal patients was that the latter 'imposed' on doctors with 'trivial ailments'. But on occasion this perception resulted in sick people dying when a doctor failed to attend them. Another problem with placing doctors on salary was that the people preferred to choose their own doctors, perhaps in part because of the problems already cited. Some felt that their expenses should be paid regardless of which doctor had provided the services.

A further grey area was created through the notion held by at least some agents that they were supposed to teach First Nations people to pay their own debts. This notion was expressed, for example, by H.J. Eade of Christian Island. Eade paid an annual salary out of band funds to a local doctor who supplied regular care to the Christian Islanders and performed operations free of charge.[73] Those who had to go to hospital were compelled to pay their own bills—usually, no doubt, out of their semi-annual interest payments. For Christian Islanders living elsewhere, Eade tried to enforce a policy of paying their medical costs out of their own interest money. By contrast, Daly took the view that these costs should be charged to band funds. The two agents clashed over this issue because Daly paid the medical bills of Christian Islanders living in his agency out of the Christian Island band fund. As he wrote to Eade, 'My understanding is that if they are in need of medical attention they must get it.'[74]

There were also no guidelines about judging whether an ailment was 'trivial' or not; this question was left to the field officials or sometimes the doctors. Given the emphasis on economizing, it was only to be expected that officials would attempt to minimize medical costs, especially the high costs of surgery. (Doctors paid on salary would also have reason to avoid performing operations.) Although Daly had stated that he believed all First Nations people must get needed medical attention, this policy still required him to make decisions about when medical care was really needed. Such decisions could be quite arbitrary—Daly's considerations included the character of an individual and his own layperson's view of their state of health. Consider the case of an elderly woman who had been recommended for surgery by a local doctor. Daly recommended against the operation on the grounds that it would be 'wasted money'.[75] Personal feelings may have been at play here: the woman in question was the wife of John Manitowaba, with whom Daly had already had disagreements, and Daly had written two years earlier, 'I have found [John Manitowaba] to be quite a trouble maker and his wife is a good second to him in this respect.'[76] The agent did not explain why he thought the operation useless, but did suggest with a kind of off-handed disdain that Aboriginal healing practices might help Mrs Manitowaba: 'Mrs. John Manitowaba may live for quite a long time with her Indian dope.'[77] It is unclear how many times Daly made these kinds of subjective decisions. On the other hand, in some cases he clearly saw to it that those who needed medical care or hospitalization received what they needed, paying their bills with band funds.

As for Lewis, his practice was similar to that of agent Eade, of Christian Island. Like Eade, he preferred to limit medical expenses to the salaries paid to local physicians for visiting the reserves and showed a general reluctance to pay other medical bills. He also shared the notion that the people had to be taught to pay their own bills. In one instance, for example, he was approached by a physician who had attended a woman in childbirth and had not yet been paid for his services. The agent first tried to recoup the money from the debtor, but when this attempt failed he forwarded the account to the DIA for payment. In a letter to the doctor, Lewis mentioned his instructions from the department that 'when an Indian leaves his reserve to earn his living as a Whiteman he must be taught to pay his own debts.'[78] Medical care was a notable area in which leaving the reserve often meant renouncing the benefits of Indian status, even without becoming officially enfranchised. In this letter, Lewis revealed that he did not pay for medical treatment for the 'Indians' around Killarney, although 'the majority of the population [of Killarney] try to crawl in under the Indian Act at times.'[79] As observed in Chapter 2, Lewis had decided that the 'Indians around Killarney' were not 'Indians' in the sense of the Indian Act and therefore should not be included in the pay lists to receive annuities. Here, another of the consequent disadvantages becomes evident: Lewis held that the department's responsibility to these people had been more or less nullified by their decision to live on surrendered land, and their medical treatment was therefore their own problem.

Margaret McLeod, a Whitefish Lake band member who lived in an isolated part of Ontario near Chapleau, experienced the effects of Lewis's attitude when she fell ill in 1926. The Whitefish Lake band had a local doctor on salary who provided for its medical needs. Since McLeod had chosen not to live on the reserve, Lewis seemed to feel that he had no responsibility to ensure her health care or pay the medical bills she might incur. As he informed the local minister who had written to advise him about McLeod's health problems, he thought it 'doubtful if the Department will bear the expense of a Doctor to visit remote parts of the district where an individual Indian feels inclined to reside.'[80] Lewis did not wish to shoulder extra burdens merely because some Aboriginal people chose to inconvenience him by living off the reserve. The department was attempting to reduce costs, including hospital expenses, and for this reason it 'may not feel disposed to pay the expense.'[81] Clearly, these kinds of decisions were almost entirely arbitrary.

Medical care and relief were two types of assistance that often overlapped, since those who were too sick to work were eligible to receive relief. Again, the operative question was always whether or not the individual was truly incapacitated, and even sometimes whether he or she 'deserved' help. For instance, Lewis demonstrated suspicion in 1929 in the case of a man who was ill and requested relief through the Jesuit missionary at Wikwemikong. Lewis claimed that this man would feel better if he took some exercise and that he was too much in the habit of obtaining assistance in the wintertime. He also stated that 'a great number of the Indians who endure misery and hardship is brought on themselves by their own misbehaviour.'[82] The comment implies that those who were the authors of their own misfortune did not deserve help when in need—they joined the well-worn category of the 'undeserving poor'. In this case, as it happened, the band's doctor certified that the man was ill and the family received relief. First Nations people often required verification from non-Aboriginal professionals before the department would extend benefits that the Indian Act stated they ought to receive.

Conclusion

Clearly, assistance from the Indian department was a double-edged sword for the Anishinabek around Georgian Bay. It was necessary because of their poverty and marginalization, and it did provide some benefits to people who had no other place to turn. But it also greatly enhanced the power of the Indian agent. While most First Nations people in the 1920s requested assistance only in case of emergencies, and on a temporary basis, the Great Depression created a radically new situation. In the worst years of the Depression (roughly 1931–5), hundreds of formerly independent First Nations people were out of work on a long-term basis and largely reliant on the meagre aid provided by their Indian agent. For the people of the Manitowaning agency, this meant prolonged periods of severe poverty with only minimal help from Robert Lewis, the agent. For the people of the Parry Sound agency, roadwork provided intermittent opportunities to earn their own money and augment relief issues, but it also occasioned serious conflicts as agent John Daly sought to discipline individuals who had defied him in the past.

The Department of Indian Affairs was supposed to provide certain benefits that were laid out in treaties and the Indian Act. In practice, however, these were attenuated both by an obsession with economy and by the pursuit of ideological imperatives such as teaching people to pay their own debts and letting the 'undeserving' suffer if their own 'misbehaviour' was perceived to have caused their troubles. Administrative inconvenience could also be a factor—people who lived far from their agent could escape his control and surveillance, but they also often experienced an effective lapse in their Indian status. Only if an outsider stepped in to contact the agent would such people have a chance of receiving services or at least having some of their debts paid. It is impossible to know how many people fell through the cracks in this way, although often someone did step in, if only because so many Aboriginal people could not pay their medical bills and the Indian department was an obvious source of money to cover them.

The Anishinabek around Georgian Bay had considerable success in their strategy of replacing services formerly provided by chiefs with the services provided by Indian agents. Agents frequently found themselves supplying not only relief and medical assistance, but also services such as dispute mediation, settlement of family quarrels, and care for orphans and widows. It was a strategy that worked, but it heightened other problems for the Anishinabek, such as their lack of economic and political autonomy. For the Indian agents, engagement in such a wide variety of community needs served to reinforce their notion that they were required and that First Nations people could not manage their own affairs. In a sense, then, the agents' provision of assistance served important needs for both parties to these transactions and further bound the agents and First Nations people together. It was an uneasy collaboration, however, especially during the miserable 1930s. To be sure, most Aboriginal people would have preferred better alternatives than accepting a measure of dependence on the agent, even for a short period of time.

6

'Always and Only an Indian':
Assimilation in Practice

'. . . the government will in time reach the end of its responsibility as the Indians progress into civilization and finally disappear as a separate and distinct people, not by race extinction but by gradual assimilation with their fellow-citizens.'[1]

'Do you know what assimilate means? It is a nice sounding word. . . . Do you know that it means the intermarriage of your sons or daughters with those who are of an alien race and of alien ideas? That is assimilation or else there is no assimilation.'[2]

In 1918, an educated young Aboriginal man named Clifford Tobias was recommended to the Department of Indian Affairs as a promising individual who might make a good teacher in an Indian school in Ontario.[3] A DIA employee in Chatham, Ontario, responded to this suggestion in a highly revealing letter. He acknowledged that the young man's academic standing might be sufficient for the job, but was adamant that only white teachers should be hired to teach Aboriginal children. Not only would an 'Indian' be unable to impart knowledge of agriculture and horticulture, but he would be incapable of performing the most important part of the teacher's job: educating for assimilation. In this official's words, 'these children require to have the "Indian" educated out of them, which only a white teacher can help to do.' He concluded bluntly, 'An Indian is always and only an Indian and has not the social, moral and intellectual standing required to elevate these Indian children, who are quite capable of improvement.'[4]

This letter speaks volumes about the contradictory but deeply ingrained notions most DIA employees held about First Nations people. On the one hand, the conviction is expressed that Aboriginal *children* are capable of change—that they can be 'improved' and 'elevated' by having the 'Indian' educated out of them. Aboriginal children apparently were not inherently unable to meet the high standards of Euro-Canadians. But in the very same sentence the 'Indian' is essentialized, demeaned, and constructed as being *incapable* of change: 'always and only an Indian'. Even an 'Indian' who had completed his high school education—entirely at the hands of

Euro-Canadian teachers, of course—was presumed to be inadequate in every important way: socially, morally, *and* intellectually.

It is instructive that the official made no effort to establish Clifford Tobias's level of assimilation, even though the young man had advanced to the level of secondary education, far beyond most of his fellows and many Euro-Canadians at the time. If white teachers were supposed to educate the 'Indian' out of the children, should Clifford Tobias not have become a model of assimilation? But no, it was assumed that he had not been improved, that he remained 'only an Indian'. This letter was unusual in its frank prejudice, in its bald rejection of an Aboriginal teacher (neither Lewis nor Daly refused Aboriginal teachers on principle, for example). Still, the writer expressed a fundamental belief in a largely unchanging 'Indian' character that was common to most DIA officials. In this chapter we will interrogate the policy of assimilation, the underlying attitudes towards it, and some of the means by which officials attempted to put it into practice.

Clearly, a man like Clifford Tobias was in a difficult position. He had gone to the trouble of obtaining a secondary education at a time when Aboriginal people received little encouragement to do so. If he grew up on a reserve, he probably had to leave his home to attend high school, and he certainly would have attended a white-dominated school where he might have been the only Aboriginal student. This course of action required determination as well as academic achievement. Somehow he had succeeded in coming to the attention of Toronto's Minister of Education, which further suggests ability and ambition. The letter does not reveal what Tobias hoped to do with his education, but it appears that the education minister believed him best suited to work among First Nations people rather than within Euro-Canadian society—in effect, sending him back to his own community. This was probably the most common attitude among Euro-Canadians at the time: cultural assimilation might be desirable, but once it was achieved First Nations people would still be expected to remain a community apart. On the other hand, an official like the one in Chatham would work to prevent a Clifford Tobias from working as a teacher within his own community. The situation was not hopeless— some Aboriginal people did find a place for themselves in mainstream society, and some Indian agents (like Lewis and Daly) were willing to hire Aboriginal teachers. But even First Nations people who were interested in becoming assimilated—and many were not—faced major obstacles if they wanted to join the larger non-Aboriginal society. That community was not particularly interested in welcoming them.

The Indian department's assimilation program suffered from a lack of clarity about its goals and, above all, about the nature of the problem it sought to remedy. What exactly was it in First Nations people that needed to be changed? Like the Euro-Canadian public in general, DIA officials were not at all clear in their thinking about First Nations people and this reality was reflected in the department's understandings and practices. In principle the desirability of assimilation was not questioned. But what did it mean, exactly? According to the *Oxford English Dictionary*, 'assimilate' is a transitive or intransitive verb meaning 'make like' or 'absorb into the system'; in its intransitive form, it means to 'be so absorbed'.[5] The last two parts of this definition echo the vision of Deputy Superintendent General Duncan Campbell

Scott, whose oft-quoted words at the outset of this chapter proclaimed the inevitability of First Nations peoples' absorption into the dominant society. Ultimately, however, this would remain impossible as long as Euro-Canadians continued to sideline and reject them. Then there was the component of 'making like'—making First Nations people similar to Euro-Canadians. In this sense, assimilation refers to acculturation, that is, inducing First Nations people to adopt the culture and especially the values of Euro-Canadians. The implicit assumption of DIA practice was that acculturation was a prerequisite for full assimilation (absorption).

Acculturating Aboriginal people to Euro-Canadian ways was presumed to be best both for the people themselves and for Canadian society as a whole, given the continuing belief that British civilization was superior to all others. But DIA records reveal persistent doubts about the feasibility of the project. Some peoples were simply considered unassimilable: all those of Asian heritage were placed in this category, for example.[6] DIA officials seemed to worry at times that First Nations people might also belong in the category of the unassimilable. After all, with the dedicated support of several churches, the department had been attempting to acculturate the people for about a century. The officials could not see much in the way of results, for First Nations people remained tangibly different from Euro-Canadians in their language, habits, values, and world views. (It is worth noting that the Aboriginal point of view on this subject was undoubtedly quite different—cultural change was highly visible to the people themselves.)

The uncertainty about assimilability was partly a result of the confusion of racial and cultural categories. Was 'Indian' a cultural or a racial category? This was never clear, and most Canadians did not attempt to distinguish carefully between the two.[7] If 'Indian' was a racial or biological category, then it was doubtful that any change was possible, except perhaps by miscegenation. If, on the other hand, 'the Indian' was defined by culture, this could be altered. In order to satisfy their superiors, Indian agents were obliged to speak as though change was possible, but in practice they often treated 'Indian' as an unchanging, racial or biological category ('always and only an Indian'). When frustrated with the lack of visible progress, agents were apt to blame this on innate (racial) qualities of First Nations people. This was a more palatable explanation than other likely reasons, such as the people's preference for their own culture, defects in the department's policies, and rejection by Euro-Canadians.

The goal of assimilation was predicated on assumptions that had long been basic to English-Canadian society: in particular, the need to establish a homogeneous society modelled on the mother country and to alter all those of non-British descent to fit into British-Canadian culture. But in addition to being an ideological imperative, assimilation had a number of obvious practical merits. Its pre-eminent value was that full absorption of First Nations people would eliminate all aspects of the 'Indian problem'. Absorption (through enfranchisement)[8] of all members of a band would break up the reserves and lead to the distribution of reserve lands as privately owned property, subject to purchase, sale, and property tax like any other lands. It would lead to the disappearance of reserve communities, and thus, presumably, of the collective ethic that was seen as standing in the way of progress.

Without these communities, Aboriginal cultures and languages could also be expected to vanish. Through miscegenation, racial differences would be erased, thus helping to eliminate the troubling heterogeneity of the Canadian population. Best of all, if bands could be dissolved, the DIA's responsibilities would disappear and the federal government's financial obligations to these entities would cease to exist. In fact, the DIA was supposed to become obsolete and be phased out. There would be no Indians left to receive annuities or any of the other benefits of treaties; thus the treaties would be terminated. The provinces, instead of the federal government, would be saddled with the responsibility for First Nations health and education. Euro-Canadians would even cease to be confronted with the potentially disturbing spectre of the original inhabitants who had been dispossessed of their lands. All of this made assimilation an ideal that most Canadians could embrace wholeheartedly.

For First Nations people, the advantages of assimilation were considerably less compelling. As we saw with Clifford Tobias, being identified as Aboriginal meant facing substantial obstacles within the dominant society, regardless of one's accomplishments and personal qualities. In addition, of course, assimilating meant losing an ancient, dynamic culture that many of the people still valued. The limited participation in Canadian society that most Aboriginal people could expect would not offset the benefits lost by renouncing Indian status, either. In short, there were serious losses involved in the process, and neither the Indian department nor Canadian society in general was offering very significant compensations. Thus, although federal policy certainly managed to erode First Nations cultures in many ways, the attempt at full assimilation was largely unsuccessful.

The Assimilation Program

In keeping with their lack of attention to developing specific assimilation policies, department officials spent little time elaborating their precise goals for acculturation. What changes were they looking for in Aboriginal communities and individuals? What traits did they wish to see Aboriginal people adopt? Officials themselves might have summed up their primary goal as inculcating the values of industry, sobriety, and thrift. Instilling an appreciation for the value of hard work was probably the pre-eminent objective. We have already seen agent Daly's relish at watching the men perform roadwork in stifling heat. Officials wanted to see the people comply with an industrial work ethic, revealed in a disciplined and sustained approach to work, rather than a pre-industrial rhythm of alternating intense effort and rest. An allied trait was the commitment to self-support, which was contrasted with 'improvidence' and perceived dependence. Finally, it was important that the people abandon their kinship- and community-oriented ethic of sharing resources, conforming instead to the heavily individualistic emphasis of Euro-Canadian society. As former Minister of the Interior Frank Oliver explained the issue in 1914, 'ownership [and] selfishness, which is foreign to the mind of the Indian in his normal condition, is really the foundation of civilization.'[9] Only by denying aid to their kin and friends, and by accumulating privately owned property whose use was confined to the nuclear family, could First Nations people become fully worthy of membership in Canadian society.

Of course, there were many other ways in which First Nations people were expected to change. Their languages, spirituality, marriage practices, and child-rearing methods were all supposed to be replaced by British-Canadian norms. The adoption of Christianity, in particular, had been regarded as critically important from the earliest days of colonialism. In the Georgian Bay area, the 1920s and 1930s witnessed the virtual disappearance of open adherence to traditional spirituality, as every member of a band adopted, at least nominally, one of the Christian churches. On Parry Island, where traditional beliefs remained alive much longer than on the area's other reserves, overt traditionalism was apparently dying out in the 1920s.[10]

Still, the acculturation process was slow and patchy. The formal adoption of Christianity had not entirely eliminated indigenous spiritual and supernatural beliefs. John Daly, for instance, was well aware that Aboriginal healing practices were still in use among some people of his agency, and he also believed that some still practised 'sorcery'—that is, that they used herbs and rituals to influence or harm others.[11] In 1929, anthropologist Diamond Jenness heard from several informants on Parry Island that people there used hunting and fishing charms and that some also practised various forms of magical or supernatural rites, such as night flying and causing illness in others.[12] Such activities and beliefs were condemned by the Christian missionaries, but clearly they had not been entirely abandoned—or at least, the Parry Islanders believed some people still adhered to them.[13] Jenness also described Tom King, of the King family of Potawatomi living on Parry Island, as being 'known to most of the whites in the vicinity as the Indian medicine-man'.[14]

There were numerous other factors that attested to the retention of culture. Virtually everyone in the Parry Sound agency spoke an Aboriginal tongue as their first language (most often Ojibway, but in some cases Odawa or Potawatomi).[15] These languages remained strong on Manitoulin Island as well. Then there were the moral and economic matters, which the agents considered important. The majority of the men were still considered to be following the 'Indian mode of life' and thus not acculturated to Euro-Canadian work habits and values. Some men and women engaged in relationships that Euro-Canadians regarded as extramarital, either because they had former spouses still living or because they cohabited without benefit of clergy. A small minority of women became involved with non-Aboriginal men, another factor viewed as a sign of inferior morality. While it is not clear that practices like divorce and unchurched cohabitation were any more prevalent among First Nations people than among the general population, they were important indicators to the officials and were considered proof that assimilation was not working—at least not in the way it was supposed to. Assimilation was intended to lead to the adoption of only those aspects of Euro-Canadian culture that department officials considered desirable.

There were obvious internal contradictions in the agents' attitudes concerning assimilation. Daly, in particular, often showed ambivalence about the adoption of 'white' values and habits, especially when these were not part of the desired set of values. In practice, he also wanted Aboriginal people to be like whites only when it suited the department's needs. A typical illustration of this phenomenon is provided by Daly's comment during the Depression, when his clients were agitating for equal treatment and relief rates that matched those of the area's Euro-Canadians. The agent was in a predicament, because the local relief agencies were providing relief to Euro-Canadians until the end of May, while his superiors were not willing to grant it for so long to First Nations people. In such a situation, Daly resorted to the rhetoric of difference, explaining to the people 'that they are Indians and should not do as the whites do, but should get out and hustle and do a little trapping.'[16] Clearly, this was another moment when 'different' was equivalent to disadvantaged. At other times, Daly had depicted the habit of 'getting out and hustling' as a positive Euro-Canadian trait.

The public rhetoric of assimilation was stripped of class references, but one of the key underlying principles of the Indian Affairs system was that First Nations people were to be assimilated at the level of the unskilled or semi-skilled working class. Any higher aspirations were believed to be inconsistent with Aboriginal abilities and, in any case, would have violated the accepted principles of Canada's racial hierarchy. The emphasis on trades rather than academic subjects at Indian residential schools is indicative of the department's class assumptions,[17] but the agents betrayed these sentiments as well. Daly, for example, once lamented the influence of wealthy tourists on his clients, for he was convinced that their habit of treating First Nations guides like equals had a detrimental effect on their sense of humility. He remarked that he continuously had to 'try and impress upon the Indian that he is still an Indian', because it was hard for the men to 'get back to earth' after going out fishing with millionaires and smoking their cigars. The tourists, in Daly's eyes, gave 'the Indian the wrong steer and a false idea of what he is'.[18]

By the 1930s, the department's approach towards assimilation had become considerably less proactive. Duncan Campbell Scott retired in 1932, eliminating one of the most avid proponents of assimilation and coercion. His successor, Harold McGill, expressed less fervour about achieving far-reaching changes in First Nations people. His description of the basic outline of Indian policy in 1939 did not suggest a very ambitious program: 'so to treat our native races that they may become self-supporting and enjoy thereby some degree of economic security and increase their welfare and happiness.'[19] Indian Affairs officials had backed away somewhat from the expectation of dissolving reserves and First Nations communities, at least in the immediate future. But the goal of acculturation, already pursued for about a century, had not been abandoned by any means.

Aboriginal Views on Assimilation

Aboriginal people have always been willing to adapt to new influences and circumstances, but they have always resisted forced assimilation. We have already seen many ways in which they actively fought DIA policies, especially their coercive aspects. Another obvious proof of the people's resistance to assimilation is their retention of many cultural traits and values. Current Aboriginal thinkers have stressed the continuity of First Nations values, contradicting the dominant society's frequent emphasis on cultural change and loss. As Wendat scholar Georges E. Sioui demonstrates in *For an Amerindian Autohistory*, a strong argument can be made that the essentials of Aboriginal thought and culture have been preserved: 'An examination of the Amerindian philosophical tradition will show the persistence, vivacity, and universality of the essential values proper to America.'[20] In her recent book *A Recognition of Being*, Kim Anderson has made a similar point.[21] Through a broad-based movement that began in the 1960s, First Nations people have also made significant gains in their effort to revive the ceremonies, customs, and spirituality of their ancestors—traditions that were kept alive in the era under examination here.

Although the specific goals that the people have pursued in the past 150 years or so have varied according to time and place, there are many consistent elements in Aboriginal strategies of adaptation to the European presence. In the treaty negotiations of the nineteenth century, for example, they presented a series of demands that reflected a reasonably coherent plan. In many ways, that strategy seems to have been intact in the 1920s and 1930s. During treaty negotiations, the chiefs usually tried to retain a land base and access to traditional resources, particularly game and fish. Those leaders located in mining areas, where prospecting was already in progress, made a great effort to ensure that their people would control the wealth generated by any minerals on their lands. They also attempted to secure a perpetual income (annuities), along with a guarantee of ongoing government support in time of need. Finally, they sought a series of provisions to help them adjust economically to the new conditions, including training in farming techniques and a variety of tools, implements, and livestock to start them off as agriculturalists. In some instances education was also mentioned, and in the West negotiators successfully pressured the government to include health care in its guarantees.[22] Taken together, these requirements suggest an adjustment program that included retention of traditional occupations along with adaptation of European methods of making a living. The people desired continuity with the past, combined with the ability to benefit from European knowledge and technology.

It is clear that First Nations people wanted, as much as possible, to control the pace of change in their lives and to choose how, when, and why they would adapt. There were always vociferous objections whenever the government passed coercive amendments to the Indian Act. There was clear recognition, for instance, that the initial introduction of enfranchisement provisions in the Gradual Civilization Act (1857) was designed to break up reserve communities and alienate land.[23] The people recognized the importance of retaining their lands and were always vigilant, even suspicious, concerning arrangements about land. They clearly wanted to maintain strong, viable Aboriginal communities in which their own cultures and customs thrived. Adjustment, in short, was something they accepted but wished to do selectively, rather than abandoning wholesale the ways of their ancestors. There is, of course, nothing surprising about this attitude.

Indian department officials clearly assumed that much of the acculturation they sought would occur automatically, presumably through a combination of schooling, interaction with Euro-Canadians, and intermarriage. It was particularly the latter step that would finalize assimilation and result in the absorption of First Nations people into mainstream society. This would, of course, require that all First Nations people sooner or later marry non-Aboriginal people and move off the reserve. As many commentators have observed, the segregation of reserve life seriously hampered that process. Heterosexual contact across racial lines did occur, but there were many barriers—not least, the simple fact that meetings were not all that common. Some First Nations people married and left the reserve, just as a few Euro-Canadians lived with their partners within reserve communities, but the vast majority in these communities were Aboriginal. As long as they were the majority on their own reserves, and as long as the languages remained alive and in use, acculturation could not proceed very far, at least not in the sense of relinquishing their own traditions. In the 1920s and 1930s, as we have seen, Aboriginal languages were very much in use and were the first language of most reserve residents. The languages carried with them a great deal of the world view and values particular to these cultures.

In this context it is important to remember the presence on most reserves of returned soldiers. These individuals had had experiences that set them apart from the rest of the community. Not only had many of them faced direct combat, but they had also had the opportunity to develop comradeship and even friendships with Euro-Canadian men. There was nothing like the experience of sharing mortal danger to forge bonds that transcended the barriers of race. Moreover, these men had gained new insights into the world view of Euro-Canadians. A number of them took advantage of their wartime connections with Euro-Canadian men in positions of authority, requesting their intervention into disputes with the DIA. Former soldiers also made use of the Canadian Legion, which willingly approached department officials to defend its members' rights, especially regarding issues specific to veterans such as pensions and the soldier settlement program.[24] The returned soldiers were often less inclined to tolerate the department's control and the condescension of its employees. Veteran Francis Pegahmagabow seems to have had a pugnacious attitude even before he went away to war, but it is likely that his wartime experiences further shaped his vision, affirming his conviction that First Nations people did not need a government department to run their affairs. Pegahmagabow also spoke and wrote fluent English, and no doubt his language skills were improved by his years in the armed forces.

Apart from the returned soldiers, most First Nations people around Georgian Bay had only certain types of interactions with Euro-Canadians. They performed wage labour for Euro-Canadians and often worked side by side with them. There were other types of economic interaction, especially purchases of goods and labour on both sides. There was a limited amount of contact related to religious observance. Then there must have been a certain amount of amorous or sexual interaction—how much is difficult to judge. But for the most part, these activities did not allow First Nations people to gain an in-depth understanding of the cultural values and expectations of Euro-Canadians. As much as Indian agents found Aboriginal people's actions inexplicable, then, the people must have found Indian agents equally difficult to comprehend, and often morally reprehensible from their own cultural perspective.

Education

Clearly, education was the primary tool of assimilation envisioned by government. It was one of the earliest methods adopted, and it remained the assimilative tool to which the greatest quantity of resources was devoted. A significant proportion of the Indian department's budget was devoted to education, and statistics and reports on Indian schools always took a prominent place in the department's annual reports. Education was something to which mainstream Canadians could relate and it was not controversial, as long as expenditures were kept to a minimum. Schooling was aimed almost exclusively at children—it was primarily an attempt to intervene at an early age to interrupt the transmission of Aboriginal cultural values and instill Euro-Canadian values in their place. If this intervention failed or was successfully counteracted, officials looked to the next generation—the next generation was perpetually the one that would be saved. There was not much intervention with adults, and even for young adults there was limited interest in going beyond a rudimentary education. Officially, DIA policy stated that deserving individuals would be helped to obtain more advanced schooling, but it was really up to the individual agent how much this policy was put into practice. Since the secondary grades were not usually provided on the reserves, advancing to high school required particular dedication on the part of a student, as well as additional resources that typically had to come from the Indian department. The records show that some young people moved on to high school, but also that the agents had diverging views on the usefulness of their doing so. By contrast, the provision of primary school was accepted as a given by all the agents.

Agents endeavoured to ensure that all the youngsters attended school either on their reserve or at a residential school. They inspected schools regularly and often spoke about the value of education. In southern Ontario in the interwar years, on-reserve day schools were the preferred method of instruction. Residential schools had long since lost their popularity with officials, given their great expense and their failure to fulfill expectations. By the 1920s, Ontario agents used residential schools more often as orphanages than as places of education—children tended to be sent there when there was no one to look after them. Occasionally parents requested that their children be accepted at boarding schools. The reasons for these requests are not always clear, but religion was a factor. Francis Pegahmagabow, for instance, agreed to have his sons sent to an orphanage for schooling after considerable urging by agent Daly. Until this time Pegahmagabow had resisted sending his children to school and even managed to prevent them from attending the reserve school, which was Protestant.[25] The purpose of sending the children to the orphanage was to obtain a Catholic education for them, and Daly had to exercise his persuasive powers to induce his superiors to assume the expense.[26] Children who lived too far from a day school to permit regular attendance might also be dispatched to residential schools.

On the more isolated reserves, it was sometimes considered more efficient to round up the school-aged children and send them to a boarding school, rather than attempt to run a local school with a small number of children (fewer than 10–12 pupils). Even so, parents sometimes succeeded in reversing the process once there were enough children. In the summer of 1921, for example, the DIA had all the school-aged youngsters on the Whitefish River Reserve placed in boarding schools.[27] Three years later, the band council passed a resolution calling for a day school to be opened on the reserve. There were now 12 children old enough to attend, with another 15 who would soon reach school age. Lewis therefore supported the move to open a school, and presumably the youngsters were now allowed home from the boarding schools.[28] This was one area in which the department's obsession with thrift could work in the people's favour, and particularly in the interests of the children. In another instance, a father from Sheguiandah, Alex Nahwaikeshik, managed to get his children home from the Chapleau school for the summer holidays in 1923.[29] After initial resistance to the visit, Lewis finally agreed, and then pointed out that the children could finish their schooling at home since there was a day school at Sheguiandah with 'a small attendance'.[30] The father had thus succeeded in liberating his offspring from the Chapleau school for good.

There are numerous examples in the records of agents rejecting the notion of educating children at a residential school. Daly wrote fellow agent A.D. Moore at Cape Croker in 1926, responding to Moore's proposal to send Louis Lamorandiere's children to the school at Spanish, on the north shore of Lake Huron. Daly opposed the idea because the Lamorandiere family lived right beside the reserve day school and the parents should be capable of providing for the children. The latter point turned the question into one of self-support. Daly added that he did not think the department would 'grant the admission' of the Lamorandiere children into a boarding school as 'the parents are well able to support them.'[31] Clearly, there is no question in this case of forcible removal of the children from their home, as often occurred in other places (especially in British Columbia and on the Prairies). This remark and others like it underline the agent's perception of the boarding schools as charity institutions, functioning primarily as homes for poor and orphaned children. It would seem that the Indian department had instructed the agents to make sparing use of residential schools on the grounds of their higher cost per student. Even the children at Moose Deer Point, an isolated reserve only reached by water, were not committed to residential schools. Instead, Daly found teachers willing to live on the reserve for the school year and maintained a day school there.[32]

The residential school experience was more common for children in the Manitowaning agency. Lewis was strongly in favour of education, and in places where there were only small numbers of children, that meant sending them to one of the boarding schools, as occurred at Whitefish River in 1921. On several occasions children escaped from a school or resisted being sent back at the end of holidays. One of these incidents proved a painful experience for the agent, as he was torn between obeying his instructions and responding compassionately to the two boys, who pleaded to be spared another stint at the school. Lewis persevered in tearing the youngsters away from their mothers, but not without grave misgivings about his role. He wrote that it was 'a severe test' for him, 'as they both sobbed bitterly and begged of me that I should let them remain at home until I almost had to use force to get them away.' Such accounts of his emotional responses are extremely rare in Lewis's correspondence, which lends this passage all the more poignancy; the agent was very much disturbed by what he had seen. He expressed concern to his superiors about the school's treatment of the children: 'judging from the way the boys acted I am lead [sic] to believe that some of the boys are not treated in the best manner.'[33] Unfortunately, the Indian department was not prepared to inquire too closely into the reasons why these children were so desperate to stay at home.

Even so, the majority of children around Georgian Bay were educated in day schools on the reserves in this period. The day schools had their own drawbacks. It was very difficult for the Indian department to find or retain teachers for them, primarily because the DIA offered a very low salary compared to other schools. Moreover, taking charge of a reserve school meant making sacrifices that few Euro-Canadian teachers were willing to contemplate—isolation, loneliness, coping with differences of language and culture, living as an outsider in small First Nations communities. In many cases, teaching on a reserve required living there as well, given the transportation of the time and the isolation of many reserves. Some teachers had to walk many miles from the railway in to the reserve where they had been appointed. Daly actually submitted a brief item on this subject to a newspaper, valorizing Emily Donald who he said braved wolves (or the possibility of meeting them) in walking 18 miles in to Moose Deer Point to reach her new job.[34]

In addition to these issues, conflict between teachers and parents was not uncommon. The documents suggest that parents expected to exercise a voice in the way the school was run and sometimes experienced disputes with teachers as a result. For instance, a major controversy broke out at Whitefish Lake Reserve under Lewis's tenure when a young woman ran afoul of the people there. The original source of the problem is unclear, but it may have been largely a question of personality (racist attitudes on her part cannot be ruled out, but neither can they be proven from the sources). In addition, the parents seem to have felt that she gave inferior instruction, and they protested that she did not teach regular hours.[35] Although Lewis initially supported this teacher, he later concluded that the students were not learning much and went up to the reserve to remove her.[36] The incident clearly illustrated the parents' interest in the teacher's work and their sense that they were entitled to intervene.

There were differing views among field officials about the advisability of hiring Aboriginal teachers for day schools. We have seen the comments of the official in Chatham who derided the abilities of Clifford Tobias merely because he was Aboriginal. On the other hand, both Lewis and Daly were willing to hire Aboriginal teachers. Daly hired Emily Donald, a young Aboriginal woman who had been raised at the Anglican residential school at Chapleau, to teach on Parry Island and subsequently at the Moose Deer Point day school for at least three years.[37] Lewis also voiced no objection to Aboriginal teachers, and responded in positive terms to an Aboriginal woman's inquiry about teaching in his agency.[38] Given the challenges they often faced in finding qualified teachers, these agents were not in a position to be overly choosy (whereas an agent in Chatham, located in more accessible southern Ontario, might have less difficulty hiring non-Aboriginal teachers). Nevertheless, there is no suggestion anywhere in their correspondence that they objected to First Nations people as teachers. In fact, Daly on one occasion noted that local non-Aboriginal teachers were often undesirable for the position because of their racist attitudes: 'they have the idea that they know the Indian bent of mind, and it is a case of familiarity breeding comtempt [*sic*].'[39]

Lewis showed more enthusiasm for education than Daly. Lewis recommended DIA assistance towards higher education on a number of occasions and declared himself generally in favour of high school education for Native children. This was an unusual attitude for the time, when primary schooling was all the DIA provided to most children. In 1925, Lewis informed Ottawa that parents at Wikwemikong had been complaining about one of the day-school teachers. The agent felt that they had grounds for complaint, as she was too inexperienced to teach senior school. He recommended that she be replaced by a more qualified teacher, 'as the Indians are now of the opinion that their children should all graduate to high schools and I would like to give them every encouragement.'[40] Clearly this agent saw potential, in at least some cases, for First Nations people to move beyond unskilled wage labour, and even beyond high school. He fought for one young woman to attend normal school (for teacher training) with DIA aid, and also successfully defended the funding for five other Wikwemikong girls to complete high school at the Pembroke convent.[41]

In Daly's case, his experience with his protege Emily Donald seemed to prejudice him permanently against further education for First Nations people. Emily Donald was raised in a residential school, and the school principal had sent her to Daly with the expectation that he would take a paternal interest in her welfare (she was an orphan).[42] She taught at two day schools in Daly's agency, and the agent tried to steer her towards teacher training at a normal school.[43] But the young woman had her own ideas about her future and though she continued to teach, she initially elected not to go to normal school.[44] Daly became bitter towards Emily Donald as a result of his disappointed hopes. In later years he used this experience to justify a general opposition to higher education for First Nations people.

In 1935, for instance, Cape Croker agent A.C. Poste proposed that a girl living in Daly's agency be helped to attend normal school. This proposal elicited a negative reaction from Daly, who now argued that First Nations people did not need further education. He claimed that he had been encouraging the children to 'high aims' and that they had developed grand aspirations such as 'to become school teachers, doctors, and professors and so forth'. But he went on to disparage their hopes, claiming that the young girls had 'a false idea of their own importance' and that it was 'all a kind of dream with them, with the expectation that the Department will foot the bill.'[45] Ultimately, he argued, higher schooling for them would be wasted money, and the department should be 'firm' in refusing help so that this 'passing phase' would end. One source of Daly's cynicism was indicated by a further remark about Emily Donald, that she 'takes for granted all that has been done for her', and the same would occur with the other young people.[46] In this case the agent clearly let his disappointment with Donald colour his treatment of others in his agency, to their great disadvantage. Despite the indications that there was some momentum in the community towards advanced education for the young, Daly allowed the opportunity to slip.

Enfranchisement Policy

Enfranchisement policy was one area in which the trend towards greater coercion became evident in the 1920s. Deputy Superintendent General Duncan Campbell Scott intensified the campaign to advance the enfranchisement process during these years, especially in the immediate post-war period. Scott had two significant changes made to the Indian Act's enfranchisement provisions immediately after World War II. The first was made in 1918, when a new section was added allowing individuals who owned no land in an Indian reserve to become enfranchised. (Ownership of reserve land had formerly been a prerequisite.) The second amendment, introduced in 1920, permitted the federal government to initiate enfranchisement proceedings for individuals against their will. The two measures were justified by the claim that the previous procedure had been too cumbersome, and further that many First Nations people were now 'quite capable of conducting their own affairs.' Scott therefore asserted that 'in such cases the government should be empowered to free itself from the guardianship which is no longer necessary or desirable.'[47]

The 1918 amendment, which became section 122A, stated that an Indian man or unmarried Indian woman over the age of 21 who held no reserve land, did not live on a reserve, and did not follow the 'Indian mode of life' could apply to be enfranchised. Successful applicants had to prove that they were fit to be enfranchised, which meant showing that they were self-supporting, morally upright, and ready for the responsibilities of citizenship. They were also required to surrender all claims to any interest in the lands and property of the band to which they belonged and to accept their share of the band funds and any treaty annuities in lieu of all future payments.[48] The patriarchal emphasis of the Indian Act greatly multiplied the efficiency of the process, for until 1924 a married man's enfranchisement automatically carried with it that of his wife and minor unmarried children, even if the couple was not living together.[49] The male head of a family received his wife's and children's shares of the band fund. Enfranchisees became, officially, ordinary citizens of Canada with full rights and responsibilities.

The amendment of 1918 resulted in a greatly increased volume of enfranchisements. By 1920, 227 persons had become enfranchised under its provisions, 212 of them from the Six Nations Reserve.[50] This was more than twice the total number from Confederation to 1918. Thereafter, a steady trickle of individuals chose to undergo the procedure: according to official statistics, the approximate average was between 100 and 115 persons enfranchised per year from 1919 to 1939.[51] Most of these came under section 122A, the 1918 amendment that was used for those who did not own any reserve land. Enfranchisees under section 107, who owned reserve land that became their private property, were a much smaller group: DIA reports show only 53 such enfranchisements between 1919 and 1939. This distinction is important, because it shows that most of those who were renouncing band membership and Indian status lived off-reserve or were willing to give up any reserve land they owned. In many cases these were probably people who had begun to loosen their ties to these communities.

Although these figures represent a considerable *relative* increase in enfranchisement rates, they were a far cry from the result that Duncan Campbell Scott was looking for. From Scott's point of view, a hundred or so people per year was entirely inadequate. Indeed, the population loss to most First Nations communities would have been relatively insignificant. Consequently, Scott had a second amendment to the Indian Act passed in 1920, this time allowing the department to initiate enfranchisement proceedings unilaterally, even against the will of the person concerned. This was part of Scott's personal mission to destroy the efforts of certain leaders to build political organizations and press for Aboriginal rights.[52] First Nations leaders were outraged, and protested vigorously against this provision. They were able to obtain the support of Liberal politicians who were offended by the amendment's anti-democratic character, and the Mackenzie King government repealed the compulsory enfranchisement provision in 1922.[53] Although it was reinstated in a slightly milder form in 1933, there is no evidence that it was ever applied, no doubt because of First Nations opposition.[54]

A noteworthy aspect of the enfranchisement policy is the gap between officials in the field and those at the top echelon of the DIA. Among the top brass, and particularly in the mind of department head Scott, there was a strong policy emphasis on enfranchising every person of Indian status. But in practice most employees showed much less interest in promoting the process. Even the officials at headquarters placed no pressure on agents to promote or approve enfranchisements, at least not in Ontario. An examination of Indian Affairs correspondence throughout the 1920s and 1930s suggests, in fact, that most officials paid little attention to the goal of enfranchisement. Directives from headquarters constantly emphasized the importance of promoting self-reliance, but never explicitly linked this strategy with the long-term objective of enfranchisement.

Moreover, there is no evidence that agents championed the procedure among their clients: if anything, they seemed more inclined to do the opposite. Since people who became enfranchised were released from both the control and the protection of the department, officials who still tended to see the people as helpless and dependent were hesitant to impose such a measure. In general, only those who had long lived off the reserve and could show steady employment were approved for the procedure—and in fact, the vast majority of applications came from this group. When applications were made, it is clear in most cases that the impetus did not come from the agent. The agents themselves referred to enfranchisement only when dealing with an application—otherwise this element of policy was entirely absent from their correspondence. They also displayed only a vague understanding of the implications of the process. Daly, for instance, once wrote the following:

'it is expected that if an Indian lives for five years apart from the Indian mode of life, then when he gets his enfranchisement he is not likely to come back on the Department of Indian Affairs.'[55] This statement implies that an individual could apply to the department for help after renouncing Indian status. Legally, however, an enfranchisee would have no claim on the DIA after completing the process—this was the whole point of the policy.

Enfranchisement cut First Nations people off from their communities of birth and kinship and cut them loose from the DIA. Given the conditions of the time, this kind of independence could be difficult to sustain and sometimes resulted in problems for those who did become enfranchised. Although Lewis initially recommended a series of enfranchisements, he later made a point of warning certain individuals against undergoing the procedure. In 1927, for instance, he wrote, 'I have noticed that a number of the Indians who have received their enfranchisement are not making a very favourable success of life, therefore, now and in future I have to be more cautious.'[56] The cash payout from band funds provided a considerable lure, especially for those who needed money, and enfranchisement files often confirm that this was the applicant's primary motivation.[57] But the money was to compensate for the withdrawal of all future interest and treaty payments, as well as department services. The semi-annual treaty and interest payments were a significant component of many people's budgets (for those belonging to bands that received them), and losing them would have a noticeable impact, especially after the cash windfall had been spent.

Indeed, it is difficult to imagine that the benefits of enfranchisement could outweigh the disadvantages, not only economically but also socially and culturally. Enfranchisees were expected to disappear into mainstream Canadian society through absorption, but virtually no one who was visibly Aboriginal could find the ready acceptance that 'absorption' implied. Those who had already lived off-reserve for many years may have been well enough established that enfranchisement involved little loss, in some cases at least. But an ill-advised enfranchisement may have condemned some enfranchisees to a life in between the two communities, formally separated from the one and barred through exclusionary social practices from the other. Although the DIA spoke about the assumption of the rights and responsibilities of Canadian citizenship, enfranchisees lost more rights than they gained. More importantly, no change in legal status could confer a corresponding change in their racial status and the marginalized social position that stemmed from it.

Implementation of Enfranchisement

Particularly on the local level, there were few signs of consistent effort towards enfranchisement of the First Nations population. Enfranchisement does not seem to have been urged on the people at all in this period. There were enfranchisements in both agencies, consisting almost entirely of people who had lived off the reserve for a long time or even for their entire lives. These applications were routinely approved on the grounds that the individuals did not live on a reserve, earned their living like Euro-Canadians, and did not live the 'Indian mode of life'.[58] But by the early 1920s, Lewis was questioning the wisdom of the whole process, and Daly also showed little enthusiasm for it. Other agents were equally dubious. Agent Nelson Stone of the Moravian agency in southwestern Ontario witnessed the ill effects of the procedure first-hand and found the experience of one enfranchised man, a returned soldier, particularly disheartening. After the DIA foreclosed his mortgage and took away this man's farm, Stone commented sadly, 'it only goes to prove that enfranchising Indian families is a decided mistake.'[59]

Lewis's correspondence shows an evolution from an initially positive attitude towards enfranchisement to the conclusion that its impact had been negative in a number of cases. Although he continued to recommend enfranchisement applications from some individuals, he also began to warn others against undergoing the process. A search of enfranchisement records in the National Archives suggests that Lewis received about 84 applications during his tenure as agent. The vast majority of these received the agent's endorsement—but these are the files of the people Lewis considered fit for enfranchisement. He also received at least five additional inquiries between 1921 and 1927. In the early 1920s he had readily recommended a series of enfranchisements, advising against only a few applicants who he felt could not support their families adequately or who might squander their children's share of the band funds. Throughout the remainder of his tenure as agent (to 1939), he continued to recommend in favour of applicants who had always lived away from the reserves and whose work lives matched his conception of the 'white man's' way of earning a living (for the most part, this meant wage labour and reasonably steady employment). It is worth noting that the number of applications he received appears to have nearly doubled in the 1930s as compared to the 1920s—another clear indication of the inducement to enfranchise provided by the cash payout.[60]

As early as 1923, however, he was having doubts about the wisdom of enfranchisement and made his first intervention to spare a man from ill consequences. He wrote of one applicant that he could probably qualify and cease to be an Indian within the meaning of the law, but that the disadvantages far outweighed the benefits: 'The only advantage he will receive, as far as I can see, is that he will draw from the funds at the credit of the Whitefish River Band somewhere in the neighbourhood of $200, and that is a small amount for him to live on the balance of his days.'[61]

Lewis counselled at least four other people not to proceed in the 1920s. In September 1923 he advised a woman that pursuing enfranchisement would be 'an unwise act', since she would receive only $60 as her final payout and it would 'deprive you from residing on any reserve in future.'[62] This was, of course, a substantial drawback. In 1925 Lewis warned another man about the benefits he would lose through enfranchisement, since it involved 'giv[ing] up all the privileges of a treaty Indian', including trapping and residing on a reserve.[63] Clearly, Lewis was determined to ensure that his clients knew what the process entailed and that those who still required these important benefits did not lose them. By 1927 he had determined that he must be cautious because past enfranchisees were not faring well. As far as Lewis was concerned, the enfranchisement policy was problematic not because First Nations people failed to make use of it, but because it had a detrimental effect on some of those who did undergo the process.

Like Lewis, Daly had no objection to enfranchisement applications from individuals who had left the reserves and established a lifestyle that he associated with Euro-Canadians. Daly received about 43 applications during his tenure as Indian agent, the great majority of which were from individuals who lived off-reserve and far from his home.[64] In these cases Daly was content to let applications go forward and did not oppose them. He also stated at one point that he was happy to see anyone enfranchise who was ready for it.[65] But he was wary of some people's intentions, suspecting that the lure of the money was their sole motivation. In any case where he believed that an individual retained ties to the reserve community, Daly recommended against enfranchisement.

The case of a young man from Parry Island is a good example of this attitude. Daniel T. applied to become enfranchised in 1931 but was blocked in the process because Daly opposed his application. He then engaged a lawyer to write Daly on his behalf, urging that the agent reconsider. Daly's response revealed the reasoning behind his decision, which rested primarily on his conviction that Daniel T. was not ready for enfranchisement because he still lived the 'Indian mode of life'. In the agent's view, T. was seeking financial gain rather than the responsibilities of citizenship, and he was only 'anxious to get the money that his enfranchisement would give him, not the status of enfranchisement.'[66] Daly was particularly annoyed at the applicant's implied questioning of his authority when he enlisted the aid of lawyers: 'About ten minutes after he was in my office, he was down at the office of the lawyers . . . trying to rush things.'[67]

At least one other man, also from Parry Island, engaged a lawyer to help him complete his enfranchisement. Unlike Daniel T., this man, Charles S., was granted his enfranchisement.[68] But he found the process too slow and attempted to hasten it, largely because he had plans for the money he would receive.[69] In this instance, too, Daly reacted angrily to the intervention of a lawyer.[70] The fact that both resorted to lawyers is instructive. First Nations people in Ontario had been working with lawyers for at least several decades to press their land claims, but the 1920s witnessed an increasing tendency to engage lawyers for personal matters in an effort to gain greater leverage in dealing with the Indian department. Of course, this was itself an indication of acculturation, at least in the sense of greater knowledge of Euro-Canadian society. The people were identifying the levers of power within the system as a means of resistance against federal control. Most of the time, the DIA and its agents successfully resisted this sort of pressure, but the tactic was sometimes embarrassing, and it was a sign of things to come.

Daly, like Lewis, observed some individuals who regretted their choice to enfranchise. One man from Gibson band (now Wahta First Nation), for example, became enfranchised in 1925. He ran into serious financial problems in 1934 and actually requested permission from the DIA to rejoin the Gibson band. Of course, enfranchisement was not a reversible process. Daly was sympathetic, commenting, 'I can plainly see this young man has found out he has made a mistake but he did not find out until after he had spent all the money.'[71] The incident probably confirmed the agent in his misgivings about the enfranchisement process. Although his tone in refusing individuals such as Daniel T. could be belittling, and the individuals in question were frustrated at having their intentions blocked, the agent was taking his usual protective, paternalistic approach. There were losses involved in renouncing Indian status.

Given the results that Lewis had observed in his agency, Daly's hesitancy about enfranchisement may have been ultimately beneficial in economic and social terms. Lewis himself certainly concluded that some people had lost out badly by giving up their Indian status and treaty rights. The right to reside on the reserve during the Depression, for example, may have helped unsuccessful applicants for enfranchisement to weather the 1930s in a less desperate state—at least they did not have to pay rent. Similarly, the Indian department remained ultimately responsible for their welfare, and thus for issuing relief to them in times of serious need. At the same time, if their intent had been to escape the paternalistic control of their agent, they were effectively thwarted.

Gender and Sexuality

Gender and sexuality were key areas of concern within the assimilation program. Conformity to Euro-Canadian sexual norms and gender roles was a crucial indicator of 'civilization', and the agents' correspondence reflects this preoccupation. Men's observance of desirable gender roles certainly attracted attention, especially in the realm of work and economics. When it came to sexuality, there was some attention to men's transgressions, but the women received the most scrutiny. DIA records for this era are notably lacking in overt, generic condemnations of Aboriginal women based on the sexualized stereotypes constructed by Euro-Canadians. Significantly, all of the department's employees assiduously avoided use of the derogatory term 'squaw', in spite of the fact that it was widely used until at least the 1960s even by nominally sympathetic Euro-Canadians.[72] But DIA officials had their own, more subtly nuanced language that embodied gendered and racialized discourses. These discourses were also reflected in a daily practice of sexual regulation. Indeed, an obvious mode of colonialism in Indian Affairs practice and ideology lies in the assumption of the right to regulate Aboriginal women's sexuality and enforce obedience to Euro-Canadian models of correct gender expression. Indian agents had a unique ability to discipline Aboriginal women, thanks to their multiple roles in First Nations communities and their ability to exercise financial control.

The agents' perceptions about Aboriginal gender patterns were coloured by Canadian racial discourses, which constructed supposedly 'racial' traits in specifically gendered ways. Initially, the racial construct of Aboriginal women (encoded in the term 'squaw') included the notion that the women were overworked drudges within their own societies.[73] Later the image was reversed, and First Nations women were re-imagined as embodiments of idleness and other related traits such as gossiping. As Sarah Carter has demonstrated, discourses of the prairie West in the late nineteenth century emphasized the dangers posed to white society by Aboriginal women. Here they were depicted as sinister and dangerous and, in terms of their sexuality, as depraved figures who symbolized promiscuity and immorality.[74] Over time, the sexual aspect of these white constructs has arguably become the most prominent.[75] These notions were operative in DIA attitudes and practices, if carefully veiled within its written documents.

One area of ambivalence among DIA officials was the question of intermarriage between Aboriginal people and Euro-Canadians. As local DIA officials, Indian agents were located within two related but competing discourses about First Nations people. On the one hand, they were socialized into the long-standing Indian Affairs ideology in which Aboriginal people were constructed as culturally inferior to Euro-Canadians but capable of 'civilization'. This ideology prescribed a future of total assimilation into the mainstream population—a project that ultimately could only be completed through intermarriage. At the same time, the agents lived in Euro-Canadian communities that nurtured their own notions about First Nations people. The local discourses of these communities have not been closely studied as yet, but it can be assumed that, typically, ideas about Aboriginal difference played an important role in the symbolic ordering of social relations and the construction of a local white identity.[76] In both Manitowaning and Parry Sound—towns located in the immediate vicinity of sizable reserves—Aboriginal people would be perceived as irrevocably different from and inferior to Euro-Canadians, and assimilation through intermarriage would be considered undesirable. These local discourses were thus, in important ways, at odds with the constructs and goals of Indian Affairs, particularly in their rejection of racial integration. The agents were careful to underline their commitment to the department's goals in their correspondence, but as members of Euro-Canadian communities they cannot have been immune to the convictions of their peers. Some features, however, were common to both local and Indian Affairs ideologies, including the assumption of Indian agents' paternalistic responsibility for First Nations people. Their role as regulators of Aboriginal women's sexuality was an implicit part of that responsibility.

This regulatory role gave rise to the expression and enactment of particular gendered notions about Aboriginal women. Indian Affairs was pursuing a major campaign in these years to confine First Nations women's sexuality within European-style patriarchal marriage, going so far as to jail women for adherence to Aboriginal customs such as divorce and remarriage.[77] Indian agents had a unique ability to enforce Euro-Canadian moral codes against women, especially through the use of financial control. For example, they could deny women their treaty and interest payments on the grounds of real or alleged sexual transgressions; they could take away their children; and they could grant or refuse relief in time of need. Indian agents' roles in controlling the people's money and dispensing social welfare greatly magnified their ability to discipline First Nations women, especially given the poverty of the 1920s and 1930s. Moreover, a series of DIA policies and Indian Act provisions had the effect of limiting Aboriginal women's access to money and resources. Federal policy had been intended to impose a European patriarchal model of gender relations on First Nations people, enforcing female dependence on men. Although women continued to be active in a number of ways as family providers, economic changes had resulted in reduced opportunities for them to contribute to family support.

Women were punished in various ways (most of them economic) for transgressions against Christian sexual morality. An agent could refuse or cancel food rations for sexually transgressive women, since this form of aid was entirely at the agent's discretion. In theory, an agent could also continue to pay an erring wife's share of interest and annuity money to her husband, or he could withhold her own and/or her children's payments. Lewis, for instance, withheld these payments from two 'immoral' women who, he argued, spent too much time travelling (both cohabited outside marriage with Euro-Canadian men as well).[78] Thus, even mobility could be construed as a sign, if not of deviant morality, then at least of behaviour inappropriate to women's domestic role. Women might have their children taken away as well, as occurred to a woman Lewis claimed was 'living an immoral life with a Whiteman' (that is, cohabiting outside of marriage). Lewis had visited the home in order to return three daughters to Shingwauk residential school against their mother's will. Finding a fourth young girl of school age, the agent took her as well, since she 'could not be left with the mother under such undesirable living conditions.'[79]

There is more evidence about sexual policing in Lewis's records than in Daly's. This may reflect the partial character of the record base in Daly's case. But it also arose from the ongoing attempt of the Jesuits on Manitoulin Island to engage Lewis in sexual policing. Lewis seemed reluctant to perform this role, and he did not tend to act very decisively. Consequently, more correspondence was generated, as priests and sometimes band councils wrote Lewis more than once about the same unresolved cases of sexual transgression. By contrast, the few relevant recorded episodes under Daly's administration were swiftly resolved. In one case, Daly promptly expelled an adulterous pair from Parry Island, and in another he moved to prevent the wedding of a woman who was still legally married to another man.[80] Daly also compelled two young couples to get married in 1932–3 'because of the conditions' (presumably both women were pregnant).[81] Unlike Lewis, then, Daly acted on his own initiative in such matters instead of waiting for complaints from others. The interventions he chose to make were effective at least in removing the source of the trouble from his own administrative aegis.

Whereas Daly responded to transgressions against the Christian moral code by rapid, informal measures, Lewis's strategies appear somewhat different. Generally he tried to contain sexuality within marriage or, for unmarried women, within the family. When one young woman was accused of prostitution, for example, he tried to arrange for her to move back into her father's home. This measure was unsuccessful because the girl was unwilling to return there. When containment within the family failed, Lewis resorted to threats and formal punishments through the law, and occasionally through confinement to institutions. His next step in the case of the young woman accused of prostitution was to seek evidence in order to 'have her convicted and placed in some institution where she will be taken care of.'[82] But a year later she was still allegedly 'leading a prostitute life'.[83] The agent had continued his efforts to return her to her father's home and had also sent the provincial constable after her, but all to no effect. His final words on the matter again suggested the possibility of taking her to court, but there is no evidence in the records that he actually did so.[84] In this case and others like it, Lewis was hampered by distance, the remoteness of some reserves, and his own apparent diffidence at this sort of intervention. He did have at least one young woman incarcerated, first in prison and then in the Hospital for the Insane at Toronto.[85] These measures followed his attempts to return her to her grandfather's control and, when this failed, to find a nearby home for the indigent where she could be kept under close surveillance and control. In the absence of such a home in the vicinity, he had resorted to the Hospital for the Insane.[86] Although Lewis's letters suggest that he viewed his actions as means of protecting the young woman from herself, clearly they could only appear highly punitive to her.

In the interwar period, women of all races and ethnicities were subject to scrutiny regarding their sexual behaviour. Two factors made the experience of First Nations women distinctive. First, they were subject to racial stereotyping that constructed them as sexually immoral and debased. Second, they were exposed to significantly intensified levels of surveillance through the Indian agents. In the agents, First Nations women experienced a designated authority whose job was to oversee their lives and promote their transformation into imitations of the ideal middle-class Euro-Canadian woman. Thanks to the multiplicity of the agents' roles in the Indian Affairs system, these men had an exceptional capacity to regulate and discipline First Nations women. To a limited extent, Aboriginal women could insulate themselves from the dominant society and thus from that society's negative opinions of them. But most had to reckon with the Indian agent and with the very real economic and social power he could wield over them.[87]

Daly and Exhibitions

A final area to explore in this chapter concerns John Daly's involvement in bringing First Nations people to fairs and exhibitions to perform as exotic, 'Indian' curiosities. Given the emphasis in federal policy on assimilating First Nations people, how was it that an agent such as Daly could participate eagerly in exhibiting them as 'Indians' at the Canadian National Exhibition? Between 1927 and 1929, Daly collaborated with the organizers of this fair to produce exhibits of 'Indians' in 'traditional' dress, performing 'traditional' activities for the benefit of non-Aboriginal spectators. While the meaning of traditional dress is unclear (quite likely it involved aspects of typical Plains warrior attire), the traditional activities concerned were things such as building canoes and teepees. For First Nations people, participation in such events was a source of income and it also permitted them to make a free trip to Toronto and its large annual exhibition. Daly, too, may have enjoyed the opportunity to visit the big city and take in the sights, while taking credit for adding a new source of wage income to his agency.

By the 1920s, there was a long history of Aboriginal participation in various sorts of shows and spectacles. The most famous of these were the Wild West shows developed by Buffalo Bill Cody in the United States in the 1880s.[88] These shows were a runaway success and inspired countless imitations in the US and Canada. Canadian spectacles such as the western rodeos also capitalized on the

Aboriginal women selling beadwork at the 1907 Canadian National Exhibition in Toronto. First Nations people participated in Canadian exhibitions from the beginning, as both merchants and performers. Archives of Ontario, F 1075-9-0-8, Acc. 6355, S 9119.

non-Aboriginal public's interest in sensational displays of Aboriginal dancing and mock fighting. The Toronto Industrial Exhibition, forerunner to the Canadian National Exhibition, had staged wild west shows in the late nineteenth century, complete with hundreds of 'natives, whites and Mexicans' who would 're-enact old battles like Little Bighorn, raid stagecoaches peopled with tourists, and perform rodeo feats.'[89] The mere physical presence of Aboriginal people evoked interest in fairgoers everywhere and was reason enough for show organizers to seek them out. The first private exhibition in Quebec, staged in 1894, included an encampment of the local Huron as one of its attractions.[90]

DIA officials regarded these spectacles with mixed emotions. On the one hand, there was no ambiguity about their opposition to public dance performances, especially when these involved the infliction of real or simulated injuries. The department had been internationally embarrassed in 1893, when a group of Kwak-waka'wakw (Kwakiutl) from the Northwest Coast performed a series of dances at the Chicago World's Fair, including the banned Hamatsa dance.[91] This dance, which was outlawed in Canada, featured feigned acts of cannibalism and the inflic-tion of knife wounds on some of the dancers (who were willing volunteers). Fair promoters in western Canada frequently engaged local First Nations groups to perform dances in traditional costume, thrilling spectators and outraging federal officials. The department was intent on demonstrating its progress towards 'civilizing' First Nations people, and nothing more effectively contradicted its image of steady advancement than these public displays of Aboriginal culture. In many cases, the rituals performed were those that most offended the sensibilities of department officials and missionaries.

In response to these pressures, the DIA actually banned such public performances in the western provinces, first by an Indian Act ban on 'giveaway dances' in 1906, and subsequently by a broader provision introduced in 1914. The latter provision, an amendment to section 149 of the Indian Act, had a wider scope in terms of the activities banned, but weakened the penalties attached to them. Historian Keith Regular has suggested that the 1914 amendment indicates the department's acceptance of 'both the difficulty and futility of much of its effort to legislate native social and religious behaviour'.[92] The new amendment banned First Nations performances at exhibitions, stampedes, and pageants, but imposed relatively modest penalties (a fine of $25 or imprisonment, or both) for encouraging Aboriginal participation in these kinds of performances.[93] Significantly, Indian agents were empowered on behalf of the Superintendent General of Indian Affairs to authorize or forbid participation of First Nations people in specific events.

While the details provided by the available records are sketchy, it appears that people from Daly's agency participated in the CNE several years running, probably at least from 1927 to 1929. They may also have performed at an exhibition in Ottawa in 1929. Apparently both exhibitions made the initial contact with Daly, who responded with great enthusiasm and took the initiative in succeeding years to ensure that his agency provided the necessary 'Show Indians'.[94] The numbers of people involved were significant—Daly noted that in 1928, 78 people from the agency had performed at the CNE. He also claimed that the exhibit had been very popular.[95] It is likely that fairgoers were indeed curious about the land's original owners, especially since Toronto had little or no Aboriginal presence in this era. In one letter, Daly attributed his interest in the exhibit to a desire to educate: 'I know the children of today have no idea of what the Indians used to be like except by story books, and for that reason I am particularly interested in giving . . . a chance to the children of seeing the Indians as they used to be.'[96] To his superiors in the Indian department he stressed that the exhibit would be as 'picturesque and realistic' as possible and that he would work hard 'to show a contented and happy Band of Indians'.[97]

Clearly, there were a number of conditions and parties to satisfy in Daly's ritualized presentation of 'the Indian'. Those hiring the actors wanted a visually interesting and exotic display that would capture the imagination of their patrons. Indeed, they may well have wanted something a little livelier than what Daly provided—the agent was prone to emphasize his ability to control the people and make sure they 'caused no trouble'.[98] The exhibit consisted primarily of demonstrations of Aboriginal manufactures such as canoes, teepees, and beadwork—there was no dancing, singing, mock warfare, or any of the other spectacular performances associated in the public mind with 'Indians'. Indeed, it was a rather tame affair.

Daly was bound by his primary affiliation with the DIA, which paid his salary and strongly disapproved of sensational performances. In addition, the long exposure to missionaries and department officials in the Georgian Bay area had severed many First Nations people from their ancestors' rituals and driven the remaining practitioners underground. Unlike the nations of the West, many of them had little remaining knowledge of indigenous dances or costumes.

The exhibits Daly designed were ritualized presentations of the Aboriginal 'Other' in a form the department could sanction. In these exhibits, the 'real Indian' was relegated to the past; he was an exotic but non-threatening figure, acted out by his domesticated descendants. Daly's contrived image of 'what the Indians used to be like'—designed allegedly with children in mind—was at best a faint, sad echo of the real people. All that was displayed were a few tools that had long ago been made emblematic of 'the Indian', without any suggestion of spirituality, ritual, or belief system. In fact, the display was stripped of cultural meaning, leaving nothing but a few artifacts. Although the people were supposed to be dressed like 'Indians', it is highly unlikely that they wore the clothing or hairstyles of the earlier Ojibway or Odawa—they were almost certainly costumed as Plains people, as Lakota or Blackfoot. They were also devoid of context, especially the political context of dispossession and treaty violation. It was a reflection of an image created and managed by whites, and the Aboriginal actors playing their parts were equally carefully controlled and managed. Daly remarked that he would need to be 'on the job most of the time' at the fair, because otherwise 'some of them would get out' and possibly even miss a performance. The entire affair was scheduled without any input from the people themselves, who merely performed the image created by their overseer and the larger society of which he was a part.

Daly's account of the exhibit and his reasoning in producing it further underscore the image of First Nations people that the department wished to present. The only elements of their past that were permitted to be on display were mundane items of everyday use that did not convey anything about the values and world view of the people. Nothing about their relations with Euro-Canadians or government entered the picture either. In other contexts, the department took pains to highlight the civilizing process and its own role as dispenser of the benefits of civilization. But for a romantic like Daly, there had to be a sentimental reminder of old times, an effort to produce a picture of a lost or vanishing culture: 'what the Indians used to be like'. There was nothing controversial and not even much to lament, given the thinness of the portrait produced. In its depiction of the past, the exhibit must have appeared as evidence of a culture reduced to fragments, serving only to confirm the Anishinabek's irrevocable abandonment of the ways of their ancestors. The exhibit was essentially about nothing more than technology, demonstrating the particular technologies that were familiar to Euro-Canadians and the picturesque quaintness of Aboriginal manufactures. The underlying message carried a moral about the superiority of white technology and the inexorable disappearance of the alien culture whose forebears had given way to the superior British 'race'. There was nothing here to which the department could object.

Conclusion

This chapter has examined some important aspects of the implementation of the assimilation policy. From today's perspective, it is obvious that assimilation was largely a failure. The assimilation policy resulted neither in the complete destruction of Aboriginal cultures nor in the integration of Aboriginal people into the mainstream of Canadian society. It is true that federal policy must bear a large part of the blame for language loss and the suppression of Aboriginal spirituality, although the churches also played a substantial role. Yet this generally broad and vague policy was not successful in fully remaking First Nations people in the image of Euro-Canadians. As for the objective of integration or absorption, the real barrier to this plan was the racial prejudice nurtured by the general public and mirrored by DIA officials. Many First Nations people rejected the concept of integration anyway, but it remained impossible as long as the majority of Euro-Canadians were unwilling to accept them as equals, as fellow citizens, co-workers, neighbours, and friends, or, for that matter, as potential marriage partners.

The DIA had no hope of achieving full assimilation in the climate of opinion that prevailed in the 1920s and 1930s. At the same time, it tended to be half-hearted even in the pursuit of the limited goals it had set itself within the context of assimilation policy. There was a widespread notion that 'civilization' would occur on its own without active intervention, that 'civilization' automatically overcame 'savagery' and the First Nations would melt away before the advance of the supposedly superior culture. Officials did try to hasten this process in some ways, particularly through subjecting Aboriginal children to schools that demeaned their cultures and taught the superiority of Euro-Canadians. Faced with the determination of many First Nations people to keep their cultural traditions alive, Indian Affairs obtained federal legislation banning certain key institutions and ceremonies. There is no question that these actions involved coercion and direct intervention. But in the day-to-day practice of Indian agents in Ontario, there is little evidence of attempts to integrate Aboriginal people into the local Euro-Canadian communities. These agents considered Aboriginal people to be fundamentally different from Euro-Canadians. Alongside the obligatory rhetoric of 'improvement' stood the constant references to the persistence of 'Indianness' and the 'Indian mode of life'. Although most officials deplored the traits they considered to be typically 'Indian', they in fact did little to replace them with the traits they attributed to 'the white man'.

Probably the most noteworthy absence in the correspondence examined here is enfranchisement. Although enfranchising every person of Indian status was the official goal of the DIA, Indian agents practically never made reference to this aim. The vast majority of their communications with headquarters dealt with routine matters that, if anything, often underlined the distance between the present reality and the future envisioned by the enfranchisement policy. They also demonstrated some hesitation about the policy. Although Lewis at first supported the concept of enfranchisement, his experience of the results led him to issue warnings to some individuals about the rights they would lose in the process. The policy could only have had positive outcomes for First Nations people if they had

had real opportunities within mainstream society. Acceptance had to come before assimilation, and it was still a long way off. In the meantime, Indian agents shared the racial prejudices of the dominant society and the assumption that most First Nations people were not yet fit to join that society. They therefore acted on the premise that federal tutelage would and should continue for the foreseeable future.

Conclusion

'. . . all the difficult times I had with the white people did not make me condemn them. I just figured I had to face whatever came along and accept how we were going to be used by the white man. I made no fuss about it for the longest time, I just took it all. Little did I know there were some good people in this world besides those who put me down and kept me low through so much of the time. We always came last in the eyes of many.'[1]

This study has examined the experiences of First Nations people with the Indian agent system during the 1920s and 1930s. Such an inquiry offers insight into the sense of grievance expressed by so many Aboriginal people today, a sense of grievance aimed particularly at the federal government. In administering the lives of First Nations people, the government was often high-handed and controlling. It paid inadequate attention to the protection of treaty rights and was excessively concerned with maintaining control over the people. The paternalistic approach taken by the Indian agents meant that they offered some limited assistance to their clients and played a role as providers of social services. At the same time, they worked hard to silence critics of the system and to prevent political organizing intended to address treaty violations and assert the right of self-determination.

The Indian department and its agents wielded tremendous power over Aboriginal people due to a combination of factors. The Indian Act was designed to give the department control, particularly over Aboriginal resources and political affairs, and it also placed First Nations people under legal disabilities that restricted their economic options. Indian policy contributed to Aboriginal poverty and poor education, crucial factors in First Nations people's social marginalization. In addition, the complexities and discriminatory attitudes of Euro-Canadian society created a need for mediation between First Nations and the dominant society, a need that was often filled by Indian agents. The result of all these factors was that the Indian agent assumed a multiplicity of roles: he exercised direct control over the community while simultaneously acting as a social worker, credit and loan officer, and intermediary with non-Native society. This powerful combination of roles helped to insinuate the DIA into the fabric of First Nations communities and allowed the department to tighten its grasp over the people.

The operation of department policy hampered the development of Aboriginal communities and at the same time helped to alleviate the symptoms of policy. For instance, the DIA failed to uphold treaty rights to harvest fish, rights that might have supplied these communities with lucrative economic opportunities. Yet it mediated protest about lost rights by ensuring access to small-scale, subsistence fishing on the basis of need. The outcome was a wholesale transfer of the fish resource to non-Aboriginal commercial interests and the institutionalization of Aboriginal exclusion from the industry. Similarly, the bands never received substantial benefits from their trust funds, even though some had considerable sums at their credit. The department parcelled out the funds in thimblefuls, mainly in relief issues, small loans, and semi-annual interest payments. While these monies thus did not improve the overall economic position of individual band members, they served as an indispensable supplement to meagre cash incomes. The department's financial interventions were minimalist, but even its puny contributions were significant to a marginalized people. By the 1920s and 1930s, both First Nations people and department officials were caught in the pitiless logic of ongoing paternalism: the system wasn't working, and yet it was required to deal with the problems it had produced.

Much of the time, Indian Affairs officials were absorbed in the petty details of administration, with little introspection about the overall direction of their activities. The failures of Indian policy were evident to department head Duncan Campbell Scott, but his subordinates did not philosophize about them. In part, this was a consequence of the strict hierarchical nature of administration, which reserved planning and policy-making for the upper echelons of the department. It was not until after World War II that Indian policy was redesigned to take into account the reality that First Nations people had made the reserves into permanent geographical and cultural bases. One reason it took so long to adjust was that the DIA's expectations for Aboriginal standards of living were so low, and thus officials apparently saw no pressing need for change. Choices about policy implementation were informed by a set of stereotypes about Aboriginal character and the 'Indian mode of life' that assumed that most First Nations people would live at the level of mere subsistence.

Aboriginal people who mounted political agitation and strove for greater autonomy faced serious obstacles in the 1920s and 1930s. Language and education were key factors. In order to make progress in voicing their grievances, knowledge of English and of the Euro-Canadian political system were crucial, but too few people possessed these skills. The vast majority had learned an Aboriginal language as their mother tongue. Some spoke only Aboriginal languages, while others, especially of the younger generation, spoke English but with varying degrees of proficiency. Some chiefs, such as John Manitowaba, spoke English poorly and could not read or write it. The rudimentary education provided by the Indian department was not designed to teach the skills needed for political organizing. It is thus no surprise that some of the strongest leadership in the period came from returned soldiers, who had developed much better language skills and had also witnessed the vast gulf between the standards of living enjoyed by their own people and those of the mainstream population. Recognition of their own disadvantages, combined with the connections some were able to make with Euro-Canadians, fuelled the challenges these men offered to the Indian Affairs system.

Band councils often beckoned those pushing for change, since they appeared as potential platforms for their campaigns. Yet here again, the barriers were substantial. Given DIA practice and the provisions of the Indian Act, band councils could only remain ineffective tools of dissent. The councils had extremely limited powers and were subject to the department's absolute veto power. Department officials tightly controlled their access to their own band funds and worked to ensure that 'troublemakers' were contained or even deposed. Chiefs often had little authority with their own people, thanks to internal divisions of religion and band membership, and also because they were perceived as servants of the DIA. The system had successfully undermined traditional leadership functions and authority, limiting the ability of elected leaders to unite their own people or speak effectively on their behalf. One consequence was that chiefs in some communities, such as Parry Island, rarely served for more than one three-year term.[2] The frequent changes of leadership further reinforced the limited influence associated with the chief's office. Thus, instead of acting as counterweights to the Indian agent and the DIA, the councils tended to limit their activities to voting small amounts of money from band funds for relief and loans, as well as passing regulations about minor matters such as school truancy.

There were efforts to unite across bands and nations to pressure the Canadian government on specific issues. Francis Pegahmagabow, as we saw, corresponded with other chiefs in his region, as well as with F.O. Loft, founder of the League of Indians, in an effort to achieve political co-operation. Several chiefs were involved at various times in attempts to remove John Daly as Indian agent. Certain Parry Islanders also reacted to adverse changes in government policy, such as the reinstatement in 1933 of compulsory enfranchisement in the Indian Act.[3] But the time was not ripe for political successes, and agitators were unable to make a substantial impact. Various avenues were available for the agent to silence or punish Aboriginal detractors. Often it was equally effective to ignore them. Hierarchical thinking about race, which presupposed the inferiority of First Nations people to Euro-Canadians, was almost universally embraced among Canadians of European descent. Mainstream Canadians accepted the principle that First Nations people should be administered by government and subject to paternalistic control. Thus, they generally were not available to support Aboriginal attempts to work towards self-determination. Finally, the financial resources necessary for large-scale political organizing were simply not available to Aboriginal people. The DIA was reluctant to permit the use of band funds for travel to meetings, and in the 1930s it ceased to approve these expenditures. The economic crisis, in fact, provided a convenient pretext for closing off access to band funds for organizing efforts. Since the

DIA had banned any soliciting of contributions from First Nations people, there was no other source of money for these purposes.

Yet this era's organizing efforts were not fruitless in a larger sense. They are indicative of the surviving tradition of Aboriginal self-determination and the sustained memory of treaty obligations. They served to create substantial records of important grievances, which can now be traced in DIA records and used to bolster Aboriginal claims cases. They also kept alive band traditions of issues that had never been resolved—a prime example is the issue of the islands in Georgian Bay, which all the Robinson Huron Treaty signatories agree they never intended to surrender. This issue is still being pressed on the government today. The organizing attempts of the interwar era were part of a long campaign to transform band councils into bodies for Aboriginal self-government, a campaign that began to bear fruit in the 1960s when members of these same councils moved successfully to abolish the Indian agents. And they overtly expressed the spirit of independence that most First Nations people evidenced more quietly through their non-compliance with assimilation policies. Thus, it is only partially true to assert that the wave of Aboriginal mobilizing after World War II arose from external factors such as the international movement for decolonization, the awakened militancy of oppressed peoples, and a stronger sense of entitlement among First Nations people due to their contribution to the war effort. Although those factors were important, the post-war resurgence also had its roots in a less publicized struggle that occurred in the pre-war period. The activists of the 1940s and 1950s picked up where their predecessors had left off.

This study has also highlighted the importance of character and attitudes as factors in the implementation of federal policy by Indian agents. Although Robert Lewis and John Daly both accepted the basic premises of Indian policy, they revealed different emphases in their work, which powerfully affected the treatment their clients could expect from them. Lewis favoured liberal individualism in his work, largely abstaining from use of his powers to control band councils. This meant that department control must have been felt in a limited way in the agency under his administration. On the other hand, Lewis was also reluctant to offer much assistance. Although he supplied paternalistic care to the old, the orphaned, and sometimes the sick, his individualistic bias made him determined to enforce self-sufficiency, particularly on men. In the Depression of the 1930s, he was significantly less active than Daly in providing aid in the form of jobs, rations, and supplies. Daly, by contrast, was a confirmed paternalist, comfortable with assuming responsibility for the welfare of the people as a whole and also with exercising power over them. Daly waged an ongoing battle to silence his opponents and enforce the dependent, largely powerless position of band councils. He worked vigorously to counter the organizing efforts of those who wanted to press for treaty rights or who sought to have him replaced as Indian agent. At the same time, he was more generous with relief, pushing the department to increase its miserly rates and helping the able-bodied unemployed more actively during the Depression. His enforcement of roadwork took on political dimensions, as he used it to discipline political challengers, but this work also relieved the drain on band funds and permitted the dignity of working for one's income.

The philosophical distinction between liberal individualism and paternalism does not explain all the differences between the two men. Each showed care and concern for his clients in certain ways, and in other ways both agents revealed themselves to be lacking in sympathy. Personality and individual experiences played a role. Daly, for example, seems to have based his opposition to higher education for his clients on his experiences with Emily Donald, who resisted his efforts to make her life choices for her. He ended up arguing that higher education was wasted on First Nations people, an attitude that affected other young people who had hoped for careers. Lewis, on the other hand, showed real enthusiasm for higher education on a number of occasions and worked to make secondary education available at Wikwemikong because the parents wanted it for their children. On the other hand, while Daly argued for special harvesting rights based on prior occupation of the country, Lewis was no defender of Aboriginal rights. Despite the history of commercial fishing among the First Nations on Manitoulin Island, Lewis argued only for a strictly constrained right of small-scale fishing for personal consumption without licences.

One of the most striking areas of contradiction in Indian Affairs policy relates to the goal of assimilation. Officially, this was the department's primary objective. Duncan Campbell Scott, Deputy Superintendent General of Indian Affairs throughout much of this period, was well-known for his zealous promotion of assimilation. Yet the Indian agents in the field rarely made reference to the project except when writing about schools. They seemed, in fact, to harbour grave doubts about the likelihood of making much progress in this area. The agents were also doubtful about the enfranchisement process, perceiving the people to be, in many cases, unprepared for the management of their own lives. In practice, paternalism took precedence over the desire to further enfranchisement. Of course, it is also true that an Indian agent's job was predicated on the presumed inability of First Nations people to run their own affairs—he had to maintain this belief to justify his own position.

Ultimately, what becomes clear is that many officials seemed to have abandoned the hope of achieving assimilation in the near future, although they still had to pay lip service to the policy. In its public pronouncements, the department itself had retreated to the position of promoting self-support *on the reserves*. This meant abandoning the notion of dissolving the reserves, as well as the goal of integrating Aboriginal people into the mainstream community. Here was a tacit acknowledgement of Aboriginal people's rejection of assimilation, and perhaps also of non-Aboriginal people's equally obvious reluctance to welcome First Nations people into their communities. It was these sorts of contradictions that led department officials to recognize the need for a policy overhaul from the 1930s on. Only the successive national crises of the Depression and World War II delayed this overhaul until 1946, when a Joint Committee of the Senate and the House of Commons was appointed to consider how best to reshape federal policy.

Lastly, the records investigated in this study permit insights into how First Nations people sought to modify policy to suit their interests and even to turn federal policies to their own advantage. Their goals were not always attainable. For example, endeavours to turn band councils into instruments of self-determination were consistently thwarted, since they ran counter to the resolve of department officials to maintain control. Other campaigns were more productive. One area in which they achieved some success was the provision of social services. Faced with the decline of indigenous leadership and kin networks, the Anishinabek worked to replace their old support systems by engaging Indian agents as resource persons. They approached agents for dispute mediation and financial aid, and to obtain care for the elderly, the sick, the orphaned, and the disabled. Although these sorts of aid were provided at a minimal level and often grudgingly, the people nevertheless were able to use government paternalism in pursuit of certain kinds of goals.

When it came to assistance, both sides agreed that the government had certain obligations, but there was an ongoing struggle over how those obligations would be defined and, more importantly, by whom. The assistance offered by the DIA more or less satisfied the provisions of treaties and the Indian Act, both of which promised government aid in time of need. But there was a constant struggle over levels of assistance and over who made the decisions. The department was always battling to hold expenditures to a minimum, while First Nations people considered its contributions thoroughly inadequate and in violation of treaty promises. Assistance was also a double-edged sword. In fulfilling its role as provider of aid, the department was simultaneously able to enhance its power position and perhaps even to legitimize its presence in Aboriginal communities. Many Aboriginal people may have abstained from criticism of the agent in recognition of the fact that he was often the only person to whom they could turn for help. In its multiple roles, the department was an omnipresent factor in the people's lives, and the agent, in particular, personified the tangible, active presence of government in Aboriginal lives. Significantly, what is remembered today is not the ways in which agents supplied social services, but rather the perception that they often denied aid to those who needed it. What is remembered is their exercise of power and their failure to use it to the advantage of the people.

One may well ask how much has changed since the days of Lewis and Daly, D.C. Scott and J.D. McLean. The Indian agents are gone, phased out in the 1960s at the instigation of First Nations people themselves. The Indian Affairs Branch then moved to a system of District Supervisors who covered larger administrative areas and to whom the band councils reported. By the 1980s, at least some of these individuals were Aboriginal,[4] but they were still bureaucrats in the employ of Indian Affairs. In the present day, band councils still spend considerable time negotiating with government officials, and most have few sources of revenue outside of federal transfer payments. They continue to be subject to the veto power of the current incarnation of the DIA, now called Indian and Northern Affairs Canada. The federal government still holds the purse strings for their band funds. Policy is still defined by Indian Affairs officials and shaped by the dictates of the Indian Act, which remains a powerful force affecting First Nations destinies. A battle is now underway, spearheaded by the Assembly of First Nations, to defeat the federal government's latest effort to refashion First Nations governments, the proposed First

Nations Governance Act. This Act would finally remove the federal veto over band council resolutions, but in other ways it is very much a colonial document, driven by the federal government's agenda and owing much of its logic to old, colonial thinking. Although it would allow First Nations some latitude to design their own forms of government, it would limit them to municipal powers, a restriction many find unacceptable. In any event, the main purpose of the proposed Act is simply to enforce greater financial accountability on First Nations governments.

Another set of ongoing issues pertains to land, the fulfillment of treaties, and harvesting rights—the same issues that Aboriginal leaders were raising unsuccessfully in the interwar period. The federal government finally established a process for the resolution of land claims in 1974, when it opened the Office of Native Claims within the Department of Indian Affairs and Northern Development. That office (now divided into Comprehensive and Specific Claims)[5] has expanded dramatically in the ensuing years and is swamped with hundreds of claims from all over the country. But the process is nearly as unsatisfactory to First Nations people as the DIA's old practice of simply denying any wrongdoing. Most obviously, it is a process in which the government investigates itself and decides whether or not it fulfilled what it deems to be its 'lawful obligations'. Despite long efforts by First Nations people to have claims submitted to impartial third parties, the Specific Claims and Comprehensive Claims branches of Indian Affairs retain a virtual monopoly over decisions. Claims take an unacceptably long time to resolve—up to 1980, for example, only eight specific claims had been settled of the 250 that had been submitted.[6] When claims are rejected (and many are), the only other recourse is to the courts, which involves further endless delays and enormous expense. Canadian courts recognize only the laws made by the colonizers and frequently dismiss oral history—the main Aboriginal form of record-keeping—as invalid evidence for the determination of land claims.[7] The most notorious instance of a judge dismissing Aboriginal evidence occurred in the 1990 decision of Justice Allan McEachern in *Delgamuukw v. British Columbia*, but this is not an isolated case: many other judges have been similarly dismissive of oral testimony or have even ruled it inadmissible as evidence. Moreover, litigation can lead to the establishment of unfavourable precedents for all other First Nations in case of a negative judgement.

The First Nations whose predecessors belonged to the Manitowaning and Parry Sound agencies are involved in numerous specific claims, including some relating to Georgian Bay islands. They are also parties to litigation involving lands. As for hunting and fishing rights, it took a series of court cases initiated by First Nations people to force governments to take treaty harvesting rights seriously. These rights are still highly contested and groups such as the Saugeen First Nation, close neighbours of the Georgian Bay communities profiled in this book,[8] have continued to battle in the courts to regain the commercial fishing rights their pre-treaty ancestors could take for granted (that is, to fish commercially without paying for a licence). To compound the difficulty, the provinces play a key role in any negotiations over harvesting rights, and for the most part, provincial governments have been singularly reluctant to recognize Aboriginal rights. Thus First Nations people trying to regain access to resources often find unsympathetic bargainers on the other side of the table.

All in all, it is not unfair to characterize the systems with which First Nations people currently deal as slightly modernized versions of the old colonial DIA system. Government control is still ever-present and Indian Affairs administrators have a powerful influence over Aboriginal lives. Those administrators know less about individual First Nations people than did men like Lewis and Daly, who spent years interacting directly with the people. In the 1920s and 1930s, the Indian agents and their superiors worked for years in the same branch of the department and represented a kind of continuity and sense of history that are now almost completely absent. In place of their essentially fossilized approach, First Nations people now confront the opposite problem, Indian Affairs employees who switch jobs often in pursuit of advancement.[9] For First Nations people, this means frequent changes in the personnel they deal with and concurrent loss of time and momentum as new employees absorb the background information they need for the job. Similarly, the minister responsible for the Indian and Northern Affairs portfolio changes with predictable regularity, most of them staying too briefly to attain a sound grasp of the issues or to undertake major initiatives before moving on to another cabinet post. These factors militate against constructive change. The system remains rigid and bureaucratic, and it is more expensive than ever; yet much of the money that goes into the Indian Affairs budget does not reach First Nations people.

In spite of it all, the people of southern Ontario have made a largely successful adaptation to the world that has grown around them since the newcomers arrived.[10] The people continue to work actively to preserve their treaty and Aboriginal rights while maintaining the full rights of Canadian citizenship that were gained in 1960. But they are still forced to cope with the Indian Act, an outdated piece of legislation that applies only to them and that retains many of its nineteenth-century provisions. They are still subject to a large, separate bureaucracy premised on the colonial notion that they cannot administer their own affairs. The Indian Affairs system still does not work well for them, and it has come to represent all that is most oppressive about the history of colonization in this country. This book serves to highlight the flawed assumptions inherent in paternalism and in the racial hierarchy that operated well past the interwar period. The problems it has brought to light may help guide us all in working to dismantle colonialism in Canada.

Appendix: Treaties

Text of the Bond Head Treaty (1836)[1]

(Seal of Sir F.B. Head, and the Wampum.)
My Children,
Seventy Snow Seasons have now passed away since we met in Council at the Crooked Place (Niagara), at which Time and Place your Great Father the King and the Indians of North America tied their hands together by the Wampum of Friendship.

Since that Period various Circumstances have occurred to separate from your Great Father many of his Red Children, and as an unavoidable Increase of White population, as well as the Progress of Cultivation, have had the natural Effect of impoverishing your Hunting Grounds, it has become necessary that new Arrangements should be entered into for the Purpose of protecting you from the Encroachments of the whites.

In all Parts of the World Farmers seek for uncultivated Land as eagerly as you my Red Children hunt in your great Forest for Game. If you would cultivate your Land it would then be considered your own Property in the same way as your Dogs are considered among yourselves to belong to those who have reared them; but uncultivated Land is like wild Animals, and your Great Father, who has hitherto protected you, has now great Difficulty in securing it for you from the Whites, who are hunting to cultivate it.

Under these Circumstances I have been obliged to consider what is best to be done for the Red Children of the Forest, and I now tell you my Thoughts.

It appears that these Islands, in which we are now assembled in Council, are, as well as all those on the North Shore of Lake Huron, alike claimed by the English, the Ottawa, and the Chippawas.

I consider, that from their Facilities, and from their being surrounded by innumerable Fishing Islands, they might be made a most desirable Place of Residence for many Indians who wish to be civilized as well as to be totally separated from the Whites; and I now tell you that your Great Father will withdraw his Claim to these Islands, and allow them to be applied for that Purpose.

Are you therefore, the Ottawa and Chippawas, willing to relinquish your respective Claims to these Islands, and make them the Property (under your Great Father's Control) of all Indians who he shall allow to reside on them? If so, affix your Marks to this my Proposal.

(Signed) F.B. Head

(Signed)

J.B. ASSEKINACK	MOSUWEKO
MOKOMMINOCK	KEWUCKANCE
WAWARPHACK	SHAWENAUSAWAY
KIMOWM	ESPANIOLE
KITCHEMOKOMOU	SNAKE
PEGA ATA WICH	PANTAUSEWAY
PAIMAUSIGAI	PARMAUGUMESHCUM
NAIMAWMUTTEBE	WAGAUMAUGUIN

Manatowaning,
9th August
1836.

Text of the Robinson Huron Treaty, No. 61 (1850)[2]

Copy of the Robinson Treaty Made in the Year 1850 with the Ojibbewa Indians of Lake Huron Conveying Certain Lands to the Crown

THIS AGREEMENT, made and entered into this ninth day of September, in the year of our Lord one thousand eight hundred and fifty, at Sault Ste. Marie, in the Province of Canada, between the Honorable WILLIAM BENJAMIN ROBINSON, of the one part, on behalf of HER MAJESTY THE QUEEN, and SHINGUACOUSE, NEBENAIGOCHING, KEOKOUSE, MISHEQUONGA, TAGAWININI, SHABOKISHICK, DOKIS, PONEKEOSH, WINDAWTEGOWININI, SHAWENAKESHICK, NAMASSIN, NAOQUAGABO, WABAKEKIK, KITCHEPOSSIGUN, PAPASAINSE, WAGEMAKI, PAMEQUONAISHEUNG, Chiefs; and JOHN BELL, PAQWATCHININI, MASHEKYASH, IDOWEKESIS, WAQUACOMICK, OCHEEK, METIGOMIN, WATACHEWANA, MINWAWAPENASSE, SHENAOQUOM, ONINGEGUN, PANAISSY, PAPASAINSE, ASHEWASEGA, KAGESHEWAWETUNG, SHAWONEBIN; and also Chief MAISQUASO (also Chiefs MUCKATA, MISHOQUET, and MEKIS), and MISHOQUETTO and ASA WASWANAY and PAWISS, principal men of the OJIBEWA INDIANS, inhabiting and claiming the Eastern and Northern Shores of Lake Huron, from Penetanguishine to Sault Ste. Maire, and thence to Batchewanaung Bay, on the Northern Shore of Lake Superior; together with the Islands in the said Lakes, opposite to the Shores thereof, and inland to the Height of land which separates the Territory covered by the charter of the Honorable Hudson Bay Company from Canada; as well as all unconceded lands within the limits of Canada West to which they have any just claim, of the other part, witnesseth:

THAT for, and in consideration of the sum of two thousand pounds of good and lawful money of Upper Canada, to them in hand paid, and for the further perpetual annuity of six hundred pounds of like money, the same to be paid and delivered to the said Chiefs and their Tribes at a convenient season of each year, of which due notice will be given, at such places as may be appointed for that purpose, they the said Chiefs and Principal men, on behalf of their respective Tribes or Bands, do hereby fully, freely, and voluntarily surrender, cede, grant, and convey unto Her Majesty, her heirs and successors for ever, all their right, title, and interest to, and in the whole of, the territory above described, save and except the reservations set forth in the schedule hereunto annexed; which reservations shall be held and occupied by the said Chiefs and their Tribes in common, for their own use and benefit.

And should the said Chiefs and their respective Tribes at any time desire to dispose of any part of such reservations, or of any mineral or other valuable productions thereon, the same will be sold or leased at their request by the Superintendent-General of Indian Affairs for the time being, or other officer having authority so to do, for their sole benefit, and to the best advantage.

And the said William Benjamin Robinson of the first part, on behalf of Her Majesty and the Government of this Province, hereby promises and agrees to make, or cause to be made, the payments as before mentioned; and further to allow the said Chiefs and their Tribes the full and free privilege to hunt over the Territory now ceded by them, and to fish in the waters thereof, as they have heretofore been in the habit of doing; saving and excepting such portions of the said Territory as may from time to time be sold or leased to individuals or companies of individuals, and occupied by them with the consent of the Provincial Government.

The parties of the second part further promise and agree that they will not sell, lease, or otherwise dispose of any portion of their Reservations without the consent of the Superintendent-General of Indian Affairs, or other officer of like authority, being first had and obtained. Nor will they at any time hinder or prevent persons from exploring or searching for minerals, or other valuable productions, in any part of the Territory hereby ceded to Her Majesty, as before mentioned. The parties of the second part also agree, that in case the Government of this Province should before the date of this agreement have sold, or bargained to sell, any mining locations, or other property, on the portions of the Territory hereby reserved for their use; then and in that case such sale, or promise of sale, shall be perfected by the Government, if the parties claiming it shall have fulfilled all the conditions upon which such locations were made, and the amount accruing therefrom shall be paid to the Tribe to whom the Reservation belongs.

The said William Benjamin Robinson, on behalf of Her Majesty, who desires to deal liberally and justly with all her subjects, further promises and agrees, that should the Territory hereby ceded by the parties of the second part at any future period produce such an amount as will enable the Government of this Province, without incurring loss, to increase the annuity hereby secured to them, then and in that case the same shall be augmented from time to time, provided that the amount paid to each individual shall not exceed the sum of one pound Provincial Currency in any one year, or such further sum as Her Majesty may be graciously pleased to order; and provided further that the number of Indians entitled to the benefit of this treaty shall amount to two-thirds of their present number, which is fourteen hundred and twenty-two, to entitle them to claim the full benefit thereof. And should they not at any future period amount to two-thirds of fourteen hundred and twenty-two, then the said annuity shall be diminished in proportion to their actual numbers.

The said William Benjamin Robinson of the first part further agrees, on the part of Her Majesty and the Government of this Province, that in consequence of the Indians inhabiting French River and Lake Nipissing having become parties to this treaty, the further sum of one hundred and sixty pounds Provincial Currency shall be paid in addition to the two thousand pounds above mentioned. Schedule of Reservations made by the above-named subscribing Chiefs and Principal Men.

FIRST—Pamequonaishcung and his Band, a tract of land to commence seven miles, from the mouth of the River Maganetawang, and extending six miles east and west by three miles north.

SECOND—Wagemake and his Band, a tract of land to commence at a place called Nekickshegeshing, six miles from east to west, by three miles in depth.

THIRD—Kitcheposkissegan (by Papasainse), from Point Grondine westward, six miles inland, by two miles in front, so as to include the small Lake Nessinassung a tract for themselves and their Bands.

FOURTH—Wabakekik, three miles front, near Shebawenaning, by five miles inland, for himself and Band.

FIFTH—Namassin and Naoquagabo and their Bands, a tract of land commencing near Lacloche, at the Hudson Bay Company's boundary; thence westerly to the mouth of Spanish River; then four miles up the south bank of said river, and across to the place of beginning.

SIXTH—Shawenakishick and his Band, a tract of land now occupied by them, and contained between two rivers, called Whitefish River, and Wanabitaseke, seven miles inland.

SEVENTH—Windawtegawinini and his Band, the Peninsula east of Serpent River, and formed by it, now occupied by them.

EIGHTH—Ponekeosh and his Band, the land contained between the River Mississaga and the River Penebewabecong, up to the first rapids.

NINTH—Dokis and his Band, three miles square at Wanabeyakokaun, near Lake Nipissing and the island near the Fall of Okickandawt.

TENTH—Shabokishick and his Band, from their present planting grounds on Lake Nipissing to the Hudson Bay Company's post, six miles in depth.

ELEVENTH—Tagawinini and his Band, two miles square at Wanabitibing, a place about forty miles inland, near Lake Nipissing.

TWELFTH—Keokouse and his Band, four miles front from Thessalon River eastward, by four miles inland.

THIRTEENTH—Mishequanga and his Band, two miles on the lake shore east and west of Ogawaminang, by one mile inland.

FOURTEENTH—For Shinguacouse and his Band, a tract of land extending from Maskinongé Bay, inclusive, to Partridge Point, above Garden River on the front, and inland ten miles, throughout the whole distance; and also Squirrel Island.

FIFTEENTH—For Nebenaigoching and his Band, a tract of land extending from Wanabekineyunnung west of Gros Cap to the boundary of the lands ceded by the Chiefs of Lake Superior, and inland ten miles throughout the whole distance, including Batchewanaung Bay; and also the small island at Sault Ste. Marie used by them as a fishing station.

SIXTEENTH—For Chief Mekis and his Band, residing at Wasaquesing (Sandy Island), a tract of land at a place on the main shore opposite the Island; being the place now occupied by them for residence and cultivation, four miles square.

SEVENTEENTH—For Chief Muckatamishaquet and his Band, a tract of land on the east side of the River Naishconteong, near Pointe aux Barils, three miles square; and also a small tract in Washauwenega Bay—now occupied by a part of the Band—three miles square.

(Signed)	W.B. ROBINSON	MEKIS	ASA WASWANAY
	SHINGUACOUSE	MAISQUASO	PAWISS
	NEBENAIGOCHING	NAOQUAGABO	OCHEEK
	KEOKOUSE	WABAKEKIK	METIGOMIN
	MISHEQUONGA	KITCHEPOSSIGUN	WATACHEWANA
	TAGAWININI	(by PAPASAINSE)	MINWAWAPENASSE
	SHABOKISHICK	WAGEMAKI	SHENAOQUOM
	DOKIS	PAMEQUONAISHEUNG	ONINGEGUN
	PONEKEOSH	JOHN BELL	PANAISSY
	WINDAWTEGOWININI	PAQWATCHININI	PAPASAINSE
	SHAWENAKESHICK	MASHEKYASH	ASHEWASEGA
	NAMASSIN	IDOWEKESIS	KAGESHEWAWETUNG
	MUCKATA	WAQUACOMICK	(by BABONEUNG)
	MISHOQUET	MISHOQUETTO	SHAWONEBIN

SIGNED, SEALED, AND DELIVERED AT SAULT STE. MARIE, THE DAY AND YEAR FIRST ABOVE WRITTEN, IN PRESENCE OF—

ASHLEY P. COOPER	ALLAN MACDONELL	J.B. ASSIGINACK
GEORGE IRONSIDE	GEO. JOHNSTON	J.W. KEATING
F.W. BALFOUR	LOUIS CADOTT	JOS. WILSON

Witness to signatures of Muckata Mishoquet, Mekis, Mishoquetto, Asa Waswanay, and Pawiss—

T.G. ANDERSON
W.B. HAMILTON
W. SIMPSON
ALFRED A. THOMPSON

Text of the Manitoulin Island Treaty, No. 94 (1862)[3]

Articles of agreement and convention made and concluded at Manitowaning or the Great Manitoulin Island in the Province of Canada, the sixth day of October, Anno Domini, 1862, between the Hon. William McDougall, Superintendent General of Indian Affairs, and William Spragge, Esq., Deputy Superintendent of Indian Affairs, on the part of the Crown and government of said Province, of the first part, and Mai-she-quong-gai, Okemah-be-ness, J.B. Assiginack, Benjamin Assiginock, Nai-be-ness-me, She-ne-tah-guw, George Ah-be-tos-o-mai, Paim-o-quo-naish-gung, Abence, Tai-bose-gai, A-to-nish-cosh, Nai-wau-dai-ge-zhik, Wau-kau-o-say, Keesh-kewanbik, Chiefs and Principal Men of the Ottawa, Chippewa and other Indians occupying the said Island, on behalf of the said Indians of the second part.

Whereas, the Indian title to said island was surrendered to the Crown on the ninth August, Anno Domini, 1836, under and by virtue of a treaty made between Sir Francis Bond Head, then Governor of Upper Canada, and the Chiefs and Principal Men of the Ottawas and Chippewas then occupying and claiming title thereto, in order that the same might 'be made the property (under their Great Father's control) of all Indians whom he should allow to reside thereon.'

And whereas, but few Indians from the mainland, who it was intended to transfer to the island, have ever come to reside thereon.

And whereas, it has been deemed expedient (with a view to the improvement of the condition of the Indians as well as the settlement and improvement of the country) to assign to the Indians now upon the island certain specified portions thereof to be held by patent from the Crown, and to sell other portions thereof fit for cultivation to settlers, and to invest the proceeds thereof, after deducting the expenses of survey and management, for the benefit of the Indians.

And whereas a majority of the chiefs of certain bands residing on that portion of the island easterly of Heywood Sound and the Manitoulin Gulf, have expressed their unwillingness to accede to this proposal as respects that portion of the island, but have assented to the same as respects all other portions thereof, and whereas the Chiefs and Principal Men of the bands residing on the island westerly of the said sound and gulf, have agreed to accede to the said proposal.

Now this agreement witnesseth that in consideration of the sum of seven hundred dollars now in hand paid (which sum is to be hereafter deducted from the proceeds of lands sold to settlers) the receipt whereof is hereby acknowledged, and in further consideration of such sums as may be realized from time to time as interest upon the purchase money of the lands to be sold for their benefit as aforesaid, the parties hereto of the second part, have, and hereby do release, surrender and give up to Her Majesty the Queen, all the right, title, interest and claim of the parties of the second part, and of the Ottawa, Chippewa and other Indians in whose behalf they act, of, in and to the Great Manitoulin Island, and also, of, in and to the islands adjacent which have been deemed or claimed to be appurtenant or belonging thereto, to have and to hold the same, and every part thereof, to Her Majesty, Her heirs and successors forever. And it is hereby agreed by and between the parties hereto as follows;—

Firstly. A survey of the said Manitoulin Island shall be made as soon as conveniently may be by or under the authority of the Department of Crown Lands.

Secondly. The Crown will, as soon as conveniently may be, grant by deed for the benefit of each Indian being the head of a family and residing on the said island, one hundred acres of land; to each single person over twenty-one years of age, residing as aforesaid, fifty acres of land; to each family of orphan children under twenty-one years of age containing two or more persons, one hundred acres of land, and to each single orphan child under twenty-one years of age, fifty acres of land to be selected and located under the following rules and conditions:—

Each Indian entitled to land under this agreement may make his own selection of any land on the Great Manitoulin Island, provided:—

1stly. That the lots selected shall be contiguous or adjacent to each other so that Indian settlements on the island may be as compact as possible.

2ndly. That if two or more Indians claim the same lot of land, the matter shall be referred to the resident Superintendent, who shall examine the case and decide between them.

3rdly. That selections for orphan children may be made by their friends subject to the approval of the resident Superintendent.

4thly. Should any lot or lots, selected as aforesaid, be contiguous to any bay or harbour, or any stream of water upon which a mill site shall be found, and should the Government be of opinion that such lot or lots ought to be reserved for the use of the public, or for village or park lots, or such mill site be sold with a view to the erection of a mill thereon, and shall signify such its opinion through its proper agent, then the Indian who has selected, or who wishes to select such lot, shall make another selection, but if he has made any improvements thereon he shall be allowed a fair compensation therefor.

5thly. The selections shall all be made within one year after the completion of the survey, and for that purpose plans of the survey shall be deposited with the resident Superintendent as soon as they are approved by the Department of Crown Lands, and shall be open to the inspection of all Indians entitled to make selections as aforesaid.

Thirdly. The interest which may accrue from the investment of the proceeds of sales of land as aforesaid, shall be payable annually, and shall be apportioned among the Indians now residing westerly of the said sound and gulf and their descendants per capita, but every Chief lawfully appointed shall be entitled to two portions.

Fourthly. So soon as one hundred thousand acres of the said land is sold, such portion of the salary of the resident Superintendent and of the expenses of his office, as the Government may deem equitable, shall become a charge upon the said fund.

Fifthly. The deeds or patents for the lands to be selected as aforesaid shall contain such conditions for the protection of the grantees as the Governor in Council may under the law deem requisite.

Sixthly. All the rights and privileges in respect to the taking of fish in the lakes, bays, creeks and waters within and adjacent to the said island, which may be lawfully exercised and enjoyed by the white settlers thereon, may be exercised and enjoyed by the Indians.

Seventhly. That portion of the island easterly of Heywood Sound and Manitoulin Gulf, and the Indians now residing there are excepted from the operation of this agreement as respects survey, sale of lots, granting deeds to Indians and payments in respect of moneys derived from sales in other parts of the island, but the said Indians will remain under the protection of the Government as formerly, and the said easterly part or division of the island will remain open for the occupation of any Indians entitled to reside upon the island as formerly, subject in case of dispute, to the approval of the Government.

Eighthly. Whenever a majority of the Chiefs and Principal Men, at a council of the Indians residing easterly of the said sound and gulf, to be called and held for the purpose, shall declare their willingness to accede to the present agreement in all respects, and the Government shall signify its approval, then that portion of the island shall be surveyed and dealt with in like manner as other portions thereof, and the Indians there shall be entitled to the same privileges in every respect from and after the date of such approval by the Government, as those residing in other parts of the island.

Ninthly. This agreement shall be obligatory and binding on the contracting parties as soon as the same shall be approved by the Governor in Council.

In Witness Whereof, the said Superintendent General of Indian Affairs, and the Deputy Superintendent, and the undersigned Chiefs and Principal Men of the Ottawa, Chippewa and other Indians, have hereto set their hands and seals at Manitowaning, the sixth day of October, in the year first above written.

Executed in the presence of
(having been first read, translated and explained).

GEO IRONSIDE, S.I. AFFRS.	SHE-WE-TAGUN
S. PHILLIPS DAY	GEORGE WEBETOOSOWN
WM. GIBBARD	PAIM-O-QUO-NAISH-KUNG
DAVID S. LAYTON	ABENCE

Jos. Wilson
John H. McDougall

F. Assiginack
Peter Jacobs, Ch. of England Missionary
McGregor Ironside
Wm. McDougall
Wm. Spragge
J.B. Assiginack
Maisheguong-gai

Okemah-beness
Benjamin Assiginack
Wai-be-nessieme

Tai-bos-egai
A-towish-cosh
Naiwotai-key-his
Wet-cow-sai
Kush-ke-wah-bie
Bai-bom-sai
Keg-hik-god-oness
Pah-tah-do-ginshing
Teh-kum-meh
Paim-sah-dung

Notes

Introduction

1. Franz Koennecke Collection, Wasauksing First Nation, John M. Daly to Department of Indian Affairs, 18 Apr. 1933. (Hereafter Koennecke Collection.)
2. 'The Politics of Indian Affairs', in Ian A.L. Getty and Antoine B. Lussier, eds, *As Long As The Sun Shines and Water Flows* (Vancouver, 1983), 169; abridged from H.B. Hawthorn, ed., *A Survey of Contemporary Indians of Canada*, Part 1 (Ottawa, 1966), ch. 17.
3. See Burton Jacobs, 'The Indian Agent System and Our Move to Self-Government', in Diane Engelstad and John Bird, eds, *Nation to Nation: Aboriginal Sovereignty and the Future of Canada* (Concord, Ont., 1992).
4. Koennecke Collection, Daly to DIA, 18 Apr. 1933.
5. The typical pattern for an Indian agent was to remain in the same agency throughout his entire career, but there were exceptions. A.D. Moore, for instance, began his career as agent at Cape Croker in 1922, was transferred to Caradoc agency in 1929, and moved once more, to Tyendinaga, in 1941, retiring in 1947.
6. Decision-making positions in the internal service were limited entirely to men, in keeping with the gender system of the era. Indian agents, too, were almost exclusively male. These positions demanded the exercise of authority, which, in the gendered assumptions of the time, was a male prerogative. In the records for Ontario I found only two women who served as Indian agents, both for short periods during World War II when men were in short supply. One of the women was the former agent's wife.
7. There were, of course, some individuals who continued to interest themselves in Indian Affairs for specific personal reasons, usually involving efforts to gain access to reserve lands or resources.
8. See clippings from local newspapers in the Brantford area, in National Archives of Canada (NAC), RG 10, vol. 7504, file 25,032-1-2, part 1.
9. Father Gaston Artus of Wikwemikong, for example, complained that Lewis was not doing enough to fight the peddling of liquor and homebrew to Aboriginal people on Manitoulin Island.
10. Brian Beaver, 'What's in a name? Anger and pride', *Globe and Mail*, 26 Nov. 1996, A20; Janet Silman, *Enough Is Enough. Aboriginal Women Speak Out* (Toronto, 1987), 22.

11. Two recent examples are Beth Brant, *I'll Sing 'Til the Day I Die: Conversations with Tyendinaga Elders* (Toronto, 1995), and The Blackfoot Gallery Committee, *Nitsitapiisinni: The Story of the Blackfoot People* (Toronto, 2001).

12. Jacobs, 'The Indian Agent System'.

13. Ibid.

14. I place the term 'traditional' in quotation marks to highlight the fact that tradition is itself a construct. In the case of Aboriginal people, the concepts of 'traditional' and 'modern' (or 'progressive', in the language of the Indian department) have been dichotomized in ways that distort the past and freeze Aboriginal cultures into static relics, denying them the dynamism characteristic of all cultures.

15. John L. Tobias, 'Protection, Civilization, Assimilation: An Outline History of Canada's Indian Policy', in J.R. Miller, ed., *Sweet Promises: A Reader on Indian-White Relations in Canada* (Toronto, 1991), 138–9.

16. In his poem 'The Onondaga Madonna', Scott described his character as a 'woman of a weird and waning race'. From *The Poems of Duncan Campbell Scott* (Toronto, 1926), cited in R.P. Bowles et al., *The Indian: Assimilation, Integration or Separation?* (Scarborough, Ont., 1972), 110. For a sensitive, nuanced exploration of Scott's poetry and career in the Department of Indian Affairs, see Stan Dragland, *Floating Voice: Duncan Campbell Scott and the Literature of Treaty 9* (Concord, Ont., 1994); see also the excellent film, *Duncan Campbell Scott: The Poet and the Indians* (Ottawa: National Film Board, 1995).

17. George Manuel, for example, discusses the means by which Indian agents pushed chiefs aside. See George Manuel and Michael Posluns, *The Fourth World: An Indian Reality* (New York, 1974), 54.

18. Peter Jones, *History of the Ojebway Indians* (London, 1861), 108–9.

19. Diamond Jenness, *The Ojibwa Indians of Parry Island, Their Social and Religious Life* (Ottawa, 1935), 2.

20. Ibid.

21. Mel Hill, in Brant, *I'll Sing 'Til the Day I Die*, 80.

22. See P.S. Schmalz, *The Ojibwa of Southern Ontario* (Toronto, 1991), 208–10.

23. I am using the term 'client' here in the older sense, referring to the hierarchical relationship between patron and client in which a wealthy, powerful patron controlled a set of clients who received benefits from him and gave loyalty and obedience in return.

24. See Silman, *Enough Is Enough*, 21–2.

25. See Rupert Ross, *Dancing with a Ghost: Exploring Indian Reality* (Markham, Ont., 1992); Ross, *Returning to the Teachings: Exploring Aboriginal Justice* (Toronto, 1996).

26. According to Ross, First Nations people from across Canada have responded positively to his writings and have tended to confirm that his conclusions apply to their own cultures. Nevertheless, it is important to acknowledge the likelihood that there were significant cultural differences among the many nations of the area that is now Canada.

27. Ross, *Dancing with a Ghost*. They are 'rules' in the sense that they are guidelines for proper conduct, but rather than being articulated or even clearly formulated, they tend to operate unconsciously.

28. Speech of Dr Clare Brant, quoted in Ross, *Dancing with a Ghost*, 12.

29. Juanita Perley has made a similar observation about her Maliseet culture, in which the word 'please' was not needed because 'nobody was ever made to beg.' When Maliseet people asked for something in English, 'they translated it literally from the way we speak and it sounded like a demand.' Juanita Perley, in Silman, *Enough Is Enough*, 51.

30. Ross, *Dancing with a Ghost*, xxv.
31. NAC, RG 10. vol. 7798, file 30001 part 1, H.J. Bury, Supervisor, Indian Timber Lands, 'Timber Resources of Indian Reserves in the Province of Ontario, 1923', 1–2.
32. For example, only one member of the Parry Island (Wasauksing) band is still living who remembers events of the 1920s and 1930s. This woman, Flora Tabobundong, is an important and engaged elder who was unable to find time to meet with me in the period in which I was conducting research. Verna Johnston, of Cape Croker, was experiencing health problems in this period, and I was only able to interview her briefly by tele-phone. I also interviewed an 84-year-old non-Aboriginal man of Parry Sound, the late Lyle Jones, who spent a good deal of time with Parry Islanders in the 1930s. Mr Jones shared many memories of the Anishinabe men who were his friends, but had had no contact with agent Daly, nor did he know much about him from rumour or report.
33. I visited Parry Island (Wasauksing) several times and spoke with people there about my project. Although they generally expressed interest, they did not seem to recall hearing stories about the agents. I interviewed Aileen Rice of Wasauksing and Donald Fisher of Wikwemikong. Both these individuals spent much of their lives off the reserve, and in spite of their best attempts to help they had little directly relevant infor-mation about the officials themselves.
34. The National Archives has never received these records, and the current Department of Indian and Northern Affairs informed the late Franz Koennecke that they could not be located in its files.
35. It is also important to note that the Koennecke Collection represents a selection of the original agency records. Mr Koennecke did not photocopy every paper he found. In some cases it has been possible to supplement his records with those found in the National Archives. But those Parry Sound agency documents that have been trans-ferred to the National Archives are dispersed throughout files, organized by topic rather than agency. There was thus a strong element of happenstance in the research process.
36. Dragland, *Floating Voice*, 110.
37. Parry Island was the subject of Koennecke's thesis, 'Wasoksing: The History of Parry Island, an Anishnabwe Community in the Georgian Bay, 1850 to 1920', MA thesis (University of Waterloo, 1984).
38. Koennecke Collection, Daly to DIA, 8 Feb. 1924.
39. The term 'First Nations' has met with some criticism for its apparent exclusion of the Métis. On the other hand, it is widely used by Aboriginal people today in the areas cov-ered by this study. As noted, I do not use it here to distinguish between those with and without non-Aboriginal ancestors. I am also not using 'Aboriginal people' in the legalis-tic sense in which it appears in the Charter of Rights and Freedoms, which specifies that the term includes 'Indians, Inuit, and Métis'. Rather, I employ it as it is used in common parlance, to refer to those whose heritage traces back to the original owners of this land.
40. The word 'Anishinabek' means 'people' in the Ojibway language. Some people use it to refer to First Nations people in general, but more often it is applied specifically to people of Odawa, Ojibway, and Potawatomi descent. The population of the Mani-towaning agency was almost entirely Anishinabek, but the Parry Sound agency con-tained Gibson (Wahta), which was a Mohawk reserve.
41. For an illuminating interrogation of the qualities by which judgements about a person's 'race' were made in Canadian courts in this period, see Constance Backhouse, *Colour-Coded: A Legal History of Racism in Canada, 1900–1950* (Toronto, 1999). See also James W. St G. Walker, *'Race,' Rights and the Law in the Supreme Court of Canada: Historical Case Studies* (Waterloo, Ont.,1997).

42. See, for example, Michel Foucault, *Discipline and Punish: The Birth of the Prison* (New York, 1979).

Chapter 1

1. Archives of Ontario (AO), MS 137, 'Parry Island Reserve Papers, 1877–1951', undated document signed Francis Pegahmagabow, Chief (*ca* 1921).
2. Another term sometimes used for these three nations is the Three Council Fires, a reference to their long history of mutual aid and alliance.
3. The 2,000–3,000 Potawatomi who moved to Upper Canada in the 1830s and 1840s came largely from Wisconsin, Michigan, and Indiana. See Edward S. Rogers, 'The Algonquian Farmers of Southern Ontario, 1830–1945', in Rogers and D.B Smith, eds, *Aboriginal Ontario: Historical Perspectives on the First Nations* (Toronto, 1994).
4. P.S. Schmalz, 'The Role of the Ojibwa in the Conquest of Southern Ontario, 1650–1701', *Ontario History* 76, 4 (1984): 326–52.
5. Victor Lytwyn, 'Ojibwa and Ottawa Fisheries around Manitoulin Island: Historical and Geographical Perspectives on Aboriginal and Treaty Fishing Rights', *Native Studies Review* 6, 1 (1990): 6.
6. Ibid.; Shelley Pearen, *Exploring Manitoulin* (Toronto, 1992), 6.
7. Among other things, the usual procedures involved informing the First Nations groups ahead of time that a surrender would be requested and then calling a meeting for the sole purpose of discussing a land cession. Normally some payment for the land would be made as well, but since it was to be held in trust for permanent Aboriginal occupation, this was probably not seen as necessary. One of Bond Head's main motives was to induce Aboriginal people living in southern Upper Canada to move to the island, thus clearing their lands for non-Aboriginal settlement.
8. This discussion of the Bond Head Treaty is based primarily on Robert J. Surtees, *Treaty Research Report: Manitoulin Island Treaties* (Ottawa: Treaties and Historical Research Centre, Indian and Northern Affairs, 1986). See also John S. Milloy, 'The Era of Civilization: British Policy for the Indians of Canada, 1830–1860', Ph.D. thesis (Oxford University, 1978), 100–64.
9. Sir Francis Bond Head to Lord Glenelg, 20 Aug. 1836, cited in Surtees, *Treaty Research Report*, 11. See appendix for full text of speech, which constitutes the Bond Head Treaty.
10. Lytwyn, 'Ojibwa and Ottawa Fisheries around Manitoulin Island', 11.
11. The Robinson Superior Treaty was signed by the Ojibway on the northern shores of Lake Superior on 7 Sept. 1850. Two days later the Robinson Huron Treaty was signed.
12. Surtees, *Treaty Research Report*, 6–8. Much of this paragraph is based on Surtees's account.
13. The group involved numbered between 30 and 100 people, and the company agent, John Bonner, chose to surrender rather than resist. Six people were arrested for this action: two Ojibway chiefs, including Garden River leader Shingwaukonse, two Euro-Canadians including entrepreneur Allan Macdonell, and two Métis men. They were sent to Toronto to be tried but were later released. See Surtees, *Treaty Research Report*, 8–9. For a more thorough account, see Nancy M. and W. Robert Wightman, 'The Mica Bay Affair: Conflict on the Upper Lakes Mining Frontier, 1840–1850', *Ontario History* 83 (1991): 193–208.
14. The number of people covered by the treaty was probably a good deal larger, since government officials typically underestimated numbers at the outset.

15. In Parry Sound: Lower French River, Henvey Inlet, Magnetawan, Shawanaga, Parry Island. In Manitowaning: Point Grondine, Spanish River No. 3, Tahgaiwenene, Whitefish Lake, and Whitefish River.

16. The Ojibway engaged in a lengthy and ultimately successful battle to activate the provision raising their annuities in the 1870 and 1880s, with the support of the federal government (the Ontario provincial government was responsible for paying Robinson Treaty annuities).

17. NAC, RG 10, vol. 1844, 'Treaty 60'. Although verbal guarantees of hunting and fishing rights had been made in earlier treaty negotiations, this was the first time that such a guarantee was included in a written treaty. See Surtees, *Treaty Research Report*, 27.

18. Wikwemikong Diary 1836–1917, Summary by Father J. Paquin, SJ, 14, cited in Surtees, *Treaty Research Report*, 22.

19. Surtees, *Treaty Research Report*, 25–6. See also David Shanahan, 'The Manitoulin Treaties, 1836 and 1862: The Indian Department and Indian Destiny', *Ontario History* 86, 1 (Mar. 1994): 13–31.

20. The only other unceded territory in the province of Ontario is Walpole Island, located on the St Clair River in the southwestern tip of the province.

21. Agnes I. Wing, *History of Parry Sound: The Place and the People* (n.p., n.d.), 47.

22. At first the fish were caught by Aboriginal fishermen, but it was not long before non-Aboriginals began encroaching on the fishing grounds. Lytwyn, 'Ojibwa and Ottawa Fisheries', 13.

23. David R. Cressman, *The Productive Capacity of the Natural Resources of Manitoulin Island* (Ottawa, 1968), 1.

24. See 'Manitoulin Island Pioneers and the Obidgewong Indians', compiled by Frank A. Myers, *Gore Bay Recorder* (1951).

25. See ibid. for stories in this vein.

26. The town of Depot Harbour sat on a 325-acre piece of land carved out of the reserve at the behest of the Ottawa, Arnprior and Parry Sound Railroad Company. The band was pressured into surrendering a portion of land for this purpose in 1895, and in 1899, when the railway wanted more land, the DIA bypassed the surrender process by expropriating the land. See Franz Koennecke, 'Wasoksing: The History of Parry Island, an Anishnabwe Community in the Georgian Bay, 1850 to 1920', MA thesis (University of Waterloo, 1984), 234, 245–6.

27. Vera King, 'First Citizens', in Gustav A. Richar, ed., *Parry Sound 1887–1987: Historical Miniatures* (Nobel, Ont., 1987), 9.

28. Ibid., 9, 12–13. The Belvedere Hotel boasted on its letterhead: 'The most beautiful Summer Resort in Canada. Fishing, Boating, Bathing, Lawn Tennis, Bowling Alley and Croquet.' AO, Parry Island Reserve Papers.

29. Koennecke, 'Wasoksing', 235.

30. NAC, RG 10, vol. 2841, file 172325, Thomas S. Walton to Hayter Reed, 29 Apr. 1896. The closest market to Christian Island was Collingwood, 25 miles away.

31. For an excellent discussion of spatial and legal means of racial segregation in Canada, see Sherene H. Razack, 'Gendered Racial Violence and Spatialized Justice: The Murder of Pamela George', in Razack, ed., *Race, Space and the Law: Unmapping a White Settler Society* (Toronto, 2002), 121–56.

32. Koennecke, 'Wasoksing', 212.

33. Lewis once noted, for instance, that he would need an interpreter to carry out a census because he did not speak Ojibway well enough to secure the necessary information

(NAC, RG 10, vol. 10591, Lewis to DIA, 18 May 1921). Daly reported of a band council meeting held in Ojibway that he 'could make out part of what he [Francis Pegah-magabow] was saying' (Koennecke Collection, Daly to DIA, 3 Mar. 1934). Fur traders, too, might learn to understand some words in Ojibway or another language spoken by their customers. But the agents were certainly not fluent enough to engage in whole conversations in Ojibway or to interpret for the people.

34. Organizers of county fairs and stampedes frequently included Aboriginal perform-ances on their rosters in the early twentieth century. See Arthur J. Ray, *I Have Lived Here Since the World Began: An Illustrated History of Canada's Native People* (Toronto, 1996), 234–5. For a related type of public performance, see Peter Geller, ' "Hudson's Bay Company Indians": Images of Native People and the Red River Pageant, 1920', in S. Elizabeth Bird, ed., *Dressing in Feathers: The Construction of the Indian in American Popular Culture* (Boulder, Colo., 1996).

35. William A. Campbell, *The French and Pickerel Rivers: Their History and Their People* (Sudbury, n.d. [*ca* 1992]), 182. The French River flows into Georgian Bay at the north end of the Parry Sound agency, near Lower French River Band No. 13. On the subject of the Canadian National Exhibition, see Chapter 6.

36. In the French River re-enactment, for example, the Native men were stripped to the waist and wore headbands over long hair (it is not clear from the photograph whether the hair was genuine or enhanced by wigs). From the waist down, they wore long pants that appear to be the everyday dress of their own time. Their appearance owed much more to the iconography of American theatre and Wild West shows than to the visual styles of their Anishinabek ancestors.

37. See, for example, Janet Chute's account of the great nineteenth-century Ojibway leader Shingwaukonse, *The Legacy of Shingwaukonse: A Century of Native Leader-ship* (Toronto, 1998).

38. Noel Dyck, *What Is the Indian 'Problem': Tutelage and Resistance in Canadian Indian Administration* (St John's, 1991), 24.

39. See Frank Tough, 'Ontario's Appropriation of Indian Hunting: Provincial Conserva-tion Policies vs. Aboriginal and Treaty Rights, ca. 1892–1930' (Ontario Native Affairs Secretariat, 1991). See also Chapter 4 in this volume for a more extensive discussion of these issues.

40. Two bands had never signed treaties. The Gibson (Wahta) band of Mohawks had moved from Oka (Kanesatake) to Georgian Bay in the 1880s and settled on land pur-chased for them in Gibson Township by the federal government. The Moose Deer Point band, also a later addition to the region, had been granted reserve status for their tiny plots of land after occupying them for some time without official status.

41. This paragraph is based primarily on Tough, 'Ontario's Appropriation of Indian Hunting'.

42. The term 'First Nation' is preferred today, but since they were universally known as 'bands' in the 1920s and 1930s (Indian Affairs terminology), I have used the term in this work.

43. In 1923 Lower French River and Henvey Inlet were formally merged and were hence-forth administered as a single band, known as the Henvey Inlet Band of Ojibwas. See 'The Henvey Inlet First Nation, as Told by the late Nellie Ashawasegai', in Campbell, *The French and Pickerel Rivers*, 203.

44. The Parry Island Reserve is now known, by choice of the community, as the Wasauks-ing First Nation. I retain the old name here simply because it was the name of the reserve in the time period studied.

45. In Parry Sound: Lower French River, Henvey Inlet, Magnetawan, Shawanaga, Parry Island. In Manitowaning: Point Grondine, Spanish River No. 3, Tahgaiwenene, Whitefish Lake, and Whitefish River.

46. James Morrison, 'The Robinson Treaties of 1850: A Case Study', prepared for the Royal Commission on Aboriginal Peoples (1993), 150–1. See also Leo G. Waisberg and Tim E. Holzkamm, 'Ojibway Agriculture in Northwestern Ontario 1805–1875: "Their Gardens Mostly on Islands"', paper presented to the annual meeting of the American Society for Ethnohistory, Toronto, 1990.

47. A brief account may be found in Charles Hamori-Torok, 'The Iroquois of Akwesasne (St Regis), Mohawks of the Bay of Quinte (Tyendinaga), Onyota'a:ka (the Oneida of the Thames), and Wahta Mohawk (Gibson), 1750–1945', in Rogers and Smith, eds, *Aboriginal Ontario*.

48. The First Nations who live at Kanesatake have been attempting to assert their legitimate ownership of the land since the late eighteenth century. Successive European and Euro-Canadian authorities have continued to deny their title and confirm the title conferred by the French Crown on the Sulpician order in 1717. See J.R. Miller, 'Great White Father Knows Best: Oka and the Land Claims Process', in Ken Coates and Robin Fisher, eds, *Out of the Background: Readings on Canadian Native History*, 2nd edn (Toronto, 1996).

49. Canada, *Sessional Papers*, 1881, Annual Report of the Department of Indian Affairs (Ottawa, 1882), liv–lv.

50. Canada, *Sessional Papers*, 1924, Annual Report of the Department of Indian Affairs (Ottawa, 1924).

51. See Cynthia C. Wesley-Esquimaux and Dr I.V.B. Johnson, 'United Anishnaabeg Elders: The Treaties Revisited [with particular emphasis on the 1923 Williams Treaty], testimony of Moose Deer Point elders', 96–103.

52. The most focused study of the Manitowaning experiment remains Ruth Bleasdale, 'Manitowaning: An Experiment in Indian Settlement', *Ontario History* 66, 3 (Sept. 1974): 147–57.

53. Canada, *Sessional Papers*, 1924, Annual Report of the Department of Indian Affairs, 24. For more information on the founding of Wikwemikong, see David Nazar, SJ, 'Nineteenth-Century Wikwemikong: The Foundation of a Community and an Exploration of Its People', *Ontario History* 86, 1 (Mar. 1994): 9–12.

54. Canada, *Sessional Papers*, Annual Report of the Department of Indian Affairs, Tabular Statements (Ottawa, 1918). Many of the people who fled the United States had previously been converted to Roman Catholicism.

55. Peter S. Schmalz, *The Ojibwa of Southern Ontario* (Toronto, 1991), 162–4.

56. Bleasdale, 'Manitowaning: An Experiment in Indian Settlement', 152.

57. Other useful articles on the history of Manitoulin Island include Douglas Leighton, 'The Manitoulin Incident of 1863: An Indian-White Confrontation in the Province of Canada', *Ontario History* 69, 2 (June 1977): 113–24; Nazar, 'Nineteenth-Century Wikwemikong'; Shanahan, 'The Manitoulin Treaties'.

58. The Spanish River band had its own reserve on the north shore of Georgian Bay, but the majority of the members lived on Manitoulin Island Unceded Territory. Tahgaiwenene was a small band, with 131 members in 1918. It appears that the majority of them lived on the unceded territory.

59. According to the agent's census in 1918, for instance, the total agency population was 2,138 and the MIU band contributed more than half that total, with 1,136 members. But its territory was also home to most of the 214 members of Spanish River No. 3, the 131

members of Tahgaiwenene, and residents from a wide variety of other Ontario bands. This would give a total resident population of more than 1,500.

60. Members of Robinson Treaty bands received annuities, as well as semi-annual interest payments if their band funds were large enough to permit this. Members of Manitoulin Island Treaty bands did not receive annuities, but they did receive interest payments from the investment fund established as part of the treaty.

61. Koennecke, 'Wasoksing', 256.

62. Ibid., 114.

63. Daly was most likely Scots Presbyterian himself, and he was much more inclined to complain about the Catholic element on Parry Island than about the Methodists. His views were consistent with the typical Protestant conviction that Catholics always sought hegemony.

64. Koennecke Collection, Daly to DIA, 13 July 1932.

65. Koennecke, 'Wasoksing', 160. These families had arrived in the 1870s and 1880s.

66. Ibid.

67. Lewis noted in 1932, for instance, that 'there [was] not any sale for bark work to enable the Indian women to buy a few groceries' (NAC, RG 10, vol. 10627, Lewis to DIA, 5 Sept. 1932). See also Lewis's annual report for 1917, in Canada, *Sessional Papers*, Annual Report of the Department of Indian Affairs (Ottawa, 1917).

68. NAC, RG 10, vol. 10627, Lewis to DIA, 5 Sept. 1932.

69. This paragraph and the next are based on the annual reports of the Department of Indian Affairs for the years 1919 to 1939 (Canada, *Sessional Papers*, Report of the Department of Indian Affairs [Ottawa]).

70. Canada, *Sessional Papers*, Report of the Department of Indian Affairs, Tabular Statements (Ottawa, 1919). The column for farm products is labelled 'Value of Farm Products including hay'. It is not clear whether this included the value of food consumed, or only the amount gained through sale. The next column is headed 'Value of Beef Sold, also of that used for food', which combines the two categories.

71. Schmalz, *The Ojibwa of Southern Ontario*, 233.

72. The house was valued at $240 a year for superannuation purposes (i.e., for the calculation of the agent's pension). NAC, RG 10, vol. 9183, 'Establishment Books (Outside Service, "H" through "M"), 1880–1955', entry for Robert John Lewis. First Nations people did not pay rent either, as long as they lived on a reserve.

73. Canada, *Sessional Papers*, 1916, Annual Report of the Department of Indian Affairs (Ottawa, 1917).

74. This figure is derived using the population reported in the census of 1934, since population statistics for 1932 are not available. The number of people reported as living in the agency did not vary greatly from one census to the next: Lewis reported 2,138 in 1918, 2,253 in 1924, and 2,113 in 1934. Canada, *Sessional Papers*, Annual Report of the Department of Indian Affairs, 1918, 1924, 1934.

75. James Struthers, *No Fault of Their Own: Unemployment and the Canadian Welfare State 1914–1941* (Toronto, 1983), App. IV (not paginated), 'Maximum monthly relief allowances for a family of five, selected Canadian cities, September 1936'. Relief allowances notoriously provided a bare minimum. The agent's salary had peaked in 1927 at $2,040 per year. It remained unchanged until his retirement. NAC, RG 10, vol. 9183, 'Establishment Books (Outside Service, "H" through "M"), 1880–1955', entry for Robert John Lewis.

76. Koennecke Collection, Daly to Prof. C.B. Grant, Dept. of Anatomy, University of Toronto, 2 May 1933.

77. Koennecke, 'Wasoksing', 97.
78. In their study of Parry Island farmers, Edward S. Rogers and Flora Tabobondung comment that 'most of the land was unusable for farming, consisting of swamp or bedrock outcroppings.' They assert nevertheless that the Odawa and Potawatomi, whose villages were further from Parry Sound than the Ojibway Upper Village, did a considerable amount of subsistence farming up to about 1930. This sort of activity might well go unrecorded in the DIA income figures, since the crops were probably not sold on the market. Edward S. Rogers and Flora Tabobondung, *Parry Island Farmers: A Period of Change in the Way of Life of the Algonkians of Southern Ontario* (Ottawa: National Museum of Man Mercury Series, Canadian Ethnology Service Paper No. 31, 1975), 307–8.
79. He also consistently left the column for 'Earned by other Industries and Occupations' blank—obviously earnings that fell outside the department's specific categories were not captured by these records.
80. The annuity and interest payments work out to $17.30 per person in 1923 and $25.72 per person in 1931. These figures are based on the populations reported in the censuses taken in 1924 and 1934, and corrected for the discrepancy in the Parry Island population. That is, the non-band members who swelled the numbers reported for Parry Island in 1924 have been subtracted, since they would not have received interest payments from Daly, nor was he responsible for paying their annuities.
81. After 1932, the agent reported the value of farm produce as $1,500, reduced from its former level of $7,450. This suggests at least that the few Aboriginal farmers' fortunes declined drastically some time around 1932.
82. Daly's figures simply record the timber income, without showing where it went. Given the complaints made by Parry Islanders that the timber company was hiring mainly white men, presumably the Parry Island people made little wage income from this source. Thus, most of the money must have taken the form of timber dues based on volume, which would have been added to the band fund. The resulting growth in the band fund resulted in significant percentage increases in interest payments, but the money did not go directly into people's pockets.
83. In 1931, $85 were earned per person, or just over $35 per month for a family of five.
84. NAC, RG 10, vol. 9182, 'Establishment Books (Outside Service, "A" through "G"), 1880–1955', entry for John McLean Daly.
85. Frederick Johnson, 'Notes on the Ojibwa and Potawatomi of the Parry Island Reservation, Ontario', *Indian Notes* 6, 3 (July 1929): 194–5.
86. Diamond Jenness, *The Ojibwa Indians of Parry Island, Their Social and Religious Life* (Ottawa, 1935), 10.
87. Koennecke Collection, A.F. MacKenzie to Daly, 10 Feb. 1934. This was a circular sent to all the Indian agents in response to the massive increase in demand for relief. In 1930 the department had ruled that the monthly relief issue should be $5, half the amount that Daly had regularly allowed in the 1920s.
88. L.M. Grayson and Michael Bliss, eds, *The Wretched of Canada: Letters to R.B. Bennett 1930–1935* (Toronto, 1971), xiv.

Chapter 2

1. *Toronto Star Weekly*, 28 Aug. 1920, quoting Frederick Ogilvie Loft, Mohawk returned soldier and founder of the League of Indians. Cited in Peter Kulchyski, ' "A Considerable Unrest": F.O. Loft and the League of Indians', *Native Studies Review* 4, 1–2 (1988): 95–117.

2. Robert Sinclair, *The Canadian Indian* (Ottawa, 1911), quoted in R.P. Bowles et al., eds, *The Indian: Assimilation, Integration or Separation?* (Scarborough, Ont., 1972), 114.

3. Harold Cardinal, quoted in Peter S. Schmalz, *The Ojibwa of Southern Ontario* (Toronto, 1991), 208.

4. By directed acculturation I mean the concerted attempt to induce Aboriginal people to adopt Euro-Canadian culture in its entirety.

5. At least as late as 1969 Prime Minister Pierre Trudeau elaborated the assimilation thesis, when his government drew up the aptly named 'White Paper'. See, for instance, the excerpt of a speech delivered by Trudeau, reprinted in Bowles et al., eds, *The Indian*, 71–2.

6. Duncan Campbell Scott, in *Proceedings of the Fourth Conference of the Institute of Pacific Relations* (Canadian Institute of International Affairs, 1931), quoted in Bowles et al., eds, *The Indian*, 112.

7. E. Brian Titley, *A Narrow Vision: Duncan Campbell Scott and the Administration of Indian Affairs in Canada* (Vancouver, 1986), 37.

8. This sketch applies to Ontario and points east of it. In the West there were more officials, including farming instructors and sometimes field matrons. Since Native people in the West were considered to be less civilized than those in the East, the department employed more individuals to move the assimilation process along.

9. John D. McLean joined the DIA in 1876, probably as a clerk, was appointed secretary in 1897, and became the Assistant Deputy Superintendent General in 1908. Canada, *Sessional Papers*, 1916, Annual Report of the Department of Indian Affairs (Ottawa, 1917).

10. Harold Cardinal, 'Hat in Hand: The Long Fight to Organize', in Cardinal, *The Unjust Society: The Tragedy of Canada's Indians* (Edmonton, 1969), 98–9.

11. See AO, Parry Island Reserve Papers.

12. See Douglas Leighton, 'The Ironside Family and the Development of Indian Administration in Upper Canada, 1796–1863', paper presented at the Western District History Conference, Windsor, Ont., 1979. Some 'dynastic' families included the Johnson, Ironside, and Claus families.

13. Entries in the department's 'Establishment Books', which contain information on employees, include notations such as 'Succeeded by G.M. Taylor pending result of competition. Samuel Devlin qualified as result of competition.' NAC, RG 10, vol. 9182, 'Establishment Books (Outside Service, "A" through "G"), 1880–1955', entry for John McLean Daly. See also Titley, *A Narrow Vision*, 39.

14. This is the opinion expressed by John Leslie of INAC's Treaties and Historical Research Centre after years of researching the department's history (personal communication). Following a post-war commission of inquiry into the Civil Service, an examination process was put in place for all civil servants, which was supposed to prevent nepotism and favouritism in appointments.

15. R.W. Dunning, 'Some Aspects of Governmental Indian Policy and Administration', *Anthropologica* 4 (1962): 209–29.

16. For comments on a later period, see 'The Politics of Indian Affairs', abridged from Chapter 17 of *A Survey of Contemporary Indians of Canada*, Part 1, edited by H.B. Hawthorn (Ottawa, 1966), in Ian A.L. Getty and Antoine S. Lussier, eds, *As Long As the Sun Shines and Water Flows: A Reader in Canadian Native Studies* (Vancouver, 1983), 173.

17. *Wiarton Echo*, 22 Aug. 1879, quoted in Schmalz, *The Ojibwa of Southern Ontario*, 196.

18. The new section read as follows: 'In the event of a band refusing to consent to the expenditure of such capital moneys as the Superintendent General may consider

advisable for any of [a number of specific] purposes . . . and it appearing to the Super-intendent General that such refusal is detrimental to the progress or welfare of the band, the Governor in Council may, without the consent of the band, authorize and direct the expenditure of such capital for such of the said purposes as may be considered reasonable and proper.' *Statutes of Canada*, 1918, ch. 26, s. 4, in Sharon Venne, ed., *Indian Acts and Amendments 1868–1975: An Indexed Collection* (Saskatoon, 1981), 206.

19. See, for example, Janet E. Chute, *The Legacy of Shingwaukonse: A Century of Native Leadership* (Toronto, 1998), 232.

20. *Revised Statutes of Canada*, 1906, ch. 81 (Indian Act), s. 92, para. 2, in Venne, ed., *Indian Acts and Amendments*, p.207.

21. Burton Jacobs, 'The Indian Agent System and Our Move to Self-Government', in Diane Engelstad and John Bird, eds, *Nation to Nation: Aboriginal Sovereignty and the Future of Canada* (Concord, Ont., 1992), 114.

22. John Leslie and Ron Maguire, eds, *The Historical Development of the Indian Act*, 2nd edn (Ottawa 1978), 97.

23. Parry Island chief Stanley Manitowaba wrote that R. had lived on the island 'for this last twenty five years, in fact, he has lived permenantly [*sic*] on this Reserve ever since his childhood.' Koennecke Collection, Stanley Manitowaba to Daly, 27 Oct. 1925.

24. Ibid., Daly to DIA, 16 Oct. 1925. The implication, though oblique, seems to be that R. was a threat to the authority and control of the Department of Indian Affairs.

25. McLean wrote, 'This man has no right or authority to reside on the reserve, in that he is not a member of the Band, and in view of his general conduct should be ordered to remove therefrom at once.' Ibid., J.D. McLean to Daly, 22 Oct. 1925.

26. Daly noted with satisfaction, 'I am hoping that the sentence meted out to him will be a warning to the other Indians that the purpose of the Indian Act will be carried out in this Agency.' Ibid., Daly to J.D. McLean, 29 Oct. 1925.

27. *Revised Statutes of Canada*, ch. 81, ss. 34, 36, 37, in Venne, ed., *Indian Acts and Amendments*.

28. Sarah Carter, 'Two Acres and a Cow: "Peasant" Farming for the Indians of the Northwest, 1889–1897', in J.R. Miller, ed., *Sweet Promises: A Reader on Indian-White Relations in Canada* (Toronto, 1991), 370. The article was originally published in *Canadian Historical Review* 70, 1 (1989).

29. 'The Politics of Indian Affairs', in Getty and Lussier, eds, *As Long As the Sun Shines and Water Flows*, 169, abridged from H.B. Hawthorn, ed., *A Survey of Contemporary Indians of Canada*, Part 1 (Ottawa 1966), ch. 17; NAC, RG 10, vol. 7141, file 1/ 3-7, part 1.

30. Helen S. Buckley, *From Wooden Ploughs to Welfare: Why Indian Policy Failed in the Prairie Provinces* (Montreal and Kingston, 1992), 43.

31. 'The Politics of Indian Affairs', in Getty and Lussier, eds, *As Long As the Sun Shines and Water Flows*, 173.

32. For example, an 1897 schedule of documents required from agents in the West shows four different kinds of monthly reports, four kinds of quarterly reports, and cites further: annual estimates; vouchers, accounts, bills, and invoices; requisitions for supplies; and store returns. All were common forms of paperwork to attend to. NAC, RG 10, vol. 3086, file 279,222, part 1, 'Schedule, showing reports, returns & c., required after 1st June, 1897, and their disposal'. This is by no means an exhaustive list.

33. Harold W. McGill, 'General Instructions to Indian Agents in Canada' (1933), 1.

34. 'The Politics of Indian Affairs', in Getty and Lussier, eds, *As Long As the Sun Shines*, 172.

35. Koennecke Collection, Daly to Duncan Campbell Scott, 18 Mar. 1930.
36. Ibid.
37. Paul Williams, 'The Chain', LLM thesis (Osgoode Hall Law School, York University, 1981), 8.
38. Daniel Francis, *The Imaginary Indian: The Image of the Indian in Canadian Culture* (Vancouver 1992), 204.
39. Ibid., 205.
40. This critical demographic change occurred in the second or third decade of the twentieth century. See J.R. Miller, *Skyscrapers Hide the Heavens* (Toronto, 1989), 213.
41. In 1929, for instance, an agent who was earning $1,680 a year reported that some Aboriginal veterans in his agency were making a 'comfortable living' in dairy farming. Their farms produced about $300 per year. It is doubtful that this agent would have considered himself 'comfortable' with such an income, but it was deemed sufficient for First Nations people. NAC, RG 10, vol. 7489, file 25008-1, part 1, Cape Croker agent A.D. Moore to DIA, 6 Feb. 1929. For Moore's salary, see ibid., vol. 9183.
42. This was section 141, passed in 1927. See Titley, *A Narrow Vision*, 59, 94–110.
43. Scott engaged the Royal Canadian Mounted Police to spy on Aboriginal leaders and organizations, and attempted to discredit the most successful. See ibid.
44. T.R.L. MacInnes, 'The History and Policies of Indian Administration in Canada', in C.T. Loram and T.F. McIlwraith, eds, *The North American Indian Today*, proceedings of a conference held 4–16 Sept. 1939 (Toronto, 1943), 158, 163.
45. D.J. Allan, 'Indian Land Problems in Canada', in Loram and McIlwraith, eds, *The North American Indian Today*, 186–9, 198.
46. H.W. McGill, 'Policies and Problems in Canada', in Loram and McIlwraith, eds, *The North American Indian Today*, 133–5. In fact, branch officials did little to 'direct' Aboriginal economic pursuits, except in the sense of encouraging farming and controlling their access to their own resources.
47. Noel Dyck, *What Is the Indian 'Problem': Tutelage and Resistance in Canadian Indian Administration* (St John's, 1991), 9.
48. An Act respecting Indians, *Revised Statutes of Canada*, 1906, chapter 81, s. 2 (g) and (e), cited in Venne, ed., *Indian Acts and Amendments*, 174. An 'irregular band' was 'any tribe, band or body of persons of Indian blood who own no interest in any reserve or lands of which the legal title is vested in the Crown, who possess no common fund managed by the Government of Canada, and who have not had any treaty relations with the Crown.'
49. Constance Backhouse, *Colour-Coded: A Legal History of Racism in Canada, 1900–1950* (Toronto, 1999), 24.
50. Ibid., 25.
51. Koennecke Collection, Daly to J.D. McLean, 15 Jan. 1927.
52. Personal conversation with Lyle Jones, Parry Sound resident, 7 Oct. 1993.
53. Cited in Francis, *The Imaginary Indian*, 210.
54. Koennecke Collection, Daly to Rev. Vale, Principal of St John's Indian Residential School, 15 Mar. 1933.
55. Angus McLaren, 'Males, Migrants, and Murder in British Columbia, 1900–1923', in Franca Iacovetta and Wendy Mitchinson, eds, *On the Case: Explorations in Social History* (Toronto, 1998), 168.
56. NAC, RG 10, vol. 10599, R.J. Lewis to the Secretary, DIA, 24 Apr. 1923. Emphasis added.
57. Ibid. Emphasis added.

58. This was a reserve in Daly's agency.

59. NAC, RG 10, vol. 10609, Lewis to Daly, 22 Nov. 1926.

60. James Morrison, Ontario Native Affairs Secretariat, *The Robinson Treaties of 1850: A Case Study*, report prepared for the Royal Commission on Aboriginal Peoples, Treaty and Land Research Section (1993), 202.

61. NAC, RG 10, vol. 10599, R.J. Lewis to Dr C.F. McLean, 13 Oct. 1923.

62. Koennecke Collection, Daly to DIA, 24 July 1934.

63. McGill, 'Policies and Problems in Canada', 136.

64. Indian Act, *Revised Statutes of Canada 1906*, ch. 81, s. 2(c), in Venne, ed., *Indian Acts and Amendments*, 174.

65. NAC, RG 10, vol. 10599, Lewis to DIA, 28 Sept. 1923.

66. Howard Adams, *Prison of Grass: Canada from a Native Point of View* (Saskatoon, 1989 [1975]), 147.

67. NAC, RG 10, vol. 7496, file 25015-6, part 1, Nelson Stone to DIA, 18 June 1926.

68. Much of the personal information about Daly's background was obtained through personal communication with his granddaughter, Nonie Bristol, 15 Nov. 1992.

69. In one letter he wrote, 'For seven years, during construction of the Transcontinental, I kept law and order from Cochrane to Doucet, with all nationalities on the construction.' Koennecke Collection, Daly to the Secretary, Department of Indian Affairs, 17 Oct. 1934. Two of the couple's four children died in Scotland when Daly was already in Canada.

70. Ibid., Daly to Rev. F. Reed, Toronto, 5 Feb. 1929. There is no indication in the records that Daly's own position was ever threatened, and dismissals of agents were relatively rare. This remark therefore remains somewhat mysterious, but should not be summarily discounted.

71. Actually, though other government employees may have faced dismissal after a government change, Indian agents typically served for long periods.

72. Koennecke Collection, Daly to E.J. Graham, 28 Jan. 1924.

73. Daly's first wife died while he was away during World War I. The second, Edith Smiley, was a schoolteacher on Parry Island Reserve until she married Daly in 1927.

74. Koennecke Collection, Daly to Arthur C. Poste, 22 Mar. 1933.

75. Personal communication with Nonie Bristol, Daly's granddaughter, 15 Nov. 1992; interview with Lyle Jones of Parry Sound, 7 Oct. 1993.

76. Personal communication with Nonie Bristol, 15 Nov. 1992.

77. Koennecke Collection, Daly to DIA, 9 Jan. 1935.

78. For example, Daly made the following complaint in 1932 about the incumbent chief and council on the Parry Island Reserve: 'Chief Judge has shown over and over again, also his councillors Peter Judge and James Miller, that they do not consider it necessary to have a white man looking after the business of the Reserve, and they have stated in public that they are quite capable of looking after their own affairs.' Daly asserted that he had been 'very patient' with the men and that his kindness had been 'misconstrued': 'Chief Frank Judge, as Chief, will have to be held tight by the head.' Ibid., Daly to DIA, 13 July 1932.

79. Ibid., Daly to Duncan C. Scott, 18 Mar. 1930.

80. Interview with Lyle Jones of Parry Sound, 7 Oct. 1993.

81. Koennecke Collection, Daly to DIA, 24 Jan. 1931; Daly to Rev. Canon Vale and Everybody, 25 Jan. 1932.

82. Thomas Peltier of Wikwemikong later claimed that Lewis was unsympathetic towards war veterans. In 1934 Peltier wrote to C.G. Power, the Minister of Pensions, requesting help in supporting his sick wife and six young children. He stated that he was unable to

get help from his agent and that 'there is no use asking for help from a man who had never enlisted during the war, and has no sympathy for returned men.' Schmalz, *The Ojibwa of Southern Ontario*, 233.

83. NAC, RG 10, vol. 10597, Lewis to Gregor McGregor, Birch Island, 23 Nov. 1922.
84. Departmental decisions and opinions were virtually always rendered in the passive voice, which tidily concealed the source of the actual opinion. Phrases such as 'it is thought' and 'it is considered' were the standard style in which such decisions were explained. In many instances these expressions undoubtedly camouflaged the fact that the letter-writer had simply made a snap decision.
85. In 1921, for example, Chief Joseph Petahtegoose of the Whitefish Lake band reported that a number of individuals on his reserve needed relief. Lewis relayed this information to the department and recommended in favour of extending assistance to all the named individuals, since he '[knew] for a fact that all these Indians [were] in trying circumstances and in need of relief.' The agent had not taken any steps on his own initiative to assist these people, but left the matter to the council. NAC, RG 10, vol. 10593, Lewis to DIA, 7 Dec. 1921.
86. Ibid., vol. 10599, Lewis to Mr Joseph Sebiswens, 18 Dec. 1923.
87. Ibid., vol. 10597, Lewis to DIA, 28 Nov. 1922.
88. Ibid., vol. 10631, Lewis to Dominic Odjig, Wikwemikong, 23 Apr. 1934.

Chapter 3

1. Koennecke Collection, Daly to DIA, 3 Mar. 1934.
2. AO, MS 137, Parry Island Reserve Papers, 1877–1951, 'Declaration Against the Agent', undated (*ca* early 1920s).
3. Koennecke Collection, Chief John Manitowaba to Daly, 11 Oct. 1934.
4. Aboriginal people living on reserves did not receive the vote until 1960.
5. See Paul Williams, 'The Chain', LLM thesis (York University, 1981), 18.
6. AO, MS 137, Parry Island Reserve Papers (including band council minutes).
7. In large part this resulted from the fragmented character of reserve communities, which were divided along lines of religion, band affiliation, Indian status, and ancestral origins.
8. Koennecke Collection, Chief Frank Judge to J.M. Daly, 17 May 1931.
9. Ibid., Daly to DIA, 8 June 1925, 31 Jan. 1934.
10. Ibid., Daly to DIA, 13 July 1932.
11. *Revised Statutes of Canada*, 1906, ch. 81, para. 4, in Sharon H. Venne, ed., *Indian Acts and Amendments 1868–1975: An Indexed Collection* (Saskatoon, 1981), 176.
12. Ibid., section 98, in Venne, ed., *Indian Acts and Amendments*, 209.
13. Ibid., sections 44 and 45.
14. Koennecke Collection, Daly to DIA, 12 Dec. 1934.
15. Telephone interview with Verna Petronella Johnston, 20 June 1993.
16. *Revised Statutes of Canada*, 1906, section 96, in Venne, ed., *Indian Acts and Amendments*, 208.
17. The council accused Odjig of immorality and neglect of duty, citing several allegations to prove the charge of immorality. Odjig's neglect of duty concerned his responsibility to oversee the cutting of ties, posts, and sawlogs on the reserve and see that the workers were paid, which he evidently did not do. NAC, RG 10, vol. 7926, file 32-19, part 1, Chief Joseph Wabegijig, Joseph Eshkakogan, Joseph Jabokwaam, John Atchitawims, Daniel Wemigwance to R.J. Lewis, 25 Aug. 1917.
18. Ibid., Lewis to DIA, 10 May 1920.

19. For a discussion of these kinds of tactics, as used by the Walpole Island agent in the 1960s to avoid his own expulsion, see Burton Jacobs, 'The Indian Agent System and Our Move to Self-Government', in Diane Engelstad and John Bird, eds, *Nation to Nation: Aboriginal Sovereignty and the Future of Canada* (Concord, Ont., 1992), 113–19.

20. Koennecke Collection, Daly to DIA, 21 Nov. 1934.

21. Ibid., Daly to DIA, 3 Mar. 1934.

22. The chiefs in question include Francis Pegahmagabow, Frank Judge, and John Manitowaba. See AO, Parry Island Reserve Papers, 'Declaration Against the Agent'; NAC, RG 10, vol. 7540, file 29022-5, Chief Judge to RCMP, Toronto, 12 Mar. 1931; Koennecke Collection, A.F. MacKenzie to Col. Cortlandt Starnes, Commissioner, RCMP, 25 Mar. 1931; MacKenzie to Daly, 25 Mar. 1931; John Manitowaba to Superintendent General of Indian Affairs, 10 Oct. 1934.

23. Complaints about poaching by the residents of Depot Harbour, the non-Aboriginal railway town located right on Parry Island, were a constant feature of the period. According to the Indian Act, only band members had the right to hunt on a reserve. See Franz M. Koennecke, 'Once Upon a Time There Was a Railway on Wasauksing First Nation Territory', in Bruce W. Hodgins, Shawn Heard, and John S. Milloy, eds, *Co-existence? Studies in Ontario-First Nations Relations* (Peterborough, Ont., 1992).

24. Koennecke Collection, Daly to DIA, 5 Aug. 1931.

25. AO, MS 137, Parry Island Reserve Papers, page in Pegahmagabow's hand entitled 'Family record and times'. This is a brief autobiographical account of his life, apparently written in the early 1930s.

26. Fred Gaffen, *Forgotten Soldiers* (Penticton, BC, 1985), 28.

27. AO, MS 137, Parry Island Reserve Papers, 'Family record and times'.

28. Ibid.

29. Canada, Veterans' Affairs, *Native Soldiers, Foreign Battlefields* (Ottawa, 1993), 10.

30. P.S. Schmalz wrote of Francis Pegahmagabow, 'Enlisting in 1914, he, as a sniper, bears the extraordinary record of having killed 378 of the enemy. After participating at Amiens, he led his company at Passchendaele through an engagement with only one casualty, and subsequently captured 300 Germans at Mount Sorrell.' Schmalz, *The Ojibwa of Southern Ontario* (Toronto, 1991), 229.

31. Local historian Agnes Wing included a noteworthy passage on Pegahmagabow's enlistment and wartime career: 'There was much interest in the enlistment of Francis Pegahmagabow and the hope expressed that he would distinguish himself as his grandfather had done [in] the War of 1812. Distinguish himself he did, for he was one of the greatest (if not the greatest) sharp-shooters in the Allied armies.' Agnes I. Wing, *History of Parry Sound: The Place and the People* (n.d.), 57.

32. Diamond Jenness, *The Ojibwa Indians of Parry Island, Their Social and Religious Life* (Ottawa, 1935), v. Pegahmagabow signed a set of council minutes in the 1920s 'Chief Pegahmagabow F., Acting Interpreter and Secretary, Next of Kin to former Late Chief Peter Megis'. (AO, MS 137, Parry Island Reserve Papers.)

33. NAC, RG 10, vol. 7502, file 25022-5, Alexander Logan to DIA, 8 Jan. 1920.

34. Ibid., vol. 8021, file 475/37-7-8-9, Samuel Devlin to Indian Affairs Branch, 1 Feb. 1945.

35. Secretary T.R.L. MacInnes, who had been hearing about the man's exploits for several decades, wrote in 1945, 'It is my personal opinion that the man is a mental case.' Koennecke Collection, T.R.L. MacInnes to J.J.S. Garner, Office of the High Commissioner for the United Kingdom, 13 Apr. 1944.

36. His writings have been preserved in the Parry Island Reserve Papers at the Archives of Ontario. See, for example, a document dated 17 Sept. 1946, in which Pegahmagabow recounts his reception of this revelation as a child.

37. NAC, RG 10, vol. 7927, file 32-22, part 2, Daly to DIA, 8 Feb. 1924.

38. AO, Parry Island Reserve Papers.

39. NAC, RG 10, vol. 8021, file 475/37-7-8-9, Francis Pegahmagabow to Chief Noganosh, 9 July 1923. The letter did not cite specific grievances.

40. Koennecke Collection, Daly to J.D. McLean, DIA, 28 May 1924.

41. Ibid., J.D. McLean to Daly, 10 June 1924.

42. Scott took this approach with 'Chief Thunderwater', an American organizer, and with F.O. Loft, founder of the League of Indians. When both men began to receive favourable media attention and appeared to be attracting Native support, Scott moved to the offensive, adopting various measures to hamper and discredit these leaders. See E. Brian Titley, *A Narrow Vision* (Vancouver, 1986), 94–110.

43. AO, MS 137, Parry Island Reserve Papers, 'Re Timber Operations on Parry Island Indian Reserve', 19 Feb. 1923.

44. Ibid., uncompleted, undated document, *ca* 1920s.

45. Ibid., 'Declaration Against the Agent'.

46. Ibid., Wallace Nesbitt, KC, to Chief Francis Pegahmagabow, 5 June 1925.

47. Schmalz, *The Ojibwa of Southern Ontario*, 230.

48. Koennecke Collection, Daly to DIA, 8 June 1925.

49. Ibid.

50. Collins Inlet was at the northernmost end of the Parry Sound agency.

51. Koennecke Collection, Daly to DIA, 8 June 1925.

52. The motion was passed by a clear majority of 14–4 (with 3 abstentions).

53. NAC, RG 10, vol. 7927, file 32-22, part 2, memo from Henry Fabien to the Deputy Superintendent General, 15 Apr. 1925. Unless otherwise noted, the background information in this paragraph is based on the memo.

54. Ibid.

55. AO, Parry Island Reserve Papers. The document is signed by 17 band members, including Francis Pegahmagabow and John Miller.

56. NAC, RG 10, vol. 7927, file 32-22, part 2, Daly to DIA, 3 Aug. 1925.

57. AO, Parry Island Reserve Papers, Francis Pegahmagabow to M.H. Ludwig, KC, Toronto, 21 Mar. 1931.

58. Koennecke Collection, Daly to DIA, 15 July 1932.

59. Judge and Daly claimed that the copy belonged to the band, not Pegahmagabow.

60. Koennecke Collection, Daly to DIA, 11 July 1932.

61. Ibid.

62. AO, Parry Island Reserve Papers, Francis Pegahmagabow to M.H. Ludwig, KC, 21 Mar. 1931.

63. Ibid.

64. Koennecke Collection, Daly to DIA, 18 Jan. 1935.

65. Ibid., Daly to DIA, 30 Oct. 1934.

66. Ibid., Daly to DIA, 18 Dec. 1930.

67. Ibid.

68. Manitowaba was born around 1857, Daly in 1873. At the bottom of a letter written to the Department, he signed his name, followed by 'Age 73'. Ibid., copy of John Manitowaba's letter to the department, undated, but sent to DIA by Daly, Apr. 1930.

69. Ibid., Daly to DIA, quoting Manitowaba, 4 Apr. 1930.

70. Ibid., Daly to Duncan Campbell Scott, 13 Mar. 1930.
71. Ibid., Daly to DIA, 18 Dec. 1930.
72. Ibid.
73. The initiative for this deposition seems to have come from the band, but certainly Daly approved it.
74. NAC, RG 10, vol. 7540, file 29022-5, Daly to DIA, 3 Mar. 1931.
75. Ibid., Daly to J.D. McLean, 18 Jan. 1927.
76. Ibid., Daly to DIA, 3 Mar. 1931.
77. Koennecke Collection, Daly to Duncan Campbell Scott, 13 Mar. 1930.
78. Ibid., Daly to Duncan Campbell Scott, 18 Mar. 1930.
79. Ibid.
80. Ibid., Daly to DIA, 4 Apr. 1930.
81. Ibid.
82. Ibid.
83. For further insights into the department's practice of ignoring the concerns of Aboriginal leaders and organizations, see Jean Goodwill and Norma Sluman, *John Tootoosis* (Winnipeg, 1984), especially chs 12–13.
84. NAC, RG 10, vol. 7927, file 32-22, part 3, John Manitowaba to DIA, 15 May 1933. In the three months since his election, the chief reported that the council had received only two answers from Ottawa, presumably responses to band council resolutions. Such delays would be normal for the department but appeared suspicious to Manitowaba, who already regarded Daly as untrustworthy and antagonistic.
85. Koennecke Collection, Daly to DIA, 31 Jan. 1934.
86. A protest note written by some band members when Manitowaba was elected chief cited four reasons why he was not suitable, including '2. He can't talk English well. 3. He can't read . . . .' NAC, RG 10, vol. 7927, file 32-22, part 3, Alfred Tabobondung, Edward Judge, Joseph Partridge to DIA, 20 Feb. 1933.
87. Ibid.
88. Koennecke Collection, Daly to DIA, 3 Mar. 1934. Daly went so far as to claim that 'the saliva was running out of his mouth.'
89. Ibid., Daly to DIA, 22 June 1935.
90. Ibid., Daly to DIA, 3 Mar. 1934.
91. Ibid.
92. Ibid. This phrase appeared twice in the letter, the words almost identical each time.
93. Ibid.
94. Ibid., Daly to DIA, 10 Mar. 1934.
95. Ibid., John Manitowaba to Superintendent General of Indian Affairs, 10 Oct. 1934. Although this letter contained spelling and grammatical errors, Manitowaba clearly had assistance in writing it from someone much more conversant with the English language. Daly noted several times in his correspondence that Manitowaba had other people write letters for him. See, for example, ibid., Daly to DIA, 4 Apr. 1930, 20 May 1932.
96. Ibid., Chief John Manitowaba to Daly, 11 Oct. 1934.
97. Ibid., Daly to DIA, 1 Oct. 1934.
98. According to the Indian Act, of course, these people would not have had the right to take part in these elections.
99. Rev. Julien Paquin, SJ, 'Modern Jesuit Indian Missions in Ontario', unpublished manuscript, n.d., located at the Jesuit Province of Upper Canada Archives at Regis College,

158. Father Paquin states that this exclusion involved 600 members of other bands who lived on the unceded territory. This was a large group of people, and a sizable portion of the population.

100. It is not difficult to understand the reluctance of non-MIU members to join the unceded band. The latter was a sizable band, and the proposed amalgamation would mean dividing relatively small amounts of money among a large population. The non-MIU members would lose financially without the members of the unceded band gaining anything of substantial value. But it was really a matter of principle more than practicality.

101. Paquin, 'Modern Jesuit Indian Missions in Ontario', 184–5.

102. By contrast, some other bands (including Parry Island, for example) had surrendered the timber on their reserves to be harvested by outside companies. In these cases the band received an initial sum of money for the timber surrender and also timber dues based on the volume of wood cut. These dues were entered into the band fund. Under this system the band lost control of forest use on its reserve, and we have already seen that some Parry Islanders were very dissatisfied, especially because the woodcutting jobs went to white men.

103. Father Artus, 'Wikwemikong Diary 1919–1937', entry for 3 Jan. 1921, photostat (Jesuit Archives 1951), author's translation. The original reads: 'Beaucoup de gens de South Bay sont ici. On discute de leur droit de faire bande à part et d'avoir des fonds qui leur soient propres.'

104. Ibid., entry for 4 Jan. 1921, author's translation. Original reads: '. . . ceux d'entre eux qui ne voudraient pas transférer leurs annuités dans le fonds commun de Wikwemikong, étaient menacés de perdre le droit non seulement de vendre du bois, mais d'en couper pour leurs propres constructions.'

105. Father Artus was convinced that the MIU band was in error, not only in their 'un-Christian' attitude, but also according to the treaty. He argued that the 1836 treaty gave the South Bay people 'le premier droit de propriété sur l'île' and wrote the department to this effect. Artus, 'Wikwemikong Diary 1919–1937', entries for 4 Jan., 7 Feb. 1921. Jesuit historian Julien Paquin has provided further details about Father Artus's intervention in this matter—the priest went so far as to deny the sacraments to the MIU band members involved in banning timber use by non-band members. He became so involved in the battle that his superiors considered it necessary to transfer him to another posting. See Paquin, 'Modern Jesuit Indian Missions in Ontario', 184–5.

106. NAC, RG 10, vol. 10591, Lewis to DIA, 7 June 1921.

107. In July 1922, at the request of the Jesuit Provincial, Inspector Charles Parker was sent from the DIA to investigate the dispute. Parker was not impressed with the claims advanced by the excluded residents and stated that the MIU council's decision was legal and justified. Artus, 'Wikwemikong Diary 1919–1937', entry for 6 July 1921.

108. According to Father Artus, Lewis had declared in conversation that the MIU band did not have the authority to forbid other residents to cut timber: 'Le père a avec [l'agent] une longue conversation sur les difficultés entre les gens. Il déclare au père qu'il n'y a ni acte ni loi qui autorise à refuser de couper du bois'. Artus, 'Wikwemikong Diary 1919–1937', entry for 18 June 1921.

109. NAC, RG 10, vol. 10591, Lewis to Rev. G.A. Artus, 8 July 1921. Lewis consistently spelled Michel's last name as Tredeau, but the correct spelling is Trudeau.

110. In addition, transferring from a richer band to a poorer one involved a long-term financial loss, while richer bands were reluctant to accept new members from poorer bands.

111. NAC, RG 10, vol. 10591, Lewis to DIA, 27 Apr. 1921.
112. Ibid. As we have seen, Jesuit historian Julien Paquin supports Lewis's interpretation, at least to a point—Artus's superiors were so annoyed with his actions that they transferred him away from Manitoulin Island, feeling that he had significantly undermined his own authority. In September 1922, Artus was appointed Superior of the Indian Residential School at Spanish, on the north shore of Lake Huron. Paquin, 'Modern Jesuit Indian Missions in Ontario', 185.
113. NAC, RG 10, vol. 10591, Lewis to DIA, 20 Sept. 1921. Members of a series of bands attempted to register their votes in the band council election but were turned away by the agent. These individuals formally belonged to various bands around Georgian Bay: Spanish River No. 3, Point Grondine, Tahgaiwenene, and Sucker Lake, all of which were reserves in the Manitowaning agency; Cockburn Island, which is part of the Manitoulin Island cluster but was located in a separate agency; and Dokis and Nipissing, which are located on the eastern shore of Georgian Bay and belonged at the time to the Nipissing agency.
114. NAC, RG 10, vol. 10597, Lewis to DIA, 12 Mar. 1923.
115. The South Bay band's population in 1924 is recorded as 75, but only 45 in 1934. Of course, the reduction in numbers may have had more than one cause; Lewis reported only that the chief and 'a certain fraction of the band' had transferred their capital fund to the account of the MIU band. NAC, RG 10, vol. 10609, Lewis to DIA, 24 Nov. 1926. Population statistics from Annual Reports of the Department of Indian Affairs (Ottawa, 1924, 1934).
116. I am grateful to Debbie Maiangowi of Wikwemikong Unceded First Nation for this information.
117. Lewis was less controlling, but Daly was not alone in his approach. Other agents of the period, for example H.J. Eade of Christian Island and A.D. Moore of Cape Croker, showed similar tendencies. Eade spoke noticeably more disparagingly than Daly about some of his clients.

Chapter 4

1. Wanda Big Canoe of the Chippewas of Georgina Island First Nation, interviewed in the 1990s, cited in Cynthia C. Wesley-Esquimaux and Dr I.V.B. Johnson, 'United Anishnaabeg Elders: The Treaties Revisited [with particular emphasis on the 1923 Williams Treaty]', 54. In possession of Chippewas of Georgina Island First Nation.
2. Angus Scelbe of Chippewas of Georgina Island First Nation, interviewed in the 1990s, ibid., 58.
3. Dalton Jacobs of Curve Lake First Nation, interviewed in the 1990s, ibid., 61–2.
4. Collins Inlet was located on the eastern shore of Georgian Bay, near the Henvey Inlet and Magnetawan reserves.
5. NAC, RG 10, vol. 10280, file 475/20-2, part 2, Joseph Traunch to DIA, 8 Jan. 1926. I have left Traunch's text unaltered, leaving spellings as they are in the original, except that I have added the occasional word in square brackets to make the meaning clearer.
6. Ibid., J.D. McLean to Joseph Traunch, 13 Jan. 1926.
7. Several of the so-called 'numbered treaties' signed in the 1870s in western Canada were also forced on the Canadian government by local First Nations groups. The Ojibway of Treaty 3 (covering a large area of northwestern Ontario), the Ojibway of Treaty 1 (in southern Manitoba), and the Plains Cree of Treaty 6 (southern Saskatchewan) all placed direct pressure on government prior to the negotiation of their agreements. See

John L. Tobias, 'Canada's Subjugation of the Plains Cree, 1879–1885', in Ken S. Coates and Robin Fisher, eds, *Out of the Background: Readings on Canadian Native History*, 2nd edn (Toronto, 1998), 150–76. The article was originally published in *Canadian Historical Review* 64, 4 (Dec. 1983).

8. 'There has been a great unrest among the Indians and I have endeavoured to explain to them that these treaties are past and done with.' Koennecke Collection, Daly to DIA, 15 July 1932.

9. H.B. Hawthorn, ed., *A Survey of the Contemporary Indians of Canada* (Ottawa, 1966), 248. Emphasis in original.

10. Sturgeon, for example, the large and flavourful fish that had once been obtainable in huge numbers in the Great Lakes, were practically wiped out by commercial overfishing in the late nineteenth century.

11. See William A. Campbell, *The French and Pickerel Rivers: Their History and Their People* (Sudbury, Ont., n.d. [*ca* 1992]). This lively local history book documents the fishing and hunting culture of the area and is full of photographs from the early twentieth century in which local non-Aboriginal people and tourists proudly display their considerable catches of fish, fur-bearing animals, and large game.

12. NAC, RG 10, vol. 1844, 'Treaty 60'.

13. Victor P. Lytwyn, 'Ojibwa and Ottawa Fisheries around Manitoulin Island: Historical and Geographical Perspectives on Aboriginal and Treaty Fishing Rights', *Native Studies Review* 6, 1 (1990): 11.

14. Lise C. Hansen, 'Treaty Fishing Rights and the Development of Fisheries Legislation in Ontario: A Primer', *Native Studies Review* 7, 1 (1991): 4.

15. The first Fisheries Act was passed in 1857. It consolidated earlier legislation, established closed seasons for certain species, and provided for the appointment of fishery overseers and superintendents to enforce the Act. This Act made no reference to Aboriginal people and was supposed to apply to 'all subjects of her Majesty'. See ibid., 6–7.

16. Ibid., 6.

17. Ibid.

18. See Frank Tough, 'Ontario's Appropriation of Indian Hunting: Provincial Conservation Policies vs. Aboriginal and Treaty Rights, ca. 1892–1930' (Ontario Native Affairs Secretariat, 1991).

19. Ibid., 2.

20. NAC, RG 10, vol. 6743, file 420-8, part 1, 23 July 1906, quoted in Tough, 'Ontario's Appropriation of Indian Hunting', 5.

21. Patricia Jasen, *Wild Things: Nature, Culture, and Tourism in Ontario, 1790–1914* (Toronto, 1995), 148. See also Tough, 'Ontario's Appropriation of Indian Hunting'.

22. Tough, 'Ontario's Appropriation of Indian Hunting', 2.

23. Ibid., 3.

24. Ibid., 6.

25. Lytwyn, 'Ojibwa and Ottawa Fisheries', 11.

26. Ibid., 17–25.

27. Franz Koennecke, 'Wasoksing: The History of Parry Island, an Anishnabwe Community in the Georgian Bay, 1850 to 1920', MA thesis (University of Waterloo, 1984), 106.

28. Ibid., 107.

29. Ibid.

30. Ibid., 108.

31. AO, MS 396, Duncan Fraser Macdonald Diaries, 1872–1919, reels 6–8.

32. Canada, *Sessional Papers*, 1920, Annual Report of the Department of Indian Affairs (Ottawa, 1920), 37–8.

33. Theoretically, any Aboriginal person could engage in commercial fishing if he or she purchased a licence to a particular fishing area. But even if the people had not objected in principle to paying for fishing rights they believed were already theirs, it would have been difficult for them to obtain or pay for a licence. They did not possess much capital, and in any event the best fishing areas were long since licensed to others.

34. Diamond Jenness, for example, wrote that 'today the Ojibwa [of Parry Island] sell their fish in the towns and villages.' Jenness, *The Ojibwa Indians of Parry Island: Their Social and Religious Life* (Ottawa, 1935), 15.

35. Koennecke, 'Wasoksing', 283.

36. NAC, RG 10, vol. 10820, file 475/20-2, part 2, Daly to J.D. McLean, 12 Jan. 1923.

37. Ibid., Alex Logan to DIA, 23 Mar. 1918.

38. Ibid., D. McDonald, Acting Deputy Minister, to DIA, 5 Sept. 1917.

39. Ibid., Logan to DIA, 23 Mar. 1918.

40. Ibid., Daly to DIA, 13 Jan. 1936.

41. AO, MS 137, Parry Island Reserve Papers, 1877–1951, Wallace Nesbitt, KC, to Chief Pegahmagabow, 5 June 1925.

42. NAC, RG 10, vol. 10599, Lewis to DIA, 24 Apr. 1923.

43. Ibid.

44. Ibid., Lewis to Chief Charles Obotossaway, 25 May 1923.

45. Ibid., Lewis to Mr G.W. Parks, District Warden, North Bay, 22 Oct. 1923.

46. Ibid., Series B-3, vol. 7225, file 8019-39, Edward Paibomsai to DIA, Timmins, Ont., 15 Mar. 1930.

47. Ibid.

48. Ibid., Lewis to DIA, 25 Mar. 1930.

49. Koennecke Collection, Daly to J.D. McLean, 25 July 1925.

50. Ibid.

51. Canada, *Sessional Papers*, 1920, Annual Report of the Department of Indian Affairs (Ottawa, 1920), 37–8.

52. Ibid.

53. Koennecke Collection, Daly to D.M. McDonald, Deputy Minister of Game and Fisheries Dept., 7 Apr. 1926.

54. Ibid., Daly to Wallace Nesbitt, KC, May 1928. This is the same lawyer whom Pegahmagabow had approached three years earlier for help in asserting fishing rights and raising complaints about Daly himself. Apparently he was known for his willingness to advocate on behalf of First Nations people.

55. Ibid.

56. Ibid.

57. Ibid., Elijah Tabobindong to Daly, 12 Aug. 1923.

58. Ibid., Daly to Deputy Minister of Game and Fisheries, 20 Aug. 1924.

59. Ibid., Daly to DIA, 11 Aug. 1929.

60. Koennecke, 'Wasoksing', 113.

61. See James Morrison, *The Robinson Treaties of 1850: A Case Study*, prepared for the Royal Commission on Aboriginal Peoples, Treaty and Land Research Section (1993), 148–52.

62. NAC, RG 10, vol. 1982, file 6174, D.F. Macdonald to DIA, 13 Oct 1911.

63. Koennecke Collection, Daly to DIA, 15 July 1932.

64. Ibid.

65. Ibid., Daly to DIA, 5 Aug. 1931.
66. Ibid., Daly to Hon. D.C. Scott, DIA, 18 Mar. 1930.
67. Robert Sinclair, *The Canadian Indian* (Ottawa, 1911), cited in R.P. Bowles et al., *The Indian: Assimilation, Integration, or Separation?* (Scarborough, Ont., 1972), 115.

Chapter 5

1. NAC, RG 10, vol. 10609, R.J. Lewis to William Kinoshameg, Secretary, Manitoulin Island Unceded band, 29 Dec. 1926.
2. AO, Francis Bond Head, in 'Memorandum to Lord Glenelg', 1837, quoted in 'Information relating to the Great Manitoulin Islands' (1884), 21–2.
3. NAC, RG 10, vol. 10631, Lewis to DIA, 3 Jan. 1934.
4. R.H.G. Bonnycastle, 'The Role of the Trader in Indian Affairs', in C.T. Loram and T.F. McIlwraith, eds, *The North American Indian Today* (Toronto, 1943), 72.
5. George Manuel and Michael Posluns, *The Fourth World: An Indian Reality* (New York, 1974), 54.
6. On Parry Island, for example, Franz Koennecke states that such expectations were transferred to the agent around the turn of the twentieth century. See Franz Koennecke, 'Wasoksing: The History of Parry Island, an Anishnabwe Community in the Georgian Bay, 1850 to 1920', MA thesis (University of Waterloo, 1984), 269, 327.
7. NAC, RG 10, vol. 10280, file 475/20-2, part 2, Joseph Traunch to DIA, 8 Jan. 1926.
8. Koennecke Collection, Daly to R.H. Coats, Dominion Statistician, Dominion Bureau of Statistics, Ottawa, 12 Dec. 1935.
9. Indian and Northern Affairs Canada, Treaties and Historical Research Centre, 'General Instructions to Indian Agents in Canada', signed by Harold W. McGill, Deputy Superintendent General of Indian Affairs, 1 Sept. 1933, 14.
10. Koennecke Collection, Daly to A.S. Anderson, 6 Mar. 1933.
11. See NAC, RG 10, vol. 7552, file 41,009-2, part 2. Apparently there were at least two 'factories' producing similar lines of products. One was started in 1936 at the McIntyre Bay Reserve on Lake Nipigon. The second was founded at Squaw Bay on the Fort William Reserve in November 1937.
12. Ibid. According to the records, one reason for the company's failure was that Burk's customers were dissatisfied with the canoes, which were too heavy for their intended uses. But the Depression may have been a factor as well.
13. Ibid., vol. 10593, Lewis to DIA, 20 Dec. 1921.
14. Ibid.
15. Ibid., vol. 10599, Lewis to DIA, 27 June 1923.
16. Ibid., vol. 10615, Lewis to Rev. Father Artus, Wikwemikong, 23 Feb. 1929.
17. Koennecke Collection, Stanley Manitowaba to John M. Daly, 3 Jan. 1925.
18. Ibid., Daly to DIA, 5 Dec. 1932.
19. Ibid.
20. Ibid., Resolution passed 9 Oct. 1934; response from T.R.L. MacInnes, DIA secretary, to Daly, 27 Oct. 1934.
21. Ibid., T.R.L. MacInnes, DIA secretary, to Daly, 27 Oct. 1934.
22. Ibid., H.J. Eade to Daly, 14 Sept. 1933.
23. J.E. Chamberlin, *The Harrowing of Eden: White Attitudes toward North American Natives* (Toronto, 1975), 191.
24. Figures taken from the Annual Reports of the Department of Indian Affairs for the years 1930 to 1933, each published in Ottawa in the yearly *Sessional Papers*.

25. Koennecke Collection, Daly to M.H. Ludwig, KC, Toronto, 22 Nov. 1930.
26. NAC, RG 10, vol. 10615, Lewis to Rev. Canon Prower, Sudbury, 9 Feb. 1929.
27. Canada, *Sessional Papers*, Report of the Department of Indian Affairs, 1918, 1924, 1934.
28. NAC, RG 10, vol. 10627, Lewis to Mr Stanley E., Whitefish Falls, Ont., 28 Sept. 1932.
29. Ibid., vol. 10631, Lewis to Mr Peter B., Sault Ste Marie, 5 Nov. 1933. It is not entirely clear whether it was true that no healthy men were on relief. Certainly, healthy men had received relief the previous winter; whether or not Lewis had cut them all off cannot be determined.
30. Ibid., vol. 10627, Lewis to Mr Louis S., 3 Oct. 1932.
31. Ibid., Lewis to DIA, 5 Sept. 1932.
32. Ibid., Lewis to DIA, 19 Jan. 1933.
33. Ibid., Lewis to DIA, 20 Jan. 1933.
34. Ibid., Lewis to DIA, 19 Jan. 1933.
35. Ibid., Lewis to DIA, 20 Jan. 1933.
36. Ibid., Lewis to Chief William McGregor, 26 Jan. 1933.
37. Ibid., vol. 10631, Lewis to William Recollet, Blind River, 7 Nov. 1933.
38. The agent's 'diaries' (really monthly journals recording his daily activities for the DIA) are included among his letterbooks and were collected from all the various volumes of those letterbooks.
39. NAC, RG 10, vol. 10629, Lewis to Mrs George Gaikesheyongai, Shawanaga, Ont., 7 Mar. 1933.
40. Ibid., Lewis to Mr E.F. Priddle, Agent, Gore Bay, 12 June 1933.
41. Koennecke Collection, Daly to DIA, 20 Jan. 1931.
42. Ibid., A.F. MacKenzie to Daly, 22 Jan. 1931.
43. Ibid., Daly to Dr L.L. Stone, Medical Director, DIA, 1 Dec. 1933.
44. Ibid., Daly to DIA, 15 Apr. 1933.
45. Daly wrote, 'The fact of the matter is that I am considered rather hard by the White people here, who don't understand the Indian mode of life.' Ibid., Daly to DIA, 15 Jan. 1927.
46. Ibid., Daly to DIA, 8 Feb. 1929.
47. Ibid., A.F. MacKenzie to Daly, 10 Feb. 1934. This was a circular sent around to all the Indian agents in response to the massively increased demand for relief issues.
48. James Struthers, *No Fault of Their Own* (Toronto, 1983), app. IV (unpaginated), 'Maximum monthly relief allowances for a family of five, selected Canadian cities, September 1936'.
49. Koennecke Collection, Daly to A.S. Anderson, Indian Agent, Rama, 9 Dec. 1932.
50. In April 1934, for example, Daly wrote that he had 'told all the Indians that their relief ends with this month, but I know it cannot because they have no means of support.' Ibid., Daly to DIA, 4 Apr. 1934.
51. Ibid., Daly to DIA, 21 Nov. 1935.
52. Ibid., Daly to DIA, 18 Dec. 1930.
53. Ibid., Daly to DIA, 26 Aug. 1931.
54. Ibid., Daly to DIA, 28 Nov. 1931.
55. All these figures were taken from a summary sent by Daly to the department in 1935. Ibid., Daly to DIA, 2 Aug. 1935. In 1933–4 there were 127 recipients and 217 dependants; in 1934–5, 110 recipients with 160 dependants.
56. Ibid.
57. Ibid., Daly to DIA, 25 Mar. 1933.
58. Ibid., Daly to DIA, 22 Nov. 1933.

59. See ibid., Daly to H.J. Eade, 14 Oct. 1933 and Daly to DIA, 5 July 1935.
60. Ibid., Daly to J.A. Allan, Christian Island, 12 Feb 1935.
61. Ibid., Daly to DIA, 14 Sept. 1931.
62. Ibid., Daly to J.A. Allen, Indian Agent, Christian Island, 12 Feb. 1935.
63. Ibid., Daly to DIA, 2 June 1934.
64. Ibid.
65. Ibid.
66. Ibid., Daly to J.A. Allen, 12 Feb. 1935.
67. Ibid., Daly to Partridge, 1 Mar. 1935.
68. Ibid., Daly to E.J. Hosking, District Engineer, Department of Northern Development, Huntsville, Ont., 20 Mar. 1935.
69. Ibid., Daly to H.J. Eade, 23 Jan. 1934.
70. Ibid., Daly to DIA, 20 Aug. 1935.
71. Indian and Northern Affairs Canada, Treaties and Historical Research Centre, H.W. McGill, 'General Instructions to Indian Agents in Canada', 7.
72. Ibid.
73. Koennecke Collection, H.J. Eade to Daly, 19 Oct. 1933.
74. Ibid., Daly to DIA, 14 Oct. 1933.
75. Ibid., Daly to Dr L.L. Stone, Medical Superintendent, DIA, 11 Jan. 1932.
76. Ibid., Daly to Duncan Campbell Scott, DIA, 13 Mar. 1930.
77. Ibid., Daly to Dr L.L. Stone, Medical Superintendent, DIA, 11 Jan. 1932.
78. NAC, RG 10, vol. 10599, Lewis to Dr C.F. McLean, Collins Inlet, 13 Oct. 1923.
79. Ibid.
80. Ibid., vol. 10607, Lewis to Rev. Lewis A. Sampson, Biscotasing, Ont., 7 Aug. 1926.
81. Ibid.
82. Ibid., vol. 10615, Lewis to Rev. Father Artus, Wikwemikong, 23 Feb. 1929.

Chapter 6

1. Duncan Campbell Scott, Deputy Superintendent General of Indian Affairs, in *Proceedings of the Fourth Conference of the Institute of Pacific Relations* (Canadian Institute of International Affairs, 1931), quoted in Richard P. Bowles et al., *The Indian: Assimilation, Integration or Separation?* (Scarborough, Ont., 1972), 112.
2. Frank Oliver, *House of Commons Debates*, 12 Apr. 1901, 2934; quoted in Ninette Kelley and Michael Trebilcock, eds, *The Making of the Mosaic: A History of Canadian Immigration Policy* (Toronto, 1998), 132.
3. This letter, addressed to the Deputy Minister in the Toronto Department of Education, is quoted in Fraser Symington, *The Canadian Indian: The Illustrated History of the Great Tribes of Canada* (Toronto, 1969). Symington does not name the author of the letter. The official is clearly replying to a letter he had received from the Toronto Department of Education about 'the Indian student, Clifford Tobias'. It seems that the Department of Education had recommended Tobias to the Indian department, either because he was considered promising or because he had applied to teach in Toronto in a non-Indian school.
4. Unnamed employee of the Department of Indian Affairs (probably an Indian agent), in a letter dated 1 Dec. 1918, written in Chatham, Ontario. Quoted in Symington, *The Canadian Indian*, 228.
5. *The Concise Oxford Dictionary of Current English*, 7th edn (Oxford, 1982), 52.

6. See, for example, Kelley and Trebilcock, eds, *The Making of the Mosaic*, 96–7.
7. Howard Palmer has made this point with reference to ideas about the superiority of Anglo-Saxons: 'Notions of racial superiority and cultural superiority were hopelessly confused.' Palmer, 'Strangers and Stereotypes: The Rise of Nativism—1880–1920', in R. Douglas Francis and Palmer, eds, *The Prairie West: Historical Readings* (Edmonton, 1985), 312.
8. The process of enfranchisement is outlined in detail below.
9. *House of Commons Debates*, 8 May 1914, 3482, cited in Constance Backhouse, *Colour-Coded: A Legal History of Racism in Canada, 1900–1950* (Toronto, 1999), 68.
10. Franz Koennecke claimed that 'the last open traditionalist died in 1923.' Koennecke, 'Wasoksing: The History of Parry Island, an Anishnabwe Community in the Georgian Bay, 1850 to 1920', MA thesis (University of Waterloo, 1984), 214, 311. Koennecke conducted extensive oral history research and can generally be assumed to be highly reliable. It is worth noting, however, that Diamond Jenness conducted research on Parry Island in 1929 and designated at least one of his informants, Jonas King, as 'a frank pagan'. Jenness, *The Ojibwa Indians of Parry Island: Their Social and Religious Life* (Ottawa, 1935), vi. It may be that open adherence to indigenous forms of spirituality on Parry Island lasted well past 1923.
11. Koennecke Collection, Daly to H.J. Eade, Christian Island, 14 Oct. 1933. Daly made references to the use of 'Indian dope' to heal, and also to a rumour that someone was trying to apply bad medicine to him.
12. Jenness, *The Ojibwa Indians of Parry Island*, vi, 83–7.
13. Informants accused others of 'sorcery' and magical rites more often than they admitted to them themselves, and their charges are not conclusive proof of any particular activities (especially given the possibility that they were spinning yarns for Jenness). But some of them did admit to using charms for hunting and fishing (ibid., 83), indicating that the resort to forms of magical or supernatural power was more than just a memory or an accusation against others.
14. Ibid., vi. The book does not give further details about his activities as medicine man or whether he performed any functions beyond the dispensing of herbal medicines. Tom King and his older cousin Jonas King were also said to be the last living practitioners on the island who had been inducted into the *Midewiwin* or Grand Medicine Society.
15. See, for example, testimony of Norman Williams, Moose Deer Point First Nation: 'My father could speak Pottawatomi but mostly he spoke Ojibway. Everyone here did when I was young.' From Cynthia C. Wesley-Esquimaux and Dr I.V.B. Johnson, 'United Anishnaabeg Elders: The Treaties Revisited [with particular emphasis on the 1923 Williams Treaty]', in possession of Chippewas of Georgina Island First Nation. The use of Ojibway by the people is also indicated by countless references in the agents' correspondence.
16. Koennecke Collection, Daly to DIA, 15 Apr. 1933.
17. For a thorough discussion of this subject, see J.R. Miller, *Shingwauk's Vision: A History of Native Residential Schools* (Toronto, 1996), 151–83.
18. Koennecke Collection, Daly to Prof. J.C.B. Grant, University of Toronto, Department of Anatomy, 11 Mar. 1932.
19. H.W. McGill, 'Policies and Problems in Canada', in C.T. Loram and T.F. McIlwraith, eds, *The North American Indian Today* (Toronto, 1943), 133–5.
20. Georges E. Sioui, *For an Amerindian Autohistory: An Essay on the Foundations of a Social Ethic*, trans. Sheila Fischman (Montreal and Kingston, 1992), 22.

21. Kim Anderson, *A Recognition of Being: Reconstructing Native Womanhood* (Toronto, 2000).
22. For a comprehensive analysis of treaty negotiations and First Nations demands, see Arthur J. Ray, Jim Miller, and Frank Tough, *Bounty and Benevolence: A History of Saskatchewan Treaties* (Montreal and Kingston, 2000), 35–44, 58–87.
23. Enfranchisement was first introduced in 1857 with the passage of the Gradual Civilization Act by the legislature of the United Canadas. For an account of Aboriginal resistance, see J.R. Miller, *Skyscrapers Hide the Heavens: A History of Indian-White Relations in Canada*, rev. edn (Toronto, 1989), 110–12.
24. For more information about Aboriginal men and the soldier settlement program, as well as the Canadian Legion's involvement in lobbying for soldier settlers, see Robin Brownlie, 'Work Hard and Be Grateful: Native Veterans and the Soldier Settlement Program in Ontario after the First World War', in Franca Iacovetta and Wendy Mitchinson, eds, *On the Case: Explorations in Social History* (Toronto, 1998).
25. Daly noted, 'he never would send his children to school and we never could get them when sending the constable for them.' Koennecke Collection, Daly to DIA, 11 Sept. 1933.
26. Ibid.
27. NAC, RG 10, vol. 10593, Lewis to DIA, 9 Jan. 1922.
28. Ibid., vol. 10601, Lewis to DIA, 29 Aug. 1924. These people had also applied in 1922 to reopen the day school, but Lewis vetoed the request on that occasion, writing, 'I consider that the Indian pupils are much better in the boarding schools.' See ibid., vol. 10595, Lewis to J.B. McDougall, Assistant Chief Inspector, North Bay, Ont., 7 June 1922.
29. Both school and department officials were often reluctant to approve summer visits home, since they had often had trouble getting the pupils back to school in the fall.
30. NAC, RG 10, vol. 10597, Lewis to DIA, 21 Mar. 1923; Lewis to Rev. R.M. Fairbairn, 4 Apr. 1923; vol. 10599, Lewis to DIA, 30 June 1923.
31. Koennecke Collection, Daly to A.D. Moore, Cape Croker, 29 July 1926.
32. For a time in the 1930s, these children were educated by an Aboriginal teacher, Emily Donald, who had been raised in the St John's Indian Residential School at Chapleau. This young woman taught there at least during the school years 1931–2 and 1934–5.
33. NAC, RG 10, vol. 10597, Lewis to DIA, 28 Nov. 1922.
34. John Daly, 'Indian School Teacher Laughs at Georgian Bay Wolves', article submitted to Toronto *Globe*, 4 Jan. 1931.
35. NAC, RG 10, vol. 10593, Lewis to DIA, 10 Mar. 1922.
36. Ibid., Lewis to DIA, 17 Dec. 1921; Lewis to DIA, 10 Mar. 1922. The dispute had somehow escalated to the point where the teacher had barricaded herself in the schoolhouse and refused to come out. Lewis eventually had to travel in by rail and accompany her out of the reserve. While this woman had presumably played a part in provoking the quarrel, the incident illustrates the isolation faced by teachers and their lack of sources for advice on how to cope with problems.
37. Donald taught for two years on Parry Island in the 1920s and at Moose Deer Point during the school years 1930–1, 1931–2, and 1934–5. Koennecke Collection, Daly, 'Indian School Teacher Laughs at Georgian Bay Wolves'; Daly to Miss E. Donald, Moose Point, Ont., 4 Apr. 1932.
38. Annie Shawanda, who was probably from Manitoulin Island, had written to inquire about teaching at the South Bay school, located on the Manitoulin Island Unceded

territory. Although the missionary in charge of the Wikwemikong mission had not accepted her application, Lewis wrote her back in friendly terms and remarked, 'I would like to let you have a chance.' NAC, RG 10, vol. 10591, Lewis to Miss Annie Shawanda, Buffalo, NY, 27 July 1921.

39. Koennecke Collection, Daly to DIA, 2 Dec. 1929.

40. NAC, RG 10, vol. 10605, Lewis to DIA, 17 Nov. 1925.

41. Ibid., vol. 10611, Lewis to DIA, 8 Aug. 1927; vol. 10627, Lewis to DIA, 10 Aug. 1932, Lewis to Rev. Chas. Belanger, SJ, 15 Aug. 1932.

42. At the age of five, the young orphan Emily Donald was brought from Moose Factory to the St John's Anglican Indian Residential School in Chapleau, where she remained until she graduated. Given her name and place of birth, she probably was from the Cree-Scots family that was based around Moose Factory and associated with the Hudson's Bay Company. My thanks to the anonymous reader who supplied the information about the Donald family.

43. Koennecke Collection, Daly to Miss E. Donald, Moose Point, Ont., 4 Apr. 1932.

44. Daly had expected her to set aside money from her meagre salary to pay for this schooling, but she probably found it impossible to save anything after paying expenses. Nevertheless, she eventually did go to Normal School, possibly in North Bay, and by 1935 she was saving money for a first-class teaching certificate. Daly, 'Indian School Teacher Laughs at Georgian Bay Wolves'; Koennecke Collection, Daly to DIA, 25 Oct. 1935.

45. Ibid.

46. Ibid.

47. Canada, *Sessional Papers*, 1918, Report of the Department of Indian Affairs (Ottawa, 1918), 20.

48. Canada, *Sessional Papers*, 1920, Report of the Department of Indian Affairs (Ottawa, 1920), 31.

49. An amendment to the Indian Act passed in 1924 added the proviso, 'Provided that where a wife is living apart from her husband, the enfranchisement of the husband shall not carry with it the enfranchisement of his wife except on her own written request to be so enfranchised.' *Statutes of Canada*, 1924, ch. 47, s. 6, in Sharon H. Venne, ed., *Indian Acts and Amendments 1868–1975: An Indexed Collection* (Saskatoon, 1981), 214.

50. These figures are taken from the Annual Reports of the Department of Indian Affairs. Judging from these reports, some 2,400 people became enfranchised between 1919 and 1939. While this is a sizable group, it was a relatively small proportion of the status Indian population. Most reports state the number of Indians enfranchised, the section under which they did so, and the total number of enfranchisements resulting when wives and unmarried children were included. On average, an individual enfranchisement resulted in a total of roughly 2.5 enfranchisements. For every two voluntary enfranchisees, in other words, there were three whose opinion may or may not have been consulted.

   The enfranchisement process picked up considerably in the 1950s. According to Aboriginal scholar Walter Currie, 7,725 people were enfranchised between 1955 and 1965. He also notes that his own mother could neither read nor write when she was enfranchised. Cited in Bowles et al., *The Indian: Assimilation, Integration or Separation*, 93.

51. The overall figures for the early years are in some doubt, since the report of 1923 fails to cite numbers for that year alone, but claims that 1,035 persons had been

enfranchised to that point. Taking into account the figures given for the other years, this would imply that 450 persons enfranchised in 1923 alone. This, however, is highly unlikely; the largest figure cited for any other single year is 227, and this may have included both 1919 and 1920. Moreover, such an impressive success for the advocates of enfranchisement would hardly have gone unmentioned in the text of the report. It seems likelier that a clerical error led to the total of 1,035 claimed in the 1923 report. The average for the whole period, assuming the accuracy of the 1923 report, is 115 per year. However, if one assumes a likelier total of approximately 150 enfranchisements in 1923, the average for the whole period would fall to approximately 100 persons per year.

52. One of his targets was F.O. Loft, a charismatic and effective organizer who was active in the early 1920s. See Peter Kulchyski, ' "A Considerable Unrest": F.O. Loft and the League of Indians', *Native Studies Review* 4, 1–2 (1988): 95–117.

53. E. Brian Titley, *A Narrow Vision: Duncan Campbell Scott and the Administration of Indian Affairs in Canada* (Vancouver, 1986), 51.

54. Long-serving department secretary T.R.L. MacInnes wrote in 1946, 'There is also a provision in the [Indian] Act for compulsory enfranchisement but its operation is complicated and restricted and it is never invoked.' It is clear that MacInnes was not taking into account the compulsory enfranchisement of the university-educated and of women who married non-status men. MacInnes, 'History of Indian Administration in Canada', *Canadian Journal of Economics and Political Science* 12, 3 (Aug. 1946): 393.

55. Koennecke Collection, Daly to D.M. Grant, 18 Feb. 1932.

56. NAC, RG 10, vol. 10609, Lewis to Miss Susan Nahwaikeshik, 13 May 1927.

57. This assessment is based on an examination of the enfranchisement files examined in more detail below.

58. These conclusions are based on a survey of all the enfranchisement files located in NAC, RG 10 for the Manitowaning and Parry Sound agencies during the years of Lewis's and Daly's administrations.

59. NAC, RG 10, vol. 7496, file 25015-6, part 1, Nelson Stone to Sec. DIA, 8 Feb. 1928. This was a complicated case. The man was a returned soldier who received a 'Soldier Settlement' loan to purchase a farm and start farming. Although he enfranchised and purchased off-reserve land, his loan was still administered by the DIA. The DIA had the power to foreclose mortgages on these farms (even when they were located on reserves) and sell off the land, livestock, and equipment to recoup the loan, which is what was done in this particular case. See Brownlie, 'Work Hard and Be Grateful'.

60. I found 29 applications dating from the period 1918–29, compared to 55 between 1930 and 1939.

61. NAC, RG 10, vol. 10599, Lewis to Mr A.M. Newby, Whitefish Falls, Ont., 19 Sept. 1923. It is worth noting that this man presumably was unable to read and write, given that he had engaged another man to write on his behalf. Lewis made no comment on the applicant's lack of literacy, which was common enough at the time.

62. Ibid., Lewis to Miss Isabelle Peltier, 24 Sept. 1923.

63. Ibid., vol. 10607, Lewis to Edward [illegible], 21 (?) June 1925.

64. There were a total of 49 applications listed in National Archives records between 1922 and 1939, but Daly was on sick leave for much of the time from late 1938 until his retirement in 1939.

65. Koennecke Collection, Daly to D.M. Grant, KC, Huntsville, Ont., 18 Feb. 1932.

66. Ibid., Daly to DIA, 22 Mar. 1932.

67. Ibid.

68. NAC, RG 10, Indian Affairs, series B-3, vol. 7231, file 8022-34, 'Parry Sound Agency—Enfranchisement—S., Chas Jr'.

69. Koennecke Collection, Edwin Pirie to Daly, 11 Apr. 1932.

70. Ibid., Daly to DIA, 12 Apr. 1932.

71. NAC, RG 10, series B-3, vol. 7230, file 8022-9, 'Parry Sound Agency—Enfranchisement—L., Thomas'.

72. For example, Symington, in *The Canadian Indian*, used 'squaw' habitually to refer to Aboriginal women. Although the book is riddled with stereotyped images and notions, Symington clearly did not intend to deride First Nations people in general.

73. See David D. Smits, 'The "Squaw Drudge": A Prime Index of Savagism', *Ethnohistory* 29, 4 (1982): 281–306.

74. For an excellent exploration of these images and discourses, see Sarah Carter, *Capturing Women: The Manipulation of Cultural Imagery in Canada's Prairie West* (Montreal and Kingston, 1997).

75. See also Sherene H. Razack, 'Gendered Racial Violence and Spatialized Justice: The Murder of Pamela George', in Razack, ed., *Race, Space and the Law: Unmapping a White Settler Society* (Toronto, 2002), 121–56.

76. For an illuminating discussion of these processes in a contemporary rural Canadian community, see Elizabeth Furniss, *The Burden of History: Colonialism and the Frontier Myth in a Rural Canadian Community* (Vancouver, 1999), esp. 104–37.

77. For a detailed analysis of the use of imprisonment and other aspects of this campaign, see Joan Sangster, *Regulating Girls and Women: Sexuality, Family, and the Law in Ontario, 1920–1960* (Toronto, 2001), 168–93.

78. NAC, RG 10, vol. 10591, Lewis to Rev. B.P. Fuller, Shingwauk Home, Sault Ste Marie, 20 June 1921.

79. Ibid., vol. 10603, Lewis to DIA, 14 Oct. 1924.

80. In 1933, Daly reported to fellow agent H.J. Eade of Christian Island that David K. was 'a pretty sore man' because 'I have ordered him off the Island [Parry Island] along with the lady that he had there.' Koennecke Collection, Daly to Eade, 14 Oct. 1933. His action to prevent the wedding was recorded in his correspondence with A.S. Anderson, the Indian agent at Rama Reserve. Daly told Anderson that he had notified the town clerk not to issue a marriage licence and was trying to contact the United Church minister to prevent him from marrying them, at least until Daly had a chance to object. He also promised to get the Parry Island constable and 'root them out of there.' Ibid., Daly to Anderson, 5 Aug 1933.

81. Ibid., Daly to DIA, 21 Apr. 1933.

82. NAC, RG 10, vol. 10591, Lewis to Chief Joseph Manitowabi, 26 Mar. 1921. The phrase 'taken care of' suggests that the agent perhaps had in mind something other than a prison, but whatever he meant, he was referring to incarceration.

83. NAC, RG 10, vol. 10593, Lewis to Rev. G.A. Artus, Wikwemikong, 18 Mar. 1922.

84. Lewis assured the Jesuit priest at Wikwemikong that the woman's troubles were not over: 'This matter will be taken up with the officials again, and she will have to bear the consequences whatever the trial will bring forth.' Ibid.

85. Ibid., vol. 10629, Lewis to DIA, 4 Mar., 15 May 1933.

86. While Lewis's letter stated that the committal to the Hospital for the Insane had been ordered by Police Magistrate Major, it appears from the overall description of events that Lewis himself had been directing the process and was determined to find some institution to take custody of the young woman. Ibid., Lewis to DIA, 15 May 1933.

87. For a more extensive discussion of the DIA's regulation of women's gender and sexuality, see Robin Jarvis Brownlie, 'Intimate Surveillance: Indian Affairs, Colonization, and the Regulation of Aboriginal Women's Sexuality', unpublished manuscript.

88. For a fascinating analysis of these shows and Aboriginal participation, see L.G. Moses, *Wild West Shows and the Images of American Indians, 1883–1933* (Albuquerque, 1996).

89. E.A. Heaman, *The Inglorious Arts of Peace: Exhibitions in Canadian Society during the Nineteenth Century* (Toronto, 1999), 297.

90. Ibid.

91. For an analysis of this event, see Paige Raibmon, 'Theatres of Contact: The Kwakwaka'wakw Meet Colonialism in British Columbia and at the Chicago World's Fair', *Canadian Historical Review* 81, 2 (June 2000): 157–90.

92. Keith Regular, 'On Public Display', *Alberta History* 34, 1 (Winter 1986): 8.

93. For performing giveaway dances, the 1906 Act had imposed higher penalties: a minimum of six months and maximum of two years in prison. Ibid.

94. The term 'Show Indians' was employed by the US Bureau of Indian Affairs to designate Aboriginal people who worked as performers. It seems appropriate for this context, too, given that what the people were performing was a particular version of 'Indianness'.

95. Koennecke Collection, Daly to C.W. Ross, Manager, Department of Attractions, Canadian National Exhibition, 26 May 1928.

96. Ibid., Daly to DIA, 6 Mar. 1929.

97. Ibid.

98. Ibid., Daly to C.W. Ross, Manager, Department of Attractions, CNE, 26 May 1928.

Conclusion

1. From Madeline Katt Theriault, *Moose to Moccasins: The Story of Ka Kita Wa Pa No Kwe* (Toronto, 1992), 116–17.

2. On smaller reserves, such as Point Grondine in the Manitowaning agency, the same chief frequently remained in office for decades at a time. But these chiefs served small communities and had little power.

3. A letter dated 10 May 1933 was sent to Hon. Chas. Stewart, House of Commons, seeking his 'good office to place on record in Parliament that we oppose the said legislation as it encroaches the rights of the Indians it means the extinction of Trible Priviledges [*sic*].' AO, MS 137, Parry Island Reserve Papers, 1877–1951.

4. Don Fisher, for example, an Aboriginal man I interviewed during my research, had been a District Supervisor for a time.

5. Comprehensive claims are those concerning territories that have never been surrendered; they are fewer in number but cover much larger areas. Specific claims are those relating to lands that were unlawfully alienated but are covered by some form of surrender (for example, surrenders taken improperly from bands who were under treaty).

6. James S. Frideres with Lilianne E. Krosenbrink-Gelissen, *Aboriginal Peoples in Canada: Contemporary Conflicts*, 5th edn (Scarborough, Ont., 1998), 74. The rate of resolution has not improved appreciably. A map of Aboriginal claims in Ontario currently posted on the Indian and Northern Affairs Canada (INAC) Web site shows 201 specific claims in various stages of negotiation. Of these, only 21 have been settled, while 36 are under litigation (26 of these are claims of the Six Nations of the Grand River). The remaining 144 claims are somewhere in the system, but many of these are

categorized as being closed files or in 'Inactive Negotiations', meaning that nothing is happening at all. See <http://www.ainc-inac.gc.ca/ps/clm/onm_e.pdf>.

7. See Robin Fisher, 'Judging History: Reflections on the Reasons for Judgment in *Delgamuukw v. B.C.*', in Ken Coates and Fisher, eds, *Out of the Background: Readings on Canadian Native History*, 2nd edn (Toronto, 1996), 391–402. See also the entire volume dedicated to this case, Frank Cassidy, ed., *Aboriginal Title in British Columbia: Delgamuukw v. the Queen. Proceedings of a Conference Held September 10 & 11, 1991* (Lantzville, BC, 1992).

8. The Saugeen First Nation is located on Lake Huron on the west side of the Bruce (Saugeen) Peninsula, almost due south of Manitoulin Island and southwest of the communities in the eastern Georgian Bay.

9. I do not mean to disparage INAC employees for this, since it is the only way for them to experience job mobility. I am merely discussing the impact on First Nations people of this general change in job market behaviour.

10. Contrary to media images that often depict reserves as places of rampant poverty, substance abuse, and violence, the reserve communities in southern Ontario are generally well-run, stable, and no more violent than any other Canadian communities.

Appendix

1. *British Parliamentary Papers*, vol. 12, Correspondence, Returns and other Papers relating to Canada and to the Indian Problem Therein, 1839, Bond Head to Glenelg, no. 31, 20 Aug. 1836, cited in Robert J. Surtees, *Treaty Research Report: Manitoulin Island Treaties* (Treaties and Historical Research Centre, Indian and Northern Affairs Canada, 1986), 10–11.

2. Reprinted from the edition of 1939 by Roger Duhamel, FRSC, Queen's Printer and Controller of Stationery, Ottawa, 1964, cited on INAC Web site at <http://www.ainc inac.gc.ca/pr/trts/rbt_e.html>.

3. From Surtees, *Treaty Research Report: Manitoulin Island Treaties*, 38–45.

Index

INDEX 201

functions, of agents, 32–3
funds, band, 29, 34–5, 59, 104–5, 151; and
    assistance, 106–9, 111, 113; and Depression,
    103, 109; and medical care, 120–1; and MIU,
    76–7

game: laws, 86, 93, wardens, 86, 87–8, 89; see also
    hunting; trapping
gardening: and income, 21; and reserve sites, 13–14
gender: and assimilation, 141–4; and assistance,
    106; and 'Indian mode of life', 45
generosity, xvi, xvii; and authority, 103
Gibson (Wahta) band, 13, 14
government: Aboriginal, xvi; Ontario, creation of,
    10
Gradual Civilization Act, 130
gratitude, xviii; and assistance, 38–9, 49
'Great Trouble, The', 18, 76
grievances: land, 68; and language, 151–2; present-
    day, 150; records of, 153; timber-cutting, 71–2;
    unresolved, 79
guiding, xiii, 94–5; as wage labour, 7, 8
gulf, cultural, xv–xix; and assistance, 102

harmony, community, xviii
Haudenosaunee, 2
Hawthorn Report, 82
Hawthorn, H.B., 38
help, expectations of, xvii; see also aid; assistance
Henvey Inlet band, 13, 46, 87
heritage: as justifying special rights, 94; mixed, and
    status, 46
hierarchy: in DIA, 31–2, 151; racial, 129, 157
history, oral, xix, 156
Howson, 43–4
hunting, xiii, 5, 10, 21, 85–6, 87–9; as 'sport', 27
Huron (Wendat), 2

imperialism, xxiii
income, 28; Manitowaning, 21–2, 24; Parry Sound,
    23, 24–7; per capita, 21, 24, 26–7
independence, political, loss of, 9–10
'Indian', xxi; and assimilation, 124, 125, 126;
    definition of, 43–4; 'historic', 9; ideas of, 42–8;
    'mode of life', 43–6, 128, 136, 140; v. 'person',
    47; 'problem', 42, 126; as racial category, 46–7
Indian Act, 10, 29, 31, 41, 79, 120, 130, 146, 155;
    and coercion, 40; and definition of Indian, 43–4,
    47; and enfranchisement, 136–7; powers of,
    34–7, and treaties, 82; and women, 141
Indian and Northern Affairs Canada, 155
individualism, 127; liberal, x, xxii, 104, 105, 111,
    153–4
industriousness, 127; importance of, 45
'ingratitude', 39; see also gratitude
integration, 149; see also assimilation
intemperance, as ground for deposition, 60, 61
interaction, between non-Aboriginal and
    Aboriginal, 7–9
intermarriage, 131, 142

Iroquois (Haudenosaunee), 2
islands, Georgian Bay: dispute over, 67–8, 70, 71,
    96, 153, 157; surrender of, 13

Jackson, Henry, 57, 74–5
Jacobs, Burton, xii, 35
Jacobs, Wesley, 67–8
James, Solomon, 90
Jenness, Diamond, 27–8, 128
Jesuits, xi, xx, 15; and sexual policing, 143
Johnson, Frederick, 27
Johnston, Verna Petronella, 60
Jones, Peter, xvi
Judge, Frank, 18, 58, 68–9, 96
Judge, Peter, 58
jurisdiction, and band councils, 59
justice, and agents, 35–6

Kanesatake, 14
Keating, John, 96
Killarney, 46, 122
King, Tom, 128
Koennecke, Franz, xx–xxi, 8
Kwakwaka'wakw (Kwakiutl), 145

labour: low-paying, 42; road, 27; seasonal, 44;
    wage, xiii, 7, 8, 20, 21, 24, 26, 27–8, 110, 111,
    131; see also employment; work
Lamorandiere, Louis, 133
land: and assimilation, 130; claims, 71, 156;
    disputes over, 67–8; distribution of, 59; and
    enfranchisement, 136–8; surrenders of, 3; and
    treaties, 95–8; use of, 83
language(s), 131, 151; as barrier, 8–9; retained, 128
lawyers, engagement of, 140
leaders: new generation of, 57; as 'servants' of DIA,
    58; traditional, 56–7; see also chiefs
leadership: Aboriginal, 151–2; and expectations,
    xv–xvii
League of Indians, 152
leases, fishing, 87; see also fees; licences; permits
legacy, Indian agents', xii–xiv
Lewis, Robert John, x, xiii, xiv, xx, 45, 46, 47, 48,
    51–5, 153–4, 155; and assistance, 99, 103, 107,
    121–2, 123; and band councils, 61, 70, 77, 78; in
    Depression, 110–14; and education, 133–5; and
    enfranchisement, 138, 139–41; and language, 8;
    and rights, 87, 90, 92, 93, 98; salary of, 24, 27
licences: fishing, 91–2; guiding, 94–5; harvesting,
    89; trapping, 92–3; and treaty rights, 80; see also
    fees, leases, permits
lifestyle, and status, 45–6; see also 'mode of life'
Loft, F.O., 152
Logan, Alexander, 65, 90, 91
Lower French River (Pickerel River) band, 13
lumbering, 6–7, 25; and MIU, 76; and wage labour,
    20; and treaties, 97; see also timber

Macdonald, D.F., 88, 89, 96
McEachern, Allan, 156

THE CANADIAN SOCIAL HISTORY SERIES

Terry Copp,
The Anatomy of Poverty:
The Condition of the Working Class
in Montreal, 1897–1929, 1974.
ISBN 0–7710–2252–2

Alison Prentice,
The School Promoters:
Education and Social Class in
Mid-Nineteenth Century
Upper Canada, 1977.
ISBN 0–7710–7181–7

John Herd Thompson,
The Harvests of War:
The Prairie West, 1914–1918, 1978.
ISBN 0–19–541402–0

Joy Parr, Editor,
Childhood and Family in Canadian History, 1982.
ISBN 0–7710–6938–3

Alison Prentice and
Susan Mann Trofimenkoff, Editors,
The Neglected Majority:
Essays in Canadian Women's History, Volume 2,
1985.
ISBN 0–7710–8583–4

Ruth Roach Pierson,
'They're Still Women After All':
The Second World War and
Canadian Womanhood, 1986.
ISBN 0–7710–6958–8

Bryan D. Palmer, Editor
The Character of Class Struggle:
Essays in Canadian Working-Class History,
1850–1985, 1986.
ISBN 0–7710–6946–4

Alan Metcalfe,
Canada Learns to Play:
The Emergence of Organized Sport, 1807–1914,
1987.
ISBN 0–19–541304–0

Marta Danylewycz,
Taking the Veil:
An Alternative to Marriage, Motherhood, and
Spinsterhood in
Quebec, 1840–1920, 1987.
ISBN 0–19–541472–1

Craig Heron,
Working in Steel: The Early Years in Canada,
1883–1935, 1988.
ISBN 0–7710–4086–5

Wendy Mitchinson and
Janice Dickin McGinnis, Editors,
Essays in the History of
Canadian Medicine, 1988.
ISBN 0–7710–6063–7

Joan Sangster,
Dreams of Equality: Women on the Canadian
Left, 1920–1950, 1989.
ISBN 0–7710–7946–X

Angus McLaren,
Our Own Master Race: Eugenics in Canada,
1885–1945, 1990.
ISBN 0–19–541365–2

Bruno Ramirez,
On the Move:
French-Canadian and Italian Migrants in the
North Atlantic Economy, 1860–1914, 1991.
ISBN 0–19–541419–5

Mariana Valverde,
The Age of Light, Soap, and Water:
Moral Reform in English Canada, 1885–1925,
1991.
ISBN 0–7710–8689–X

Bettina Bradbury,
Working Families:
Age, Gender, and Daily Survival in
Industrializing Montreal, 1993.
ISBN 0–19–541211–7

Andrée Lévesque,
Making and Breaking the Rules:
Women in Quebec, 1919–1939, 1994.
ISBN 0–7710–5283–9

Cecilia Danysk,
Hired Hands: Labour and the Development of
Prairie Agriculture, 1880–1930, 1995.
ISBN 0–7710–2552–1

Kathryn McPherson,
Bedside Matters: The Transformation
of Canadian Nursing, 1900–1990, 1996.
ISBN 0–19–541219–2

Edith Burley,
Servants of the Honourable Company: Work,
Discipline, and Conflict in the Hudson's Bay
Company, 1770–1870, 1997.
ISBN 0–19–541296–6

Mercedes Steedman,
Angels of the Workplace: Women and the
Construction of Gender Relations in the
Canadian Clothing Industry, 1890–1940, 1997.
ISBN 0–19–541308–3

Angus McLaren and
Arlene Tigar McLaren,
The Bedroom and the State: The Changing
Practices and Politics of Contraception and
Abortion in Canada, 1880–1997, 1997.
ISBN 0–19–541318–0

Kathryn McPherson, Cecilia Morgan, and
Nancy M. Forestell, Editors,
Gendered Pasts: Historical Essays in Femininity
and Masculinity in Canada, 1999.
ISBN 0–19–541449–7

Gillian Creese,
Contracting Masculinity: Gender, Class, and
Race in a White-Collar Union, 1944–1994, 1999.
ISBN 0–19–541454–3

Geoffrey Reaume,
Remembrance of Patients Past: Patient Life at
the Toronto Hospital for the Insane, 1870–1940,
2000.
ISBN 0–19–541538–8

Miriam Wright,
A Fishery for Modern Times: The State and the
Industrialization of the Newfoundland Fishery,
1934–1968, 2001.
ISBN 0–19–541620–1

Judy Fudge and Eric Tucker,
Labour Before the Law: The Regulation of
Workers' Collective Action in Canada,
1900–1948, 2001.
ISBN 0–19–541633–3

Mark Moss,
Manliness and Militarism: Educating Young
Boys in Ontario for War, 2001.
ISBN 0–19–541594–9

Joan Sangster,
Regulating Girls and Women: Sexuality, Family,
and the Law in Ontario 1920–1960, 2001.
ISBN 0–19–541663–5

Reinhold Kramer and Tom Mitchell,
Walk Towards the Gallows: The Tragedy of
Hilda Blake, Hanged 1899, 2002.
ISBN 0–19–541686–4

Mark Kristmanson,
Plateaus of Freedom: Nationality, Culture, and
State Security in Canada, 1940–1960, 2002.
ISBN 0–19–541866–2

Robin Jarvis Brownlie,
A Fatherly Eye: Indian Agents, Government
Power, and Aboriginal Resistance in Ontario,
1918–1939, 2003.
ISBN 0–19–541891–3